MCSA 70-740 Cert Guide: Installation, Storage, and Compute with Windows Server 2016

Anthony Sequeira

800 East 96th Street
Indianapolis, Indiana 46240 USA

MCSA 70-740 Cert Guide: Installation, Storage, and Compute with Windows Server 2016

ISBN-10: 0-7897-5697-8

ISBN-13: 978-0-7897-5697-8

Library of Congress Control Number: 2017935907

Printed in the United States of America

2   18

Trademarks

All terms mentioned in this book that are known to be trademarks or service marks have been appropriately capitalized. Pearson IT Certification cannot attest to the accuracy of this information. Use of a term in this book should not be regarded as affecting the validity of any trademark or service mark.

Warning and Disclaimer

Every effort has been made to make this book as complete and as accurate as possible, but no warranty or fitness is implied. The information provided is on an "as is" basis. The author and the publisher shall have neither liability nor responsibility to any person or entity with respect to any loss or damages arising from the information contained in this book.

Special Sales

For information about buying this title in bulk quantities, or for special sales opportunities (which may include electronic versions; custom cover designs; and content particular to your business, training goals, marketing focus, or branding interests), please contact our corporate sales department at corpsales@pearsoned.com or (800) 382-3419.

For government sales inquiries, please contact governmentsales@pearsoned.com.

For questions about sales outside the U.S., please contact intlcs@pearson.com.

Editor-in-Chief
Mark Taub

Product Line Manager
Brett Bartow

Managing Editor
Sandra Schroeder

Development Editor
Christopher Cleveland

Project Editor
Mandie Frank

Copy Editor
Kitty Wilson

Technical Editor
Vince Averello

Editorial Assistant
Vanessa Evans

Cover Designer
Chuti Prasertsith

Composition
Studio Galou

Indexer
Ken Johnson

Proofreader
The Wordsmithery LLC

Contents at a Glance

Elements Available on the Book Website

Table of Contents

About the Author

Anthony Sequeira (CCIE #15626) began his IT career in 1994 with IBM in Tampa, Florida. He quickly formed his own computer consultancy, Computer Solutions, and then discovered his true passion—teaching and writing about Microsoft and Cisco technologies. Anthony has lectured to massive audiences around the world while working for Mastering Computers. He has never been happier in his career than he is now as a full-time trainer for CBT Nuggets. He is an avid tennis player, a private pilot, and a semi-professional poker player, and he enjoys getting beaten up by women and children at the martial arts school he attends with his daughter.

Dedication

This book is dedicated to all my fellow employees at CBT Nuggets. Thank you for your tireless efforts in enriching the lives of students all over the world.

Acknowledgments

Thanks so much to my technical reviewer, Vince Averello. Vince carefully stepped through the hefty contents of this book to ensure that the information is as accurate as possible. Thanks also to Michelle Newcomb for her patience with me as I struggled to get this book completed on time. Finally, as always, thanks to Chris Cleveland for his incredible work to ensure that this book is as awesome as possible!

About the Technical Reviewer

Vince Averello has been a professional geek for more than 30 years. During those often funny, sometimes frightening but always interesting years, he's worked for more than 10 organizations, lending his expertise to a variety of projects. Every one of them has been a learning experience, so now he knows a little bit about a lot of things, ranging from the Internet to garment trucking. Vince lives in lovely midtown Bayonne, New Jersey with his loving wife, daughter, and two cats with delusions of grandeur.

We Want to Hear from You!

As the reader of this book, you are our most important critic and commentator. We value your opinion and want to know what we're doing right, what we could do better, what areas you'd like to see us publish in, and any other words of wisdom you're willing to pass our way.

We welcome your comments. You can email or write to let us know what you did or didn't like about this book—as well as what we can do to make our books better.

Please note that we cannot help you with technical problems related to the topic of this book.

When you write, please be sure to include this book's title and author as well as your name and email address. We will carefully review your comments and share them with the author and editors who worked on the book.

Email: feedback@pearsonitcertification.com

Mail: Pearson IT Certification
ATTN: Reader Feedback
800 East 96th Street
Indianapolis, IN 46240 USA

Reader Services

Register your copy of *MCSA 70-740 Cert Guide* at www.pearsonitcertification.com for convenient access to downloads, updates, and corrections as they become available. To start the registration process, go to www.pearsonitcertification.com/register and log in or create an account*. Enter the product ISBN 9780789756978 and click **Submit**. When the process is complete, you will find any available bonus content under Registered Products.

*Be sure to check the box that you would like to hear from us to receive exclusive discounts on future editions of this product.

Introduction

Congratulations! If you are reading this, you have in your possession a powerful tool that can help you do the following:

- Install Windows Servers in host and compute environments

- Implement storage solutions

- Implement Hyper-V

- Implement Windows containers

- Implement high availability

- Maintain and monitor server environments

- Prepare for the Exam 70-740 Installation, Storage, and Compute with Windows Server 2016 certification exam from Microsoft

Whether you are preparing for the MCSA or MCSE certifications from Microsoft or changing careers to server administration, this book will help you gain the knowledge to get started and prepared.

This text covers every single objective the 70-740 exam has to offer and also provides the step-by-step guidance you need in production server environments.

The Exam 70-740 Installation, Storage, and Compute with Windows Server 2016 exam is required for the MCSA and MCSE certifications from Microsoft. This book covers all the topics listed in Microsoft's exam blueprint, and each chapter includes key topics and preparation tasks to assist you in mastering this information. Reviewing tables and practicing test questions will help you practice your knowledge in all subject areas.

About the 70-740 Installation, Storage, and Compute with Windows Server 2016 Exam

This exam focuses primarily on the installation, storage, and compute features and functionality available in Windows Server 2016. It covers general installation tasks and considerations and the installation and configuration of Nano Server, in addition to the creation and management of images for deployment. It also covers local and server storage solutions, including the configuration of disks and volumes, data deduplication, high availability, disaster recovery, Storage Spaces Direct, and Failover Clustering solutions. The exam also covers Hyper-V and containers, along with the maintenance and monitoring of servers in physical and compute environments. For a complete review of the exam structure and types of questions you will face, visit www.ajsnetworking.com/70-740-review.

You can take the exam at Pearson VUE testing centers. Register with VUE at www.vue.com.

70-740 Exam Topics

Table I-1 lists the topics of the 70-740 exam and indicates the chapter in the book where each is covered.

Table I-1 70-740 Exam Topics

Exam Topic	Chapter
Install Windows Servers in host and compute environments	
Install, upgrade, and migrate servers and workloads	Chapter 1
Install and configure Nano Server	Chapter 2
Create, manage, and maintain images for deployment	Chapter 3
Implement storage solutions	
Configure disks and volumes	Chapter 4
Implement server storage	Chapter 5
Implement data deduplication	Chapter 6
Implement Hyper-V	
Install and configure Hyper-V	Chapter 7
Configure virtual machine (VM) settings	Chapter 8
Configure Hyper-V storage	Chapter 9
Configure Hyper-V networking	Chapter 10
Implement Windows Containers	
Deploy Windows containers	Chapter 11
Manage Windows containers	Chapter 12
Implement High Availability	
Implement high availability and disaster recovery options in Hyper-V	Chapter 13
Implement failover clustering	Chapter 14
Manage failover clustering	Chapter 15
Implement Storage Spaces Direct	Chapter 16
Manage VM movement in clustered nodes	Chapter 17
Implement Network Load Balancing (NLB)	Chapter 18
Maintain and Monitor Server Environments	
Maintain server installations	Chapter 19
Monitor server installations	Chapter 20

About the MCSA 70-740 Cert Guide

This book maps to the topic areas of the 70-740 exam and uses a number of features to help you understand the topics and prepare for the exam.

Objectives and Methods

This book uses several key methodologies to help you discover for which exam topics you need more review, to help you fully understand and remember those details, and to help you prove to yourself that you have retained your knowledge of those topics. This book does not try to help you pass the exams only by memorization but by truly learning and understanding the topics. This book is designed to help you pass the 70-740 exam by using the following methods:

- Helping you discover which exam topics you have not yet mastered

- Providing explanations and information to fill in your knowledge gaps

- Supplying exercises that enhance your ability to recall and deduce the answers to test questions

- Providing practice exercises on the topics and the testing process via test questions on the companion website

Book Features

To help you customize your study time using this book, the core chapters have several features that help you make the best use of your time:

- **"Do I Know This Already?" quiz:** Each chapter begins with a quiz that helps you determine how much time you need to spend studying that chapter.

- **Foundation Topics:** These are the core sections of each chapter. They explain the concepts for the topics in that chapter.

- **Exam Preparation Tasks:** After the "Foundation Topics" section of each chapter, the "Exam Preparation Tasks" section lists a series of study activities that you should do at the end of the chapter. Each chapter includes the activities that make the most sense for studying the topics in that chapter:

  - **Review All the Key Topics:** The Key Topic icon appears next to the most important items in the "Foundation Topics" section of the chapter. The Review All the Key Topics activity lists the key topics from the chapter, along with their page numbers. Although the contents of the entire chapter could be on the exam, you should definitely know the information listed in each key topic, so you should be sure to review these.

- **Complete the Tables and Lists from Memory:** To help you memorize some lists of facts, many of the most important lists and tables from the chapter are included in a document on the companion website. This document lists only partial information, allowing you to complete the table or list.

- **Define Key Terms:** Although the exam may be unlikely to ask a question such as "How do you define the term x?" the 70-740 exam does require that you learn and know a lot of networking terminology. This section lists the most important terms from the chapter, asking you to write a short definition and compare your answer against the glossary at the end of the book.

- **Q&A:** This section helps you confirm that you understand the content that you just covered.

- **Web-based practice exam:** The companion website includes the Pearson Test Prep practice test software, which allows you to take practice exam questions. Use them to prepare with a sample exam and to pinpoint topics for which you need more study.

How This Book Is Organized

This book contains 20 core chapters:

- **Chapter 1, "Installing, Upgrading, and Migrating,"** covers installation requirements and methods as well as upgrade scenarios and migration approaches.

- **Chapter 2, "Installing and Configuring Nano,"** covers how to determine appropriate usage scenarios and requirements for Nano Server as well as how to install Nano Server, including the implementation of roles and features on Nano Server. The chapter also covers the management and configuration of Nano Server, including the use of Windows PowerShell.

- **Chapter 3, "Working with Images,"** covers the important planning and implementation steps involved in virtualization.

- **Chapter 4, "Disks and Volumes,"** covers basic and advanced disk and volume creation and management, including the use of NFS and SMB shares for a network.

- **Chapter 5, "Server Storage,"** covers more advanced storage topics such as storage pools and Storage Area Network (SAN)–related topics.

- **Chapter 6, "Data Deduplication,"** covers implementation of data deduplication.

- **Chapter 7, "Installing Hyper-V,"** covers requirements for Hyper-V as well as its implementation and management.

- **Chapter 8, "Working with Virtual Machines,"** covers advanced topics in VM creation and management.

- **Chapter 9, "Hyper-V Storage,"** covers the ins and outs of VHDs and VHDX files.

- **Chapter 10, "Hyper-V Networking,"** covers networking concepts from virtual NICs to RDMA.

- **Chapter 11, "Deploying Containers,"** covers container basics and their creation.

- **Chapter 12, "Managing Containers,"** covers container management, including the use of Docker in the Windows Server 2016 environment.

- **Chapter 13, "High Availability in Hyper-V,"** covers important high-availability topics such as Hyper-V Replica, live migration, and shared-nothing live migration.

- **Chapter 14, "Failover Clustering,"** covers the creation of various Failover Clustering models that are possible in Windows Server 2016.

- **Chapter 15, "Managing Failover Clustering,"** moves deeper into the subject of failover cluster management, including advanced topics such as VM monitoring and node fairness.

- **Chapter 16, "Storage Spaces Direct,"** includes a discussion of deployment scenarios and step-by-step instructions for implementation.

- **Chapter 17, "Managing VM Movement,"** includes features such as Live Migration; Quick Migration; Storage Migration; importing, exporting, and copying; and VM Network Health Protection, and Drain on Shutdown.

- **Chapter 18, "Network Load Balancing (NLB),"** details NLB design and implementation and provides step-by-step instructions and management guidelines.

- **Chapter 19, "Maintaining Servers,"** covers WSUS and Windows Defender.

- **Chapter 20, "Monitoring Servers,"** focuses on properly monitoring a server using Resource Monitor and Performance Monitor.

Companion Website

Register this book to get access to the Pearson Test Prep practice test software and other study materials plus additional bonus content. Check this site regularly for new and updated postings written by the author that provide further insight into the most troublesome topics on the exam. Be sure to check the box indicating that you would like to hear from us to receive updates and exclusive discounts on future editions of this product or related products.

To access this companion website, follow these steps:

1. Go to www.pearsonITcertification.com/register and log in or create a new account.

2. Enter the ISBN **9780789756978**.

3. Answer the challenge question as proof of purchase.

4. Click the **Access Bonus Content** link in the Registered Products section of your account page to be taken to the page where your downloadable content is available.

If you are unable to locate the files for this title by following these steps, please visit www.pearsonITcertification.com/contact and select the **Site Problems/Comments** option. Our customer service representatives will assist you.

Please note that many of our companion content files can be very large, especially image and video files.

Pearson Test Prep Practice Test Software

As noted previously, this book comes complete with the Pearson Test Prep practice test software, containing two full exams. These practice tests are available to you either online or as an offline Windows application. To access the practice exams that were developed with this book, please see the instructions in the card inserted in the sleeve in the back of the book. This card includes a unique access code that enables you to activate your exams in the Pearson Test Prep software.

Accessing the Pearson Test Prep Software Online

The online version of this software can be used on any device that has a browser and connectivity to the Internet, including desktop machines, tablets, and smartphones. To start using your practice exams online, simply follow these steps:

1. Go to www.PearsonTestPrep.com.

2. Select **Pearson IT Certification** as your product group.

3. Enter your email/password for your account. If you don't have an account on PearsonITCertification.com or CiscoPress.com, you need to establish one by going to PearsonITCertification.com/join.

4. In the **My Products** tab, click the **Activate New Product** button.

5. Enter the access code printed on the insert card in the back of your book to activate your product.

6. The product is now listed in your My Products page. Click the **Exams** button to launch the exam settings screen and start your exam.

Accessing the Pearson Test Prep Software Offline

If you wish to study offline, you can download and install the Windows version of the Pearson Test Prep software. There is a download link for this software on the book's companion website, or you can just enter this link in your browser: www.pearsonitcertification.com/content/downloads/pcpt/engine.zip.

To access the book's companion website and the software, simply follow these steps:

1. Register your book by going to www.pearsonITcertification.com/register and entering the ISBN **9780789756978**.

2. Respond to the challenge questions.

3. Go to your account page and select the **Registered Products** tab.

4. Click the **Access Bonus Content** link under the product listing.

5. Click the **Install Pearson Test Prep Desktop Version** link under the Practice Exams section of the page to download the software.

6. When the software finishes downloading, unzip all the files on your computer.

7. Double-click the application file to start the installation and follow the onscreen instructions to complete the registration.

8. When the installation is complete, launch the application and click the **Activate Exam** button on the My Products tab.

9. Click the **Activate a Product** button in the Activate Product Wizard.

10. Enter the unique access code found on the card in the sleeve in the back of your book and click the **Activate** button.

11. Click **Next** and then click **Finish** to download the exam data to your application.

12. You can now start using the practice exams by selecting the product and clicking the **Open Exam** button to open the exam settings screen.

Note that the offline and online versions sync together, so saved exams and grade results recorded on one version are available to you on the other as well.

Customizing Your Exams

Once you are in the exam settings screen, you can choose to take exams in one of three modes:

- **Study mode:** Study mode allows you to fully customize your exams and review answers as you are taking the exam. This is typically the mode you use first to assess your knowledge and identify information gaps.

- **Practice Exam mode:** Practice Exam mode locks certain customization options in order to present a realistic exam experience. Use this mode when you are preparing to test your exam readiness.

- **Flash Card mode:** Flash Card mode strips out the answers and presents you with only the question stem. This mode is great for late-stage preparation, when you really want to challenge yourself to provide answers without the benefit of seeing multiple-choice options. This mode does not provide the detailed score reports that the other two modes provide, so you should not use it if you are trying to identify knowledge gaps.

In addition to these three modes, you can select the source of your questions. You can choose to take exams that cover all the chapters, or you can narrow your selection to just a single chapter or the chapters that make up specific parts in the book. All chapters are selected by default. If you want to narrow your focus to individual chapters, simply deselect all the chapters and then select only those on which you wish to focus in the Objectives area.

You can also select the exam banks on which to focus. Each exam bank comes complete with a full exam of questions that cover topics in every chapter. The two exams printed in the book are available to you, along with two additional exams of unique questions. You can have the test engine serve up exams from all four banks or just from one individual bank by selecting the desired banks in the exam bank area.

There are several other customizations you can make to your exam from the exam settings screen, such as the time of the exam, the number of questions served up, whether to randomize questions and answers, whether to show the number of correct answers for multiple-answer questions, and whether to serve up only specific types of questions. You can also create custom test banks by selecting only questions that you have marked or questions on which you have added notes.

Updating Exams

If you are using the online version of the Pearson Test Prep software, you should always have access to the latest version of the software as well as the exam data. If you are using the Windows desktop version, every time you launch the software, it will check to see if there are any updates to your exam data and automatically download any changes made since the last time you used the software. This happens only if you are connected to the Internet at the time you launch the software.

Sometimes, due to many factors, the exam data may not fully download when you activate your exam. If you find that figures or exhibits are missing, you may need to manually update your exams.

To update a particular exam you have already activated and downloaded, simply select the **Tools** tab and click the **Update Products** button. Again, this is only an issue with the desktop Windows application.

To check for updates to the Pearson Test Prep exam engine software, Windows desktop version, simply select the **Tools** tab and click the **Update Application** button. This way, you can ensure that you are running the latest version of the software engine.

This chapter covers the following subjects:

- **What's New in Windows Server 2016**: This section details many of the exciting new features in the latest version of Microsoft's premier server operating system. As you might guess, we cover many of these new features in this text.

- **Installation Requirements**: This part of the chapter ensures that you have the correct hardware in place for your Windows Server 2016 installation.

- **Windows Server 2016 Editions**: This section helps you select exactly the Windows Server 2016 edition that is right for your organization.

- **Installing Windows Server 2016**: This area makes sure you can easily install Windows Server 2016 and perform the installation of Windows Server 2016 features and roles. This section also details the installation and configuration of Windows Server Core. Finally, this part of the chapter covers the implementation of Windows PowerShell Desired State Configuration (DSC) to install and support the integrity of installed environments.

- **Performing Upgrades and Migrations**: This part details upgrades and migrations of servers and core workloads from Windows Server 2008 and Windows Server 2012 to Windows Server 2016.

- **Determining the Appropriate Activation Model**: This area of the chapter ensures that you can select the appropriate activation model for your server installation. It covers options like Automatic Virtual Machine Activation (AVMA), Key Management Service (KMS), and Active Directory-based Activation.

## CHAPTER 1

Installing, Upgrading, and Migrating

With all the great new features of Windows Server 2016, it is very tempting to download your copy from Microsoft and set about quickly building your new servers. This chapter certainly walks you through that process, but it also ensures that you prepare properly for your installations and upgrades. You must pause to examine hardware requirements and editions of Windows Server 2016 and consider important topics like activation.

This chapter begins with a bang with an overview of just some of the exciting new features of Windows Server 2016.

"Do I Know This Already?" Quiz

The "Do I Know This Already?" quiz allows you to assess whether you should read the entire chapter. Table 1-1 lists the major headings in this chapter and the "Do I Know This Already?" quiz questions covering the material in those headings so you can assess your knowledge of these specific areas. The answers to the "Do I Know This Already?" quiz appear in Appendix A, "Answers to the 'Do I Know This Already?' Quizzes and Q&A Questions."

Table 1-1 "Do I Know This Already?" Foundation Topics Section-to-Question Mapping

Foundation Topics Section	Questions
What's New in Windows Server 2016	1, 2
Installation Requirements	3, 4
Windows Server 2016 Editions	5
Installing Windows Server 2016	6, 7
Performing Upgrades and Migrations	8, 9
Determining the Appropriate Activation Model	10

CAUTION The goal of self-assessment is to gauge your mastery of the topics in this chapter. If you do not know the answer to a question or are only partially sure of the answer, you should mark your answer as incorrect for purposes of the self-assessment. Giving yourself credit for an answer you correctly guess skews your self-assessment results and might provide you with a false sense of security.

1. What new version of Windows Server 2016 offers the smallest footprint for Windows Server yet?

    a. Server Core

    b. Nano Server

    c. Container Server

    d. VM-only Server

2. What well-known and trusted technology for supporting containers now integrates into Windows Server 2016?

    a. Chef

    b. Puppet

    c. Zen Server

    d. Docker

3. What is the minimum RAM required for the Server with Desktop Experience type of Server 2016 Standard installation?

    a. 512 MB

    b. 2 GB

    c. 4 GB

    d. 8 GB

4. You plan to use BitLocker Drive Encryption on your Windows Server 2016 installation to encrypt all partitions. What do you need?

    a. TPM chip

    b. 8 GB of RAM

    c. A 64 GB system partition

    d. An ATA boot drive

5. What edition of Windows Server 2016 supports an unlimited number of Hyper-V containers?

    a. Windows Server 2016 Essentials

    b. Windows Server 2016 Standard

    c. Windows Server 2016 Professional

    d. Windows Server 2016 Datacenter

6. When installing Windows Server 2016 from DVD using the Windows Setup Wizard, which is not an option from the **Select the operating system window?**

   a. Windows Server 2016 Standard

   b. Windows Server 2016 Datacenter

   c. Nano Server

   d. Windows Server 2016 Standard (Desktop Experience)

7. When installing Windows Server 2016 from DVD using the Windows Setup Wizard, what option should you choose from the Type of installation window if you want a clean install?

   a. Clean

   b. Custom

   c. Upgrade

   d. Wipe

8. You are now running Windows Server 2012 Standard. What version options exist for an upgrade to Windows Server 2016? Choose all that apply.

   a. Windows Server 2016 Essentials

   b. Windows Server 2016 Standard

   c. Windows Server 2016 Ultimate

   d. Windows Server 2016 Datacenter

9. What are two examples of license conversions you can perform with Windows Server 2016? Choose two.

   a. Converting from Windows Server 2016 32-bit to 64-bit

   b. Converting from the evaluation software to retail

   c. Converting from Standard to Datacenter

   d. Converting from Essentials to Ultimate

10. What is an alternative to volume activations of Windows Server 2016 besides using Active Directory-based Activation?

   a. WSUS

   b. KMS

   c. LDAP

   d. MS Exchange

Foundation Topics

What's New in Windows Server 2016

While this is by no means a complete list, here are some of the exciting new features and improvements offered with Windows Server 2016:

- **Nano Server**: Nano Server offers another exciting installation option for Windows Server 2016. This incredibly small service image offers no graphical or command prompt interface. Hardware requirements are much smaller than even for Server Core. Microsoft targeted Nano Server as a superb platform for Hyper-V, Hyper-V cluster, Scale-Out File Server, and cloud service applications.

- **Windows Server containers and Hyper-V containers**: Containers are certainly a buzz in IT today. They allow an application to run with everything it needs in one small and nimble container. This is a virtualization of the operating system itself and is much more efficient and lightweight than a full-blown virtual machine (VM) approach. Windows Server 2016 features two types of containers—Windows Server containers and Hyper-V containers. Windows Server containers are isolated from each other, but they run directly on the Windows Server 2016 OS. Hyper-V containers offer enhanced isolation by running the containers from a Hyper-V VM. Containers enable you to isolate your apps from the operating system environment. This improves security and reliability. Containers are also very portable.

- **Docker**: Docker is a well-known and trusted technology for managing containers. Although Docker is usually associated with Linux, Windows Server 2016 provides support for Docker as a means for managing Windows containers and Hyper-V containers.

- **Rolling upgrades for Hyper-V and storage clusters**: Thanks to this new feature, you can add Windows Server 2016 nodes to an existing Windows Server 2012 R2 failover cluster. The cluster continues to run at a Windows Server 2012 R2 functional level until you upgrade all nodes.

- **Hot add/hot remove of virtual memory/network adapters from virtual machines**: Hyper-V now supports adding or removing virtual memory and network adapters while the virtual machines are running.

- **Nested virtualization**: Now you can run Hyper-V virtual machines within a virtual machine.

- **PowerShell Direct**: You can run Windows PowerShell commands against a guest operating system in a virtual machine without handling security policies, host network settings, or firewall settings.

- **Shielded virtual machines**: This new VM feature helps protect the data on virtual machines from unauthorized access.

- **Windows Defender**: This feature helps protect your server against malware.

- **Storage Spaces Direct**: This feature enables you to build highly available storage with directly attached disks on each node in a cluster. The Server Message Block 3 (SMB3) protocol provides resiliency for this feature.

- **Storage Replica**: This feature allows you to synchronously or asynchronously replicate volumes at the block level.

- **Microsoft Passport**: Passport replaces passwords with two-factor authentication that consists of an enrolled device and a Windows Hello (biometric) or PIN.

- **Windows Server Essentials Experience server role**: This role offers easy access to cloud service integration features.

While there are many other improvements and enhancements to Windows Server 2016 compared to earlier versions, this list covers many of the most exciting ones for today's network administrators.

Installation Requirements

Before you decide on deployments of those wonderful new Windows Server 2016 systems with their incredible new features, you need to pause and study the installation requirements this powerful OS demands.

Hardware Requirements

One of the key areas of concern as you are ramping up to deploy Windows Server 2016 is, of course, the hardware resources you need to have in place for a successful installation and later usage. Let us examine these requirements now.

NOTE Unless otherwise specified, these minimum system requirements apply to all installation options (Server Core, Server with Desktop Experience, and Nano Server) and both the Standard and Datacenter Editions of Windows Server 2016. Also note that these bare minimums will not be acceptable for many installations you want to perform since resource needs could increase dramatically based on your use case.

Remember that Hyper-V runs within Windows Server 2016, as do certain non-Microsoft virtualization platforms. Thus, you should also note that virtualized deployments of Windows Server 2016 must meet the same hardware specifications as those needed for physical deployments.

The Processor

Remember that your processor performance depends not only on the clock frequency of the processor but also on the number of processor cores and the size of the processor cache. Here are the strict requirements for the Windows Server 2016 processor:

- 1.4 GHz
- 64-bit processor
- Compatible with x64 instruction set
- Supports NX (No-eXecute) and DEP (Data Execution Prevention)
- Supports CMPXCHG16b, LAHF/SAHF, and PrefetchW
- Supports Second Level Address Translation (SLAT)

NOTE The simple and easy-to-use Coreinfo tool ensures that your CPU meets the preceding requirements. You can find this tool at https://technet.microsoft.com/en-us/sysinternals/cc835722.aspx.

Random Access Memory (RAM)

The following are the RAM requirements for Windows Server 2016:

- 512 MB (2 GB for Server with Desktop Experience)
- ECC (Error Correcting Code) type or similar technology

NOTE When installing on a Hyper-V virtual machine using the minimum single-processor requirement, you should allocate at least 800 MB of RAM to the VM. Following the installation, you can give less. Another workaround to this minimum RAM exception is to create a paging file in the installation partition.

Storage Controllers and Disk Space

Computers that run Windows Server 2016 must include the following:

- A storage adapter that is compliant with the PCI Express architecture specification

  32GB

- Persistent storage devices on servers classified as hard disk drives that are not PATA

- No ATA/PATA/IDE/EIDE for boot, page, or data drives

- System partition of 32 GB

Network Adapters

Network adapters used with Windows Server 2016 should include the following:

- An Ethernet adapter capable of at least gigabit throughput

- Compliance with the PCI Express architecture specification

- Preboot Execution Environment (PXE) support

Other Requirements

You should also consider these various other potential requirements:

- DVD drive (if you intend to install the operating system from DVD media)

- UEFI 2.3.1c-based system and firmware that supports secure boot

- Trusted Platform Module version 2.0 with preprovisioned EK certificate or available on first boot; SHA-256 PCR banks

- Graphics device and monitor capable of Super VGA (1024 × 768) or higher resolution

- Keyboard and mouse

- Internet access

NOTE   While you do not require a Trusted Platform Module (TPM) chip to install Windows Server 2016, it is necessary to use certain features such as BitLocker Drive Encryption on the system partition.

Windows Server 2016 Editions

(There are three primary editions of Windows Server: Datacenter, Standard, and Essentials.) You choose an edition based on the size of your organization as well as virtualization and datacenter requirements. Windows Server 2016 Datacenter includes unlimited virtualization rights plus new features to build a software-defined datacenter. Windows Server 2016 Standard offers enterprise-class features with limited virtualization rights. Windows Server 2016 Essentials is an ideal cloud-connected first server for your organization.

Table 1-2 outlines specific details you should be aware of for each edition.

Table 1-2   Characteristics of Windows Server 2016 Editions

Windows Server 2016 Datacenter Edition	Windows Server 2016 Standard Edition	Windows Server 2016 Essentials Edition
Ideal for highly virtualized and software-defined datacenter environments	Ideal for low-density or nonvirtualized environments	Ideal for small businesses with up to 25 users and 50 devices
Core-based licensing model	Core-based licensing model	Processor-based licensing model
Windows Server Client Access Licenses (CALs) needed	Windows Server CALs needed	No Windows Server CALs needed
Unlimited containers supported	A maximum of two Hyper-V containers supported	
Host Guardian and Nano Server support	Host Guardian and Nano Server support	
Advanced storage features such as Storage Spaces Direct and Storage Replica		
Shielded virtual machine support		

Installing Windows Server 2016

While there are many options for Windows Server 2016 installation, let us examine the attended installation from the ISO step by step:

Step 1.   Launch the Windows Setup executable from the DVD/ISO.

Step 2.   From the Windows Server 2016 page, select your **language**, **time format**, and **keyboard**, as shown in Figure 1-1, and then click **Next**.

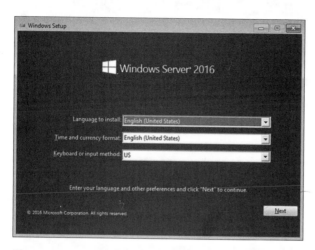

Figure 1-1   Selecting Language, Time, and Keyboard Settings

Step 3.   Click **Install Now** to begin the installation (see Figure 1-2). Note that you can also start a repair from this window.

Figure 1-2   Initiating the Installation

Step 4.   Select the desired version of the installation, as shown in Figure 1-3. Click **Next**.

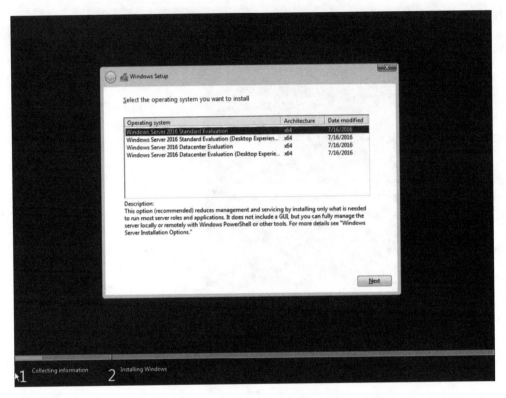

Figure 1-3   Selecting the Version of Server 2016 to Install

Step 5.   Accept the license agreement and click **Next**.

Step 6.   To perform a clean install, choose **Custom** (see Figure 1-4).

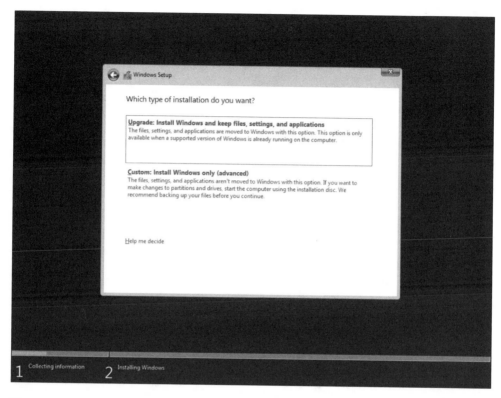

Figure 1-4   Choosing Upgrade or Custom for the Type of Installation

Step 7.   Select the partition for the installation and click **Next,** as shown in
Figure 1-5. The Installing Windows screen appears, and the system
reboots several times.

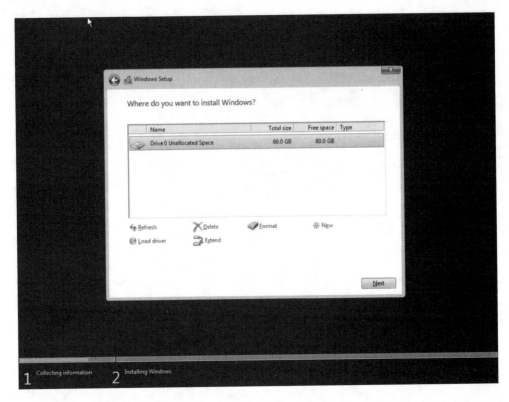

Figure 1-5   Choosing the Installation Partition

Step 8.   Set the administrator password when the installation completes.

PowerShell and Desired State Configuration (DSC)

Windows PowerShell includes a built-in tool called Desired State Configuration (DSC). You use DSC to script the intended configuration of a Windows Server. This allows the use of Windows PowerShell to not only configure a server but also restore the server settings in case "configuration drift" occurs.

You can even use automation to periodically compare a server's configuration against the desired configuration and automatically make any required changes. Because DSC is Windows PowerShell based, it can scale to manage configurations for as many servers as necessary. This is critically important if your enterprise is going to rely on many Nano Server installations in precise configurations in the datacenter.

While Microsoft had introduced this functionality previously in Windows Server 2012, it was much more cumbersome and needed more coding. In Windows Server 2016, Microsoft allows the definition of classes within PowerShell; developers can therefore produce a series of reusable DSC building blocks that they can combine to form a DSC configuration. This approach requires a minimal amount of coding.

Performing Upgrades and Migrations

Before covering the specifics of upgrades and migrations that are possible, you should review some key terms for this area:

- **Clean installation:** This refers to deleting the previous version of Windows Server before installing Windows Server 2016. Obviously, no applications or settings are kept from the previous version.

- **Migration:** This refers to moving your existing Windows Server operating system to Windows Server 2016 and hosting it on new hardware or on a new virtual machine. You can also migrate roles and features. Later in this chapter, we offer guidance on these options.

- **Cluster OS rolling upgrade:** As discussed in the "What's New in Windows Server 2016" section of this chapter, this is a new feature in Windows Server 2016 that enables you to upgrade the operating system of the cluster nodes from Windows Server 2012 R2 to Windows Server 2016 without stopping the Hyper-V or the Scale-Out File Server workloads. This feature dramatically reduces downtime you might otherwise experience.

- **License conversion:** This refers to the ability to easily convert from one edition of Windows Server 2016 to another. For example, you might convert Windows Server 2016 Standard Edition to Windows Server 2016 Datacenter Edition based on changing requirements in your environment. This also refers to converting from an evaluation edition to a retail edition.

- **Upgrade:** This refers to moving from a version of Windows Server to Windows Server 2016 on the same hardware. You can keep applications and user-configured settings in this approach.

Upgrading

Table 1-3 details the upgrade paths that are available with a licensed (non-evaluation) version of Windows Server.

Table 1-3   Upgrade Options

Current Version	Upgrade Options
Windows Server 2012 Standard	Windows Server 2016 Standard or Datacenter
Windows Server 2012 Datacenter	Windows Server 2016 Datacenter
Windows Server 2012 R2 Standard	Windows Server 2016 Standard or Datacenter
Windows Server 2012 R2 Datacenter	Windows Server 2016 Datacenter
Windows Server 2012 R2 Essentials	Windows Server 2016 Essentials
Windows Storage Server 2012 Standard	Windows Storage Server 2016 Standard
Windows Storage Server 2012 Workgroup	Windows Storage Server 2016 Workgroup
Windows Storage Server 2012 R2 Standard	Windows Storage Server 2016 Standard
Windows Storage Server 2012 R2 Workgroup	Windows Storage Server 2016 Workgroup

In addition to the upgrade paths outlined in Table 1-3, you should also be aware of the following guidelines:

- All editions of Windows Server 2016 are 64-bit only; therefore, you cannot upgrade from earlier 32-bit versions.

- You cannot upgrade from one language version to another.

- You cannot upgrade and switch from a Server Core installation to a Server with Desktop Experience installation (or vice versa).

- Direct upgrades from Windows Server 2008 are not supported; you must first upgrade to Windows Server 2012 before performing the Windows Server 2016 upgrade.

- Even if an upgrade is supported per Table 1-3, keep in mind that certain server roles might need reconfiguration to run properly in the new version.

Performing License Conversions

You can easily convert the evaluation version of Windows Server 2016 Standard to either Windows Server 2016 Standard (retail) or Datacenter (retail). You can also convert the evaluation version of Windows Server 2016 Datacenter to the retail version. Keep in mind that for this license conversion to function, you must have installed the Desktop Experience option, not the Server Core option.

Follow these steps for license conversion:

Step 1.   From an elevated command prompt, determine the current edition name with the command **DISM /online /Get-CurrentEdition.** Make note of the edition ID, an abbreviated form of the edition name.

Step 2.   Run **DISM /online /Set-Edition:<edition ID> /ProductKey:XXXXX-XXXXX-XXXXX-XXXXX-XXXXX /AcceptEula**, providing the edition ID and a retail product key. The server restarts twice.

NOTE   If the server is a domain controller, you cannot convert it to a retail version. In this case, install an additional domain controller on a server that runs a retail version and remove AD DS from the domain controller that runs on the evaluation version.

If you need to convert a current retail edition to a different current retail edition, follow these steps:

Step 1.   For Windows Server 2016 Standard, you can convert the system to Windows Server 2016 Datacenter as follows: From an elevated command prompt, determine the current edition name with the command **DISM /online /Get-CurrentEdition**.

Step 2.   Make note of the edition ID, an abbreviated form of the edition name.

Step 3.   Run **DISM /online /Set-Edition:<edition ID> /ProductKey:XXXXX-XXXXX-XXXXX-XXXXX-XXXXX /AcceptEula**, providing the edition ID and a retail product key. The server restarts twice.

At any time after installing Windows Server 2016, you can convert it between a retail version, a volume-licensed version, and an OEM version. The edition stays the same during this conversion.

Follow this simple step to perform this conversion. From an elevated command prompt, run **slmgr /ipk <key>,** where **<key>** is the appropriate volume-licensed, retail, or OEM product key.

Migrations

Table 1-4 details what server roles can migrate from Server 2012 and whether these migrations can occur without downtime.

Table 1-4 Server Role Migrations

Server Role	Downtime?
Active Directory Certificate Services	No
Active Directory Domain Services	Yes
Active Directory Federation Services	No
Active Directory Lightweight Directory Services	Yes
Active Directory Rights Management Services	No
DHCP server	Yes
DNS server	No
Failover cluster	Yes
File and storage services	No
Hyper-V	Yes
Print and Fax Services	No
Remote Desktop Services	No
Web Server (IIS)	No
Windows Server Essentials Experience	No
Windows Server Update Services	No
Work Folders	Yes

Determining the Appropriate Activation Model

Windows Server 2016 offers several activation model technologies:

- **Volume Activation Services server role**: This role enables you to automate and simplify the issuance and management of Microsoft software volume licenses for a variety of scenarios and environments. With the Volume Activation Services role, you can install and configure the Key Management Service (KMS) and enable Active Directory-based Activation.

- **Automatic Virtual Machine Activation (AVMA)**: This technology allows you to install virtual machines on a properly activated Windows server without having to manage product keys for each individual virtual machine, even in disconnected environments. The virtual machine activates and continues to work even when it is migrated across an array of virtualization servers. This provides benefits such as activating virtual machines in remote locations; activating virtual machines with or without an Internet connection; and tracking virtual machine usage and licenses from the virtualization server, without requiring any access rights on the virtualized systems.

- **Key Management Service (KMS)**: This role service allows you to activate systems in your network from a server where you have installed a KMS host. With KMS, you can complete activations on the local network, which means you do not need individual computers to connect to Microsoft for product activation. By default, volume editions of Windows clients and server operating systems connect to a system that hosts KMS to request activation. No action is needed from the end user.

- **Active Directory-based Activation**: This role service allows you to use Active Directory Domain Services (AD DS) to store activation objects, which can further simplify the task of supporting volume activation services for a network. With Active Directory-based Activation, no added host server is needed, and activation requests are processed during computer startup. Any computers running a client or server operating system with a Generic Volume License Key (GVLK) that connect to the domain activate automatically and transparently. They stay activated if they stay members of the domain and maintain periodic contact with a domain controller. Activation takes place after the licensing service starts.

Exam Preparation Tasks

As mentioned in the section "How to Use This Book" in the Introduction, you have a couple choices for exam preparation: the exercises here, Chapter 21, "Final Preparation," and the exam simulation questions in the Pearson Test Prep Software Online.

Review All Key Topics

Review the most important topics in this chapter, noted with the Key Topics icon in the outer margin of the page. Table 1-5 lists these key topics and the page number on which each is found.

Table 1-5 Key Topics for Chapter 1

Key Topic Element	Description	Page Number
List	Processor requirements for Windows Server 2016	8
List	RAM requirements for Windows Server 2016	8
Table 1-2	Characteristics of Windows Server 2016 editions	10
List	Upgrade and migration terms	15
List	Additional upgrade considerations	16
List	Activation technology options	18

Complete Tables and Lists from Memory

Print a copy of Appendix B, "Memory Tables" (found on the book website), or at least the section for this chapter, and complete the tables and lists from memory. Appendix C, "Memory Tables Answer Key," also on the website, includes completed tables and lists you can use to check your work.

Define Key Terms

Define the following key terms from this chapter and check your answers against the glossary:

Server Core, Server with Desktop Experience, Nano Server, Datacenter, Standard, Essentials, PowerShell and Desired State Configuration (DSC), Volume Activation Services server role, Automatic Virtual Machine Activation, Key Management Service (KMS), Active Directory-based Activation

Q&A

The answers to these questions appear in Appendix A. For more practice with exam format questions, use the Pearson Test Prep Software Online.

1. What is the term for running Hyper-V virtual machines within a virtual machine?

2. What system partition size is required for Windows Server 2016?

3. What edition of Server 2016 supports a maximum of two Hyper-V containers?

4. What two options are provided in the Type of Installation window during Windows Server 2016 installation?

5. What is the term for easily converting from Standard Edition to Datacenter Edition?

6. What two types of activation technology involve a Generic Volume License Key (GVLK)?

This chapter covers the following subjects:

- **Determining Appropriate Usage Scenarios:** Nano Server is certainly unlike any other version of Windows Server ever created. This section studies ideal scenarios for this version per Microsoft.

- **Requirements for Nano Server**: This section ensures that you have the correct hardware in place for your Nano Server installation.

- **Installing Nano Server**: This section guides you through the simple installation process for Nano Server.

- **Implementing Roles and Features on Nano Server**: This area ensures that you can easily install different roles and features in Nano Server to get the most from your implementation.

- **Managing and Configuring Nano Server**: This part of the chapter covers the management and configuration of Nano Server.

- **Managing Nano Server Remotely Using Windows PowerShell**: This section ensures that you can manage your Nano Server from anywhere, using Windows PowerShell. Because Nano Server lacks a user interface, this section is quite critical.

## CHAPTER 2

Installing and Configuring Nano

One of the most exciting new features in Windows Server 2016 is, without a doubt, Nano Server. This chapter helps you get up and running with this ultra-lightweight version of Server quickly and efficiently. It also ensures that you can manage and configure Windows Server 2016 in the Nano Server deployment model.

"Do I Know This Already?" Quiz

The "Do I Know This Already?" quiz allows you to assess whether you should read the entire chapter. Table 2-1 lists the major headings in this chapter and the "Do I Know This Already?" quiz questions covering the material in those headings so you can assess your knowledge of these specific areas. The answers to the "Do I Know This Already?" quiz appear in Appendix A, "Answers to the 'Do I Know This Already?' Quizzes and Q&A Questions."

Table 2-1 "Do I Know This Already?" Foundation Topics Section-to-Question Mapping

Foundation Topics Section	Questions
Determining Appropriate Usage Scenarios	1
Requirements for Nano Server	2, 3
Installing Nano Server	4, 5
Implementing Roles and Features on Nano Server	6
Managing and Configuring Nano Server	7, 8
Managing Nano Server Remotely Using Windows PowerShell	9, 10

CAUTION The goal of self-assessment is to gauge your mastery of the topics in this chapter. If you do not know the answer to a question or are only partially sure of the answer, you should mark your answer as incorrect for purposes of the self-assessment. Giving yourself credit for an answer you correctly guess skews your self-assessment results and might provide you with a false sense of security.

1. Which of the following would not be a typical use case scenario for Nano Server?

    a. As a storage host for a Scale-Out File Server

    b. As a DNS server

    c. As a web server running Internet Information Services (IIS)

    d. As an Active Directory domain controller

2. What is the minimum RAM requirement for Nano Server?

    a. 4 GB

    b. 512 MB

    c. 1 GB

    d. 2 GB

3. What is the footprint of the VHD for Nano Server Datacenter Edition?

    a. 1 GB

    b. 2.4 GB

    c. 4.6 GB

    d. 509 MB

4. What PowerShell command do you use to create the Nano Server VHD?

    a. **Fetch-NanoServerImage**

    b. **New-NanoServerImage**

    c. **Create-NanoServerImage**

    d. **VHD-NanoServerImage**

5. What do you connect to in Hyper-V when you connect to and start Nano Server?

    a. Recovery Console

    b. Server Manager

    c. Nano Desktop

    d. Nano PowerShell ISE

6. How do you add a service package to Nano Server?

    a. -Add

    b. -Install

    c. -ServicingPackagePath

    d. -Package

7. Which of the following is not an option for Nano Server management?

    a. Terminal Services

    b. Windows Management Instrumentation (WMI)

    c. Windows Remote Management

    d. Emergency Management Services (EMS)

8. From what section of the Recovery Console can you find the IP address?

    a. Networking

    b. Addressing

    c. Management

    d. Remote Control

9. Why might you not need to add your management station to the list of trusted hosts?

    a. You are in the same AD Forest.

    b. Your system is not part of a domain.

    c. You are logged in as the Nano Server admin.

    d. The trusted host feature is never required.

10. What command allows you to end a remote session with Nano Server?

    a. Quit-PSSession

    b. End-PSSession

    c. Kill-PSSession

    d. Exit-PSSession

Foundation Topics

Determining Appropriate Usage Scenarios

Nano Server is a purpose-built OS from Microsoft that is headless—which means no user interface! Specifically, Nano Server is a remotely administered server operating system perfected for private clouds and datacenters.

This might confuse you. Surely this is the job of Windows Server in Server Core mode? Nano Server is unique, offering the following features that Server Core mode cannot compete with:

- Nano Server is significantly smaller than Server Core mode

- Nano Server has no local logon capability

- Nano Server only supports 64-bit applications, tools, and agents

- Nano Server needs little disk space

- You can build Nano Server significantly faster than any other version of Server

- Nano Server needs far fewer updates and restarts than any other version of Windows Server

- Nano Server restarts faster than any other Microsoft OS

Nano Server is ideal for several different usage scenarios:

- As a compute host for Hyper-V virtual machines (clustering is possible when needed)

- As a storage host for a Scale-Out File Server

- As a DNS server

- As a web server running Internet Information Services (IIS)

- As a host for applications that you or your team develop using cloud application patterns and that run in a container or virtual machine guest operating system

Requirements for Nano Server

The Nano Server installation option is available for Standard and Datacenter Editions of Windows Server 2016.

Hardware Requirements

Nano Server needs the same hardware as other versions of Server 2016, although the minimum requirements become amazingly slight for the small footprint and requirements of Nano.

The Processor

Processor requirements are as follows:

- 1.4 GHz

- 64-bit processor

- Compatible with x64 instruction set

- Supports NX (No-eXecute) and DEP (Data Execution Prevention)

- Supports CMPXCHG16b, LAHF/SAHF, and PrefetchW

- Supports Second Level Address Translation (SLAT)

NOTE   The simple and easy-to-use Coreinfo tool ensures that your CPU meets the preceding requirements. You can find this tool at https://technet.microsoft.com/en-us/sysinternals/cc835722.aspx.

RAM (Random Access Memory)

The following are the RAM requirements for Nano Server:

- 512 MB

- ECC (Error Correcting Code) type or similar technology

Storage Controllers and Disk Space

Computers that run Nano Server must include the following:

- Storage adapter that is compliant with the PCI Express architecture specification

- Persistent storage devices on servers classified as hard disk drives that are not PATA

- No ATA/PATA/IDE/EIDE for boot, page, or data drives

- A small storage space area for the Nano Server footprint; for example, the VHD is just 509 MB in size

Remember these important distinctions with Nano Server, some of which we mentioned earlier in this chapter:

- Nano Server is headless; there is no local logon capability or graphical user interface (GUI).

- Nano Server only supports 64-bit applications, tools, and agents.

- Nano Server cannot serve as an Active Directory domain controller.

- Nano Server does not support Group Policy; Desired State Configuration can apply settings to scale.

- You cannot configure Nano Server to use a proxy server to access the Internet.

- You cannot configure Nano Server for NIC Teaming (load balancing and failover).

- Nano Server does support Switch Embedded Teaming (SET).

- There is no support for System Center Configuration Manager and System Center Data Protection Manager.

- The version of Windows PowerShell offered with Nano Server is unique in important ways. We elaborate on this more later in the chapter.

- Nano Server uses the Current Branch for Business (CBB) model only.

Installing Nano Server

You can download an EXE from the TechNet Evaluation Center that extracts the Datacenter Nano VHD to a location of your choosing.

You can also manually create Nano Server in a virtual machine using these steps:

Step 1.   Copy the **NanoServerImageGenerator** folder from the \NanoServer folder in the Windows Server 2016 ISO to a folder on your hard drive.

Step 2.   Start Windows PowerShell as an administrator, change the directory to the folder where you have placed the **NanoServerImage-Generator** folder, and then import the module with **Import-Module .\NanoServerImageGenerator -Verbose.** Here is the complete syntax for the **Import-Module** cmdlet:

```
Import-Module [-Global] [-Prefix <String>] [-Name] <String[]>
   [-Function <String[]>] [-Cmdlet <String[]>]

[-Variable <String[]>] [-Alias <String[]>] [-Force]
   [-PassThru] [-AsCustomObject] [-MinimumVersion <Version>]

[-MaximumVersion <String>] [-RequiredVersion <Version>]
   [-ArgumentList <Object[]>] [-DisableNameChecking]

[-NoClobber] [-Scope <String>] [<CommonParameters>]
```

Step 3.   Create a VHD for the Standard Edition that sets a computer name and includes the Hyper-V guest drivers by running the following command, which prompts you for an administrator password for the new VHD: **New-NanoServerImage -Edition Standard -DeploymentType Guest -MediaPath <path to root of media> -BasePath .\Base -TargetPath .\NanoServerVM\NanoServerVM.vhd -Computer-Name <computer name>.**

  - **-MediaPath**: Specifies a path to the root of the contents of the Windows Server 2016 ISO; for example, if you have copied the contents of the ISO to d:\NANO, you use that path.

  - **-BasePath** (optional): Specifies a folder that will be created to copy the Nano Server WIM and packages to.

  - **-TargetPath**: Specifies a path, including the filename and extension, where the resulting VHD or VHDX is created.

  - **-ComputerName**: Specifies the computer name for the Nano Server virtual machine.

Here is the complete syntax of this command, followed by an example:

```
New-NanoServerImage [-DeploymentType] <String> {Host | Guest}
  [-Edition] <String> {Standard | Datacenter} -AdministratorPassword
  <SecureString> -TargetPath <String> [-BasePath <String> ]
  [-Clustering] [-Compute] [-ComputerName <String> ] [-Containers]
[-CopyFiles <String[]> ] [-DebugMethod <String> {Serial | Net
  | 1394 | USB} ] [-Defender] [-Development] [-DomainBlobPath
  <String> ] [-DomainName <String> ] [-DriversPath <String> ]
  [-EMSBaudRate <UInt32> ] [-EMSPort <Byte> ] [-EnableEMS]
  [-EnableRemoteManagementPort] [-InterfaceNameOrIndex <String> ]
  [-Ipv4Address <String> ] [-Ipv4Dns <String[]> ] [-Ipv4Gateway
  <String> ] [-Ipv4SubnetMask <String> ] [-Ipv6Address <String> ]
  [-Ipv6Dns <String[]> ] [-MaxSize <UInt64> ] [-MediaPath <String> ]
  [-OEMDrivers] [-Packages <String[]> ] [-RamdiskBoot]
  [-ReuseDomainNode] [-ServicingPackages <String[]> ]
  [-SetupCompleteCommands <String[]> ] [-Storage] [-UnattendPath
  <String> ] [ <CommonParameters>]
```

```
New-NanoServerImage -Edition Standard -DeploymentType Guest
  -MediaPath f:\ -BasePath .\Base -TargetPath .\Nano1\Nano.vhd
  -ComputerName MyNano1
```

Notice that this example creates a VHD from an ISO mounted as f:\. When creating the VHD, it uses a folder called Base in the same directory where you ran **New-NanoServerImage**. It places the VHD (called Nano.vhd) in a folder called Nano1 in the folder from where the command is run. The computer name is MyNano1. The resulting VHD contains the Standard Edition of Windows Server 2016 and is suitable for Hyper-V virtual machine deployment. If you want

a Generation 1 virtual machine, create a VHD image by specifying a .vhd extension for **-TargetPath**. For a Generation 2 virtual machine, create a VHDX image
by specifying a .vhdx extension for **-TargetPath**. You can also directly generate a
WIM file by specifying a .wim extension for **-TargetPath**.

When you have the VHD, you can create a virtual machine, as shown in the following steps:

Step 1. Launch **Hyper-V Manager**, shown in Figure 2-1.

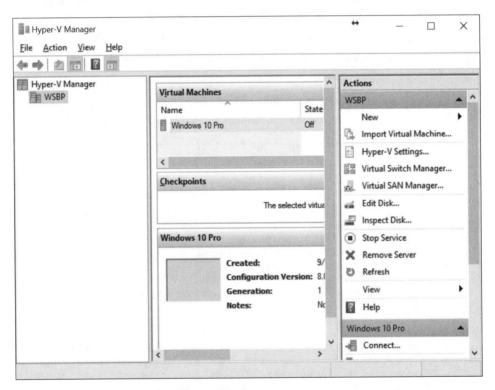

Figure 2-1   The Hyper-V Manager for the Nano Server Installation

Step 2.   In the **Specify Name and Location** window, name your server and specify where you want the virtual machine to be stored (see Figure 2-2).

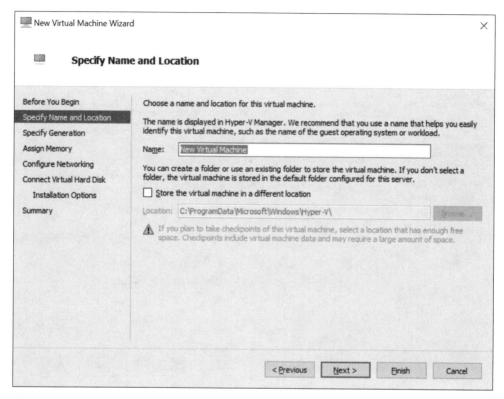

Figure 2-2   Choosing the Name and Location of the Virtual Machine

Step 3.   Choose the generation of virtual machine you want to build from the
Specify Generation window.

Step 4.   Specify the amount of virtual memory you want assigned to your VM in the **Assign Memory** window (see Figure 2-3).

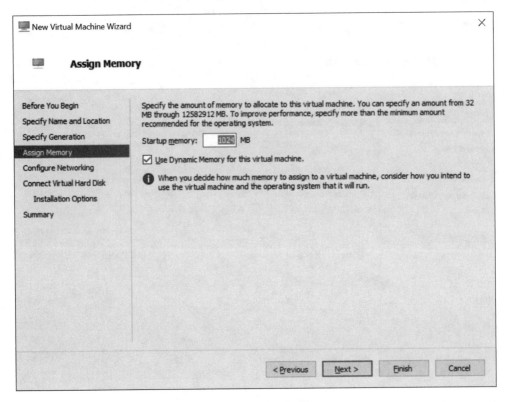

Figure 2-3   Assigning Virtual Memory to the Virtual Machine

Step 5.   In the **Configure Networking** window, select a virtual switch for the virtual machine to use.

Step 6.   In the **Connect Virtual Hard Disk** window (see Figure 2-4), select the **Use an existing virtual hard disk** option and navigate to the **VHD** or **VHDX** you downloaded or created.

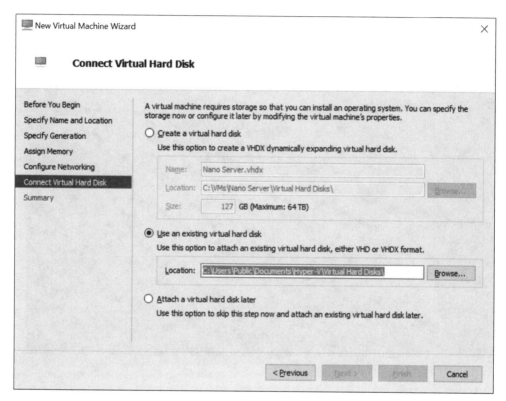

Figure 2-4   Selecting the VHD or VHDX

Step 7.   Review the options you have selected and click **Next** and then **Finish.**

Step 8.   Boot the virtual machine and use Hyper-V Manager to connect to it.

Step 9. Log on to the Recovery Console (see Figure 2-5), using the administrator and password you supplied while running the script to generate your virtual machine.

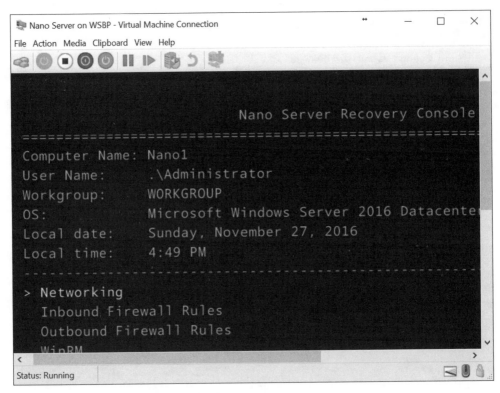

Figure 2-5 The Recovery Console of Nano Server

Step 10. Obtain the IP address of the Nano Server virtual machine and use Windows PowerShell remoting or another remote management tool to connect to and remotely manage the virtual machine.

Of course, installing on a physical machine is also possible. Follow these steps:

Step 1. Copy the NanoServerImageGenerator folder from the \NanoServer folder in the Windows Server 2016 ISO to a folder on your hard drive.

Step 2. Start Windows PowerShell as an administrator, change directory to the folder where you have placed the NanoServerImageGenerator folder, and then import the module with **Import-Module .\ NanoServerImageGenerator -Verbose**.

Step 3. Create a VHD that sets a computer name and includes the OEM drivers and Hyper-V by running the following command, which prompts you for an administrator password for the new VHD: **New-NanoServerImage -Edition Standard -DeploymentType Host -MediaPath <path to root of media> -BasePath .\Base -TargetPath .\ NanoServerPhysical\NanoServer.vhd -ComputerName <computer name> -OEMDrivers -Compute -Clustering**. (For specifics on this command, see step 3 under "Installing Nano Server.")

Step 4. Log in as an administrator on the physical server where you want to run the Nano Server VHD.

Step 5. Copy the VHD that the script creates to the physical computer and configure it to boot from this new VHD; mount the generated VHD (for example **bcdboot d:\windows**).

Step 6. Unmount the VHD.

Step 7. Boot the physical computer into the Nano Server VHD.

Step 8. Log on to the Recovery Console using the administrator and password you supplied while running the script.

Step 9. Obtain the IP address of the Nano Server computer and use Windows PowerShell remoting or another remote management tool to connect to and remotely manage the virtual machine.

Implementing Roles and Features on Nano Server

Remember that because Nano Server is headless, this exam objective can be a bit misleading. You do not add roles and features as you typically would in Server 2016. Instead, you add features through the creation of the server image.

For example, here is how you add Windows Defender as well as Internet Information Server capabilities to the Nano Server in PowerShell:

```
New-NanoServerImage -MediaPath 'D:\' -TargetPath .\mynano.vhd
  -Edition Datacenter -DeploymentType Guest -ComputerName MYNANOIIS
  -AdministratorPassword P@$$w0rd -EnableRemoteManagementPort
  -Defender -Packages 'Microsoft-NanoServer-IIS-Package'
```

You can browse the available packages in the Nano Server–Packages directory of the ISO. You can also use the Get-Package cmdlet in order to confirm what capabilities have been installed in a Nano Server.

If you want to install a servicing package, use the -ServicingPackagePath parameter (passing an array of paths to .cab files if desired), as in this example:

```
New-NanoServerImage -DeploymentType Guest -Edition Standard
  -MediaPath \\Path\To\Media\en_us -BasePath .\Base -TargetPath .\
  NanoServer.wim -ServicingPackagePath \\path\to\kb123456.cab
```

Managing and Configuring Nano Server

Remember that you manage Nano remotely, and there is no local logon capability with this ultra-lightweight version of server. Nano Server does not even support Terminal Services!

Fortunately, there are a wide variety of options for managing Nano Server from a remote workstation, including the following:

- Windows PowerShell

- Windows Management Instrumentation (WMI)

- Windows Remote Management

- Emergency Management Services (EMS)

As you learned in the "Installing Nano Server" section of this chapter, it is critical to obtain the IP address of your Nano Server following installation so that you can use the listed options for management. There are several methods for finding the IP address of your Nano Server:

- Use the Nano Recovery Console to obtain the address; you find this in the Networking section, under the adapter you are using.

- Connect a serial cable to the system and use EMS.

- Use the following command with the computer name you created: **ping MYNANOIIS /4**.

Managing Nano Server Remotely Using Windows PowerShell

Before diving in to Nano Server management using PowerShell, be aware that Nano Server does not support the following features:

- ADSI, ADO, and WMI type adapters

- **Enable-PSRemoting, Disable-PSRemoting**

- Scheduled jobs and **PSScheduledJob** module

- Computer cmdlets for joining a domain { **Add** | **Remove** }

- **Reset-ComputerMachinePassword, Test-ComputerSecureChannel**

- Profiles

- Clipboard cmdlets

- **EventLog** cmdlets { **Clear** | **Get** | **Limit** | **New** | **Remove** | **Show** | **Write** }

- **Get-PfxCertificate** cmdlet

- **TraceSource** cmdlets { **Get** | **Set** }

- **Counter** cmdlets { **Get** | **Export** | **Import** }

- Some web-related cmdlets { **New-WebServiceProxy**, **Send-MailMessage**, **ConvertTo-Html** }

- Logging and tracing using **PSDiagnostics** module

- **Get-HotFix**

- Implicit remoting cmdlets { **Export-PSSession** | **Import-PSSession** }

- **New-PSTransportOption**

- PowerShell transactions and **Transaction** cmdlets { **Complete** | **Get** | **Start** | **Undo** | **Use** }

- PowerShell Workflow infrastructure, modules, and cmdlets

- **Out-Printer**

- **Update-List**

- WMI v1 cmdlets: **Get-WmiObject**, **Invoke-WmiMethod**, **Register-WmiEvent**, **Remove-WmiObject**, **Set-WmiInstance**

Microsoft omitted many of these options to help keep the image small and the attack surface even smaller for this nimble Windows Server version.

Use the techniques listed in the "Managing and Configuring Nano Server" section of this chapter to obtain the IP address of your Nano Server and then follow these steps:

Step 1.   Add the IP address of the Nano Server to your management computer's list of trusted hosts; if the target Nano Server and your management computer are in the same AD DS forest (or in forests with a trust relationship), you should not add the Nano Server to the trusted hosts list. You can connect to the Nano Server by using its fully qualified domain name—for example, **PS C:> Enter-PSSession -ComputerName nanoserver.pearsonitcertification.com -Credential (Get-Credential).**

Step 2.   Add the account you are using to the Nano Server's administrators.

Step 3.   Enable CredSSP if you plan to use that feature.

To add Nano Server to the list of trusted hosts, run this command at an elevated PowerShell prompt:

```
Set-Item WSMan:\localhost\Client\TrustedHosts "<IP address of Nano
    Server>"
```

To start the remote PowerShell session, run the following commands from an elevated PowerShell session:

```
$ip = "\<IP address of Nano Server>"
$user = "$ip\Administrator"
Enter-PSSession -ComputerName $ip -Credential $user
```

When you are ready to exit the session, use **Exit-PSSession.**

Exam Preparation Tasks

As mentioned in the section "How to Use This Book" in the Introduction, you have a couple choices for exam preparation: the exercises here, Chapter 21, "Final Preparation," and the exam simulation questions in the Pearson Test Prep Software Online.

Review All Key Topics

Review the most important topics in this chapter, noted with the Key Topics icon in the outer margin of the page. Table 2-2 lists these key topics and the page number on which each is found.

Table 2-2 Key Topics for Chapter 2

Key Topic Element	Description	Page Number
List	Nano Server usage scenarios	26
List	Processor requirements for Nano Server	27
List	RAM requirements for Nano Server	27
List	Installing Nano Server	28
Command	Adding features to Nano Server	35
List	Remote management options for Nano Server	36
List	Steps for remote PowerShell management of Nano Server	37

Complete Tables and Lists from Memory

This chapter does not have any memory tables.

Define Key Terms

Define the following key terms from this chapter and check your answers against the glossary:

Nano Server, Second Level Address Translation, Headless, NIC Teaming, VHD

Q&A   *Answer these*

The answers to these questions appear in Appendix A. For more practice with exam format questions, use the Pearson Test Prep Software Online.

1. Name at least three usage scenarios for Nano Server.

2. Name at least three important distinctions for Nano Server.

3. What extension is used for a Generation 2 virtual machine image? *VHDX*

4. What parameter installs Windows Defender in Nano Server?

5. Name four options for management of Nano Server.

6. What three steps are used for remote management through PowerShell?

This chapter covers the following subjects:

- **Planning for Windows Server Virtualization:** Deploying Windows Server 2016 in a virtualized environment can entail more planning than in traditional environments. This section walks you through the many considerations for a virtualized datacenter.

- **The Microsoft Assessment and Planning (MAP) Toolkit**: This section details a powerful tool from Microsoft that can help you in planning a heavily virtualized datacenter environment.

- **Considerations for Deploying Workloads into Virtualized Environments**: Creating a successful virtualized datacenter involves many considerations. This section provides valuable guidance on the many aspects involved.

- **Updating Images with Patches, Hotfixes, and Drivers:** Are you familiar with the Deployment Image Servicing and Management (DISM) tool? You should be. This section describes how easy it is to update images with valuable components.

- **Installing Roles and Features in Offline Images**: This section describes how to use DISM to change features of offline images.

- **Managing and Maintaining Windows Server Core, Nano Server Images, and VHDs Using Windows PowerShell**: PowerShell Direct makes management of images a snap. This section describes the process.

## CHAPTER 3

Working with Images

Microsoft continues to enhance Windows Server in many ways for the virtualized world. This chapter focuses on that aspect of the popular server-based OS.

"Do I Know This Already?" Quiz

The "Do I Know This Already?" quiz allows you to assess whether you should read the entire chapter. Table 3-1 lists the major headings in this chapter and the "Do I Know This Already?" quiz questions covering the material in those headings so you can assess your knowledge of these specific areas. The answers to the "Do I Know This Already?" quiz appear in Appendix A, "Answers to the 'Do I Know This Already?' Quizzes and Q&A Questions."

Table 3-1 "Do I Know This Already?" Foundation Topics Section-to-Question Mapping

Foundation Topics Section	Questions
Planning for Windows Server Virtualization	1, 2, 3
The Microsoft Assessment and Planning (MAP) Toolkit	4
Considerations for Deploying Workloads into Virtualized Environments	5, 6, 7
Updating Images with Patches, Hotfixes, and Drivers	8
Installing Roles and Features in Offline Images	9
Managing and Maintaining Windows Server Core, Nano Server Images, and VHDs using Windows PowerShell	10

CAUTION The goal of self-assessment is to gauge your mastery of the topics in this chapter. If you do not know the answer to a question or are only partially sure of the answer, you should mark your answer as incorrect for purposes of the self-assessment. Giving yourself credit for an answer you correctly guess skews your self-assessment results and might provide you with a false sense of security.

1. What Windows OS is not Generation 2 capable?

    a. Windows 10

    b. Server 2008

    c. Windows 8

    d. Server 2012

2. What virtual switch does not offer networking between the host and the virtual machine?

    a. Internal

    b. External

    c. Distributed Virtual Switch

    d. Private

3. What is the memory maximum for a Windows Server 2016 Hyper-V host?

    a. 10 TB

    b. 5 TB

    c. 24 TB

    d. 1 TB

4. Which is not a common Hyper-V report in MAP?

    a. Server Consolidation Report

    b. VM Memory Utilization Report

    c. VMware Discovery Report

    d. Microsoft Workload Discovery

5. What is the term for a VM if it writes no unique information to the local hard disk after it is initially provisioned and assigned a unique computer name and address?

    a. Headless

    b. Stateful

    c. Stateless

    d. Classful

6. Why might a VM not perform well in a virtualized environment? Choose two.

    (a) It needs physical access to peripherals.

    b. It requires consistent network access.

    c. It requires static RAM assignments.

    (d.) It has massive resource requirements.

7. Which is not a typical concern when planning for the virtualization architecture?

    a. Reserve capacity

    b. Maintenance domains

    (c.) Networking stack

    d. Physical fault domains

8. What tool allows simple updating of images with drivers?

    (a) DISM

    b. MAP

    c. SYSMAN

    d. sysprep

9. What option permits you to obtain the index number for an image?

    a. Get-Index

    b. Get-Name

    (c.) Get-ImageInfo

    d. Get-ID

10. What options exist for PowerShell Direct? Choose two.

    (a) PSSession cmdlets

    b. DISM

    c. sysprep

    (d.) Invoke-Command

Foundation Topics

Planning for Windows Server Virtualization

Virtualization is a commonality in information technology today, and it just keeps getting hotter and more pervasive. Virtualization is appearing in about every facet of IT. This chapter focuses on the concept of server virtualization. Here are just some of the reasons that server virtualization technologies are taking the world by storm:

- **Lack of hardware driver issues:** Drivers for hardware can be some of the most frustrating aspects for datacenter administrators; virtualization of servers nearly ends this concern.

- **Environmental factors:** A heavy dose of virtualization in a datacenter results in smaller physical space, lower power costs, and reduced cooling requirements—if you implement server virtualization properly, of course.

- **Resource allocation:** Virtualization makes it easy to distribute resources like memory and CPU power to virtual machines that need it as workloads and demands change.

- **Ease of server provisioning:** Server virtualization makes deploying new servers a simple task, often as simple as clicking a few buttons.

- **Operational efficiency:** It is amazing to see (even with the naked eye) server performance on very small amounts of virtualized memory, storage, and CPU.

- **Increased availability:** Virtualization technologies like Live Migration (which this text covers in detail) allow never-before-achieved levels of availability and reliability for server workloads.

- **Reduced maintenance:** With physical hosts accommodating many virtual machines, your maintenance costs and maintenance windows for the physical hosts reduce dramatically.

- **Improved disaster recovery:** This text covers technologies that enable entire datacenters to fail over in different geographic locations, making disaster recovery more effective than ever before.

- **Lab testing:** Building a pilot or a prototype is easy, thanks to server virtualization.

- **Siloed applications:** Creating virtual machines for certain applications is simple and cost-effective in a virtualized world.

- **Cloud integration:** Virtualized workloads are very simple to move off premises to cloud locations; these can be private, public, or hybrid clouds. Tools even exist now to make integration between cloud providers simple and efficient.

There are many potential decisions you should plan for before launching a virtualized datacenter. The following sections review many of these key concerns.

Generation 1 Versus Generation 2 Virtual Machines

You should always try and create the feature-rich Generation 2 virtual machines, which benefit from many new and improved features, including Secure Boot and larger boot volumes. However, Generation 2 virtual machines might not work in your deployment. Any of these factors could force you into a Generation 1 choice:

- The VHD for boot is not UEFI compatible.

- The virtual machine is to be migrated to Azure.

- Your OS for the VM does not support Generation 2.

- Generation 2 does not support your boot method; Gen 2 supports PXE boot using a standard adapter and boot from a SCSI virtual hard disk (.VHDX) or virtual DVD (.ISO).

> **NOTE**   Remember that you cannot switch between Generation 1 and Generation 2 after creation. Remember also that Generation 2 requires a 64-bit OS.

Table 3-2 shows the supported 64-bit Windows operating systems for Generation 2.

Table 3-2   Windows Generation 2 Support

64-Bit Windows Version	Generation 2 Support?
Windows Server 2012 R2	Yes
Windows Server 2012	Yes
Windows Server 2008 R2	No
Windows Server 2008	No
Windows 10	Yes
Windows 8.1	Yes
Windows 8	Yes
Windows 7	No

Table 3-3 shows other supported 64-bit operating systems.

Table 3-3 Other Generation 2 Supported Operating Systems

Other 64-Bit OS	Generation 2 Support?
RHEL/CentOS 7.x series	Yes
RHEL/CentOS 6.x series	No
RHEL/CentOS 5.x series	No
Debian 7.x series	No
Debian 8.x series	Yes
FreeBSD 10 and 10.1	No
FreeBSD 9.1 and 9.3	No
FreeBSD 8.4	No
Oracle Linux 7.x series	Yes
Oracle Linux 6.x series	No
Oracle Linux UEK R3 QU3	No
Oracle Linux UEK R3 QU2	No
Oracle Linux UEK R3 QU1	No
Oracle Linux UEK R4	Yes
SUSE Linux Enterprise Server 12 series	Yes
SUSE Linux Enterprise Server 11 series	No
Open SUSE 12.3	No
Ubuntu 14.04 and later versions	Yes
Ubuntu 12.04	No

Networking

To network the VM in Hyper-V, you use a virtual network adapter and a virtual switch. Here are the options of which you should be aware:

- **External virtual switch**: Connects to a wired physical network through a physical adapter

- **Internal virtual switch**: Connects to a network that can be used only by the virtual machines running on the host that has the virtual switch; also, offers a communication path between the host and the virtual machines

- **Private virtual switch**: Connects to a network that can be used only by the virtual machines running on the host that has the virtual switch; does not allow networking between the host and the virtual machines

- **Hyper-V-specific network adapter**: Recommended and supported for Generation 1 and Generation 2 VMs

- **Legacy network adapter**: Available only for Generation 1 VMs; emulates an Intel 21140-based PCI Fast Ethernet Adapter and can be used to boot to a network so you can install an operating system from a service such as Windows Deployment Services

Scalability

Hyper-V is now much more scalable than ever before, as shown in Table 3-4 and Table 3-5.

Table 3-4   Maximums for Virtual Machines

Component	Maximum
Checkpoints	50
Memory	12 TB G2; 1 TB G1
Serial (COM) ports	2
Size of physical disks	Varies by guest OS
Virtual Fibre Channel adapters	4
Virtual floppy devices	1
Virtual hard disk capacity	64 TB for VDHx; 2040 GB for VHD
Virtual IDE disks	4
Virtual processors	240 G2; 64 G1
Virtual SCSI controllers	4
Virtual SCSI disks	256
Virtual network adapters	12: 8 Hyper-V and 4 legacy

Table 3-5   Maximums for Hyper-V Hosts

Component	Maximum
Logical processors	512
Memory	24 TB
Network adapter teams (NIC Teaming)	No limit
Physical network adapters	No limit

Component	Maximum
Running virtual machines per server	1024
Storage	Varies by host OS
Virtual network switch ports per server	No limit
Virtual processors per logical processor	No limit
Virtual processors per server	2048
Virtual storage area networks (SANs)	No limit
Virtual switches	No limit

Security

Security in a virtualization environment needs a two-pronged approach. You must secure the Hyper-V host as well as the virtual machines.

The following are best practices for securing a Hyper-V host:

- Keep the host OS secure.
- Minimize the attack surface by limiting the use of the host workstation.
- Keep the Hyper-V host operating system, firmware, and device drivers up to date with the latest security updates.
- Remotely manage the Hyper-V host.
- Enable code integrity policies.
- Use a secure network; consider using a separate network.
- Secure storage migration traffic.
- Configure hosts to be part of a guarded fabric.
- Secure devices.
- Secure the hard drive.
- Harden the Hyper-V host operating system.
- Grant proper permissions.
- Add users that need to manage the Hyper-V host to the Hyper-V administrators group.
- Do not grant virtual machine administrators permissions on the Hyper-V host operating system.
- Configure antivirus exclusions and options for Hyper-V.

- Do not mount unknown VHDs.

- Do not enable nesting in your production environment unless it is required.

- For very high-security environments, use hardware with a Trusted Platform Module (TPM) 2.0 chip to set up a guarded fabric.

The following are best practices for securing virtual machines:

- Create Generation 2 virtual machines for supported guest operating systems.

- Enable Secure Boot.

- Keep the guest OS secure.

- Install the latest security updates.

- Install integration services for the supported guest operating systems.

- Harden the operating system that runs in each virtual machine.

- Use a secure network.

- Store virtual hard disks and snapshot files in a secure location.

- Secure devices.

- Configure antivirus, firewall, and intrusion detection software in virtual machines as appropriate.

- Enable virtualization-based security for guests that run Windows 10 or Windows Server 2016.

- Enable Discrete Device Assignment only if needed for a specific workload.

- For very high-security environments, deploy virtual machines with shielding enabled and deploy them to a guarded fabric.

The Microsoft Assessment and Planning (MAP) Toolkit

The Microsoft Assessment and Planning (MAP) Toolkit is an agentless, automated, multi-product planning and assessment tool. We bring it up in this chapter because it can help you with quicker and easier desktop, server, and cloud migrations, especially in virtualized environments.

The MAP Toolkit provides detailed readiness assessment reports and executive proposals with extensive hardware and software information. It also offers actionable recommendations to help you accelerate your IT infrastructure planning process. It enables you to gather more details on assets in the current environment.

The MAP Toolkit provides server utilization data for Hyper-V server virtualization planning. With it, you can identify server placements and perform virtualization candidate assessments with relative ease.

The MAP Toolkit includes the following components:

- **MAPSetup.exe**: The installation package, which has the tool itself and the SQL LocalDB that helps power the tool

- **readme_en.htm**: Gives information to read before installing the MAP Toolkit, including installation prerequisites, and known issues

- **MAP_Sample_Documents.zip**: Has sample reports and proposals

- **MAP_Training_Kit.zip**: Holds a sample database and instructions for completing various exercises

You should be aware of the following specific reports around Hyper-V:

- **Server Consolidation Report**: Offers a detailed inventory of the Windows Server and Linux servers on the network and the potential efficiency gained by combining them into fewer physical servers using Hyper-V

- **VMware Discovery Report**: Shows virtualized servers running under VMware that can be managed with the Microsoft System Center Virtual Machine Manager platform or migrated to Hyper-V hypervisor

- **Microsoft Workload Discovery**: Identifies workloads deployed on VMware guests for migration to Hyper-V (because SQL Server, SharePoint Server, and Exchange Server run optimally on Hyper-V)

Considerations for Deploying Workloads into Virtualized Environments

Planning for a virtualized environment is critical. This section looks at some valuable considerations.

Resource Requirements

An excellent starting point is virtual machine resource requirements. You should consider the following at the very least:

- **Processor**: What processor speed, architecture, or number of processors is required?

- **Network**: What network bandwidth is needed for inbound and outbound traffic? What is the maximum amount of network latency the workload can tolerate to function properly?

- **Storage**: How much storage do the application and operating system files of the workload require? How much storage is needed for data? How many input/output operations per second (IOPS) does the workload require to its storage?

- **Memory**: How much memory does the workload need? Is the workload non-uniform memory access (NUMA) aware?

- **Peak and average requirements**: What are the peak and average requirements for each of the hardware requirements on an hourly, daily, weekly, monthly, or annual basis?

- **Downtime**: What is the number of minutes of downtime per month that is acceptable for the workload and the workload's data?

- **Encryption**: Are the workload files and/or their data encrypted on disk? Does the data have to be encrypted between the virtual machines and its end users?

Workload Characteristics

It is also important to define workload characteristics as you are planning, including the following:

- **Stateless**: The virtual machines write no unique information to their local hard disk after they are initially provisioned and assigned unique computer names and network addresses; they may however, write unique information to separate storage, such as a database.

- **Stateful**: The virtual machines write unique information to their local hard disk after they are initially provisioned and assigned unique computer names and network addresses; they also might write information to separate storage of course.

- **Shared stateful**: The virtual machines need shared state with other virtual machines; this might require a Failover Clustering design.

- **Virtualization Exceptions**: Are there aspects of the workloads that might not perform well in virtualized environments? This might exclude workloads that must access physical peripherals or very high resource requirements.

VM Configurations

You should also plan for your virtual machine configurations. Issues here include the following:

- Virtual machine generation
- Static or dynamic memory assignment
- Processor assignments
- Supported operating systems
- Virtual machine naming conventions
- Network configuration (which includes network adapters, security, and IP addressing)
- Storage configurations
- Availability configurations
- Disaster recovery
- Virtual machine types

Host Planning

You might also plan for server virtualization host groups. These are named collections of servers that are grouped together to meet common IT goals. Tasks might include the following:

- Defining physical locations
- Defining host group types (including resource requirements and workload characterizations)
- Determining clustering requirements

Next, it is common to plan for your server virtualization hosts themselves. Tasks typically include the following:

- Defining compute configurations
- Defining networking configurations
- Defining storage configurations
- Defining server virtualization host scale units (collections of servers)
- Defining the server virtualization host availability strategy

Architecture and Capability Planning

Another aspect is planning for the virtualization architecture. Tasks might include the following:

- Defining maintenance domains

- Defining physical fault domains

- Defining reserve capacity

Finally, it is common to plan for the initial capability characteristics. This typically includes the following:

- Defining initial service level agreement (SLA) metrics

- Defining startup costs

Updating Images with Patches, Hotfixes, and Drivers

The Deployment Image Servicing and Management (DISM) tool is a command-line/PowerShell tool that is used to modify Windows images. You use DISM to update Windows images with patches, hotfixes, and drivers.

Note that the following operating system package-servicing options are available for an offline image:

```
DISM.exe /Image:<path_to_image_directory> [/Get-Packages |
  /Get-PackageInfo | /Add-Package | /Remove-Package ] [/Get-Features
  | /Get-FeatureInfo | /Enable-Feature | /Disable-Feature ] [/
  Cleanup-Image]
```

For adding drivers to an offline image, use the **/Add-Driver** option, as shown in this example:

```
Dism /Image:C:\sample\offline /Add-Driver /Driver:C:\drivers\
  mydriver.inf /ForceUnsigned
```

Installing Roles and Features in Offline Images

You can enable or disable Windows features offline on a WIM or VHD file, or of course you can do so online on a running operating system. This text does not demonstrate the use of an answer file, but you can visit https://msdn.microsoft.com/en-us/windows/hardware/commercialize/manufacture/desktop/enable-or-disable-windows-features-using-dism for complete instructions.

Use the following steps to perform this process:

Step 1.   Open a command prompt with administrator privileges.

Step 2.   Use the **/Get-ImageInfo** option to retrieve the name or index number for the image that you want to modify; an index or a name value is required for most operations that specify an image file (for example, **Dism /Get-ImageInfo /ImageFile:C:\sample\images\install.wim**).

Step 3.   Mount the offline Windows image (for example, **Dism /Mount-Image /ImageFile:C:\sample\images\install.wim /Name:"Base Windows Image" /MountDir:C:\sample\offline**).

Step 4.   List all the features available in the operating system (for example, **Dism /Image:C:\sample\offline /Get-Features**).

Step 5.   Enable a specific feature in the image (for example, **Dism /Image:C:\ sample\offline /Enable-Feature /FeatureName:TFTP /All**).

> **NOTE** You can also use /Disable-Feature to disable Windows features in offline images.

Managing and Maintaining Windows Server Core, Nano Server Images, and VHDs Using Windows PowerShell

You can use PowerShell Direct to remotely manage Windows Server 2016 virtual machines from a Windows Server 2016 Hyper-V host. PowerShell Direct allows Windows PowerShell management inside a virtual machine, regardless of the network configuration or remote management settings on either Hyper-V host or the virtual machine.

You need to ensure the following before you can create a PowerShell Direct session on a virtual machine:

- The virtual machine must be running locally on the host.

- You must be logged into the host computer as a Hyper-V administrator.

- You must supply valid user credentials for the virtual machine.

- The host operating system must run at least Windows 10 or Windows Server 2016.

- The virtual machine must run at least Windows 10 or Windows Server 2016.

There are two ways to run PowerShell Direct:

- Create and exit a PowerShell Direct session by using **PSSession** cmdlets:
  - To connect, use **Enter-PSSession -VMName** *<VMName>* or **Enter-PSSession -VMGUID** *<VMGUID>*.
  - To close the session, use **Exit-PSSession**.

- Run scripts or commands with the **Invoke-Command** cmdlet (for example, **Invoke-Command -VMName PSTest -FilePath C:\myscripts\cool.ps1**).

NOTE   If you are tasked with managing older virtual machines, use Virtual Machine Connection (VMConnect) or configure a virtual network for the virtual machine you must manage.

Exam Preparation Tasks

As mentioned in the section "How to Use This Book" in the Introduction, you have a couple choices for exam preparation: the exercises here, Chapter 21, "Final Preparation," and the exam simulation questions in the Pearson Test Prep Software Online.

Review All Key Topics

Review the most important topics in this chapter, noted with the Key Topics icon in the outer margin of the page. Table 3-6 lists these key topics and the page number on which each is found.

Table 3-6 Key Topics for Chapter 3

Key Topic Element	Description	Page Number
List	Generation 1 versus Generation 2 VMs	45
Table 3-4	Scalability of VMs	47
Table 3-5	Scalability of Hyper-V hosts	47
List	MAP reports	50
List	VM resources	50
List	PowerShell Direct	54

Complete Tables and Lists from Memory

Print a copy of Appendix B, "Memory Tables" (found on the book website), or at least the section for this chapter, and complete the tables and lists from memory. Appendix C, "Memory Tables Answer Key," also on the website, includes completed tables and lists you can use to check your work.

Define Key Terms

Define the following key terms from this chapter and check your answers against the glossary:

Generation 1, Generation 2, External Virtual Switch, Internal Virtual Switch, Private Virtual Switch, MAP Toolkit, DISM

Q&A

The answers to these questions appear in Appendix A. For more practice with exam format questions, use the Pearson Test Prep Software Online.

1. Name three reasons you might need a Generation 1 VM.

2. What tool assists with server utilization data for Hyper-V?

3. What are three planning concerns for the processor in a virtualized datacenter?

4. What tool permits the updating of offline images with patches?

5. What parameter permits the addition of a role or feature to an offline image?

6. What are two tools for running PowerShell Direct?

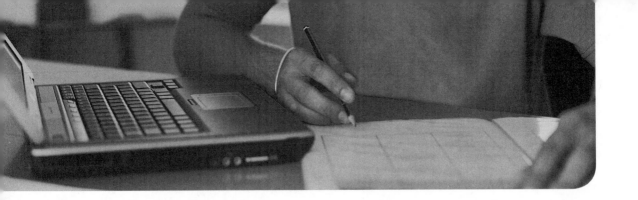

This chapter covers the following subjects:

- **Creating Disks:** This section includes tasks such as configuring sector sizes appropriate for various workloads, configuring GUID partition table (GPT) disks, creating VHD and VHDX files using Server Manager or Windows PowerShell, and mounting virtual hard disks. This part of the text also discusses the NTFS and ReFS file systems.

- **NFS and SMB Shares:** This section details the creation of these shared using tools like Server Manager and PowerShell.

- **File and Folder Permissions:** This section ensures that you are comfortable controlling important file and folder permissions in Windows Server 2016.

## CHAPTER 4

Disks and Volumes

Storage is all about physical and virtual disks and volumes. Server Manager and PowerShell are very valuable tools for managing both disks and volumes. This chapter examines these important storage topics in detail.

"Do I Know This Already?" Quiz

The "Do I Know This Already?" quiz allows you to assess whether you should read the entire chapter. Table 4-1 lists the major headings in this chapter and the "Do I Know This Already?" quiz questions covering the material in those headings so you can assess your knowledge of these specific areas. The answers to the "Do I Know This Already?" quiz appear in Appendix A, "Answers to the 'Do I Know This Already?' Quizzes and Q&A Questions."

Table 4-1 "Do I Know This Already?" Foundation Topics Section-to-Question Mapping

Foundation Topics Section	Questions
Creating Disks	1,2
NFS and SMB Shares	3,4
File and Folder Permissions	5,6

CAUTION The goal of self-assessment is to gauge your mastery of the topics in this chapter. If you do not know the answer to a question or are only partially sure of the answer, you should mark your answer as incorrect for purposes of the self-assessment. Giving yourself credit for an answer you correctly guess skews your self-assessment results and might provide you with a false sense of security.

1. Your Windows Server 2016 is working with Advanced Format disks. How many bytes exist per physical sector?

    a. 512

    b. 1024

    c. 2048

    d. 4096

2. What partition style lets you to use disk space beyond 2 TB?

    a. EUFI

    b. MBR

    c. GPT

    d. SMB

3. What type of share do you typically use with UNIX-based systems?

    a. SMB

    b. MBR

    c. GPT

    d. NFS

4. What PowerShell command permits the creation of a new SMB share?

    a. **Create-SmbShare**

    b. **Get-SmbShare**

    c. New-SmbShare

    d. **Build-SmbShare**

5. Which of the following is not a basic NTFS folder permission?

    a. Full control

    b. List folder contents

    c. Modify

    d. Write attributes

6. Which statement about file ownership in an NTFS permission system is not correct?

    a. The owner can always change the permissions on a file.

    b. By default, the creator of the file is the owner.

    c. There is a special permission called Take Ownership.

    d. No user accounts are granted Take Ownership by default.

Foundation Topics

Creating Disks

Thanks to new features and capabilities with Windows Server 2016, you must become expert regarding many aspects of disk creation. The following sections make these topics clear and concise for you.

Configuring Sector Sizes Appropriate for Various Workloads

Most people are unaccustomed to worrying about sector sizes in storage. Today, however, there are three options: 512 bytes, 512e, and 4K.

Windows Server 2016 supports Standard Format and Advanced Format hard disks. Here are key distinctions:

- Standard Format:

    - Use 512 bytes per physical sector

    - Often referred to as *512 native sector drives*

    - Sometimes referred to simply as *512b drives*

- Advanced Format:

    - Use 4096 bytes per physical sector

    - Available in 4K native and 512 emulation (512e) versions

    - Allow for the use of huge multi-terabyte drives

Remember that Windows Server 2016 handles media updates with the granularity of their physical sector size. Standard Format disks work with 512 bytes at a time, while Advanced Format disks use 4096 bytes at a time. For best performance, update your workloads to read and write at the 4096 bytes with your new, massive disk drives.

You can use the **fsutil** tool at the command prompt to check sector size information. Here is an example:

```
fsutil fsinfo sectorinfo c:
```

Figure 4-1 shows this tool in action.

```
Administrator: Command Prompt                                                 —    □    ×
Microsoft Windows [Version 10.0.14393]
(c) 2016 Microsoft Corporation. All rights reserved.

C:\Windows\system32>fsutil fsinfo sectorinfo c:
LogicalBytesPerSector :                                512
PhysicalBytesPerSectorForAtomicity :                   4096
PhysicalBytesPerSectorForPerformance :                 4096
FileSystemEffectivePhysicalBytesPerSectorForAtomicity : 4096
Device Alignment :                                     Aligned (0x000)
Partition alignment on device :                        Aligned (0x000)
Performs Normal Seeks
Trim Supported
Not DAX capable

C:\Windows\system32>
```

Figure 4-1   Using **fsutil** to Check Sector Size

When you are performing volume creation in the Windows Server 2016 Disk Management tool, you set the allocation unit size as shown in Figure 4-2.

All file systems that are used by Windows organize a hard disk based on cluster size (also known as allocation unit size). Cluster size is the smallest amount of disk space that can be used to hold a file. When file sizes do not come out to an even multiple of the cluster size, more space must be used to hold a file. On the typical hard disk partition, the average amount of space that is lost in this manner can be calculated by using the equation Cluster Size / 2 × Number of Files.

If you specify no cluster size when you format a partition, Windows Server 2016 defaults are based on the size of the partition. A server selects these defaults to reduce the space lost and to reduce the fragmentation that occurs on the partition.

For some specific workloads, Microsoft has best-practice recommendations for the allocation unit size. For example, when formatting a data disk for Microsoft SQL Server, Microsoft recommends that you use a 64 KB allocation unit size for data and log files, as well as TempDB.

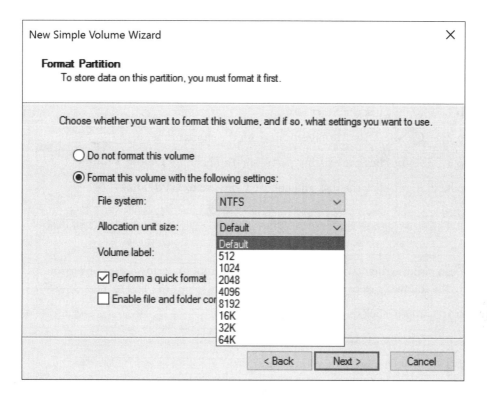

New Simple Volume Wizard   ✕

Format Partition
To store data on this partition, you must format it first.

Choose whether you want to format this volume, and if so, what settings you want to use.

○ Do not format this volume

◉ Format this volume with the following settings:

File system: NTFS   ⌄

Allocation unit size: Default   ⌄

Volume label:

☑ Perform a quick format

☐ Enable file and folder cor

Default
512
1024
2048
4096
8192
16K
32K
64K

< Back   Next >   Cancel

Figure 4-2   Setting the Allocation Unit Size

Configuring GUID Partition Table (GPT) Disks

Remember that the disks in Windows Server 2016 can use the older Master Boot Record (MBR) partition style or the new and improved GUID Partition Table (GPT) partition style. GPT is very common these days as it allows the use of disk space beyond 2 TB. GPT uses the new and improved UEFI boot mode.

It is super simple to check your partition style in Windows Server 2016. Use the following steps to check your settings using Disk Management:

Step 1.   Right-click the **Start** button.

Step 2.   Choose **Disk Management** from the shortcut menu.

Step 3.   Right-click your disk.

Step 4.   Choose **Properties**.

Step 5.   Click the **Volumes** tab and check the **Partition Style** field.

Windows Server 2016 allows the conversion of disks to GPT from MBR and vice versa. A disk must be empty and can hold no partitions or volumes. Obviously, it is important to back up your data before performing such a conversion.

Follow these steps to convert within Disk Management:

Step 1.   Right-click the **Start** button.

Step 2.   Choose **Disk Management** from the shortcut menu.

Step 3.   Right-click the existing partition(s) and choose **Delete Volume**.

Step 4.   Right-click the disk and choose **Convert to GPT Disk**.

NOTE   Third-party tools can perform this conversion without the deletion of data.

You can also use the **diskpart** command prompt tool to perform the conversion, using the following steps:

Step 1.   Right-click the **Start** menu.

Step 2.   Choose the **Command Prompt (Admin)**.

Step 3.   Type **diskpart** and press **Enter**.

Step 4.   Type **list disk** and press **Enter**.

Step 5.   Type **select disk #** and press **Enter**.

Step 6.   Type **clean** and press **Enter**.

Step 7.   Type **convert gpt** and press **Enter**.

Creating and Mounting VHD and VHDX Files Using Server Manager or Windows PowerShell

Virtual hard disks are growing in popularity in our heavily virtualized datacenter environments, and it is no surprise that their creation is simple both in the GUI of Windows Server 2016 and in PowerShell. Using Server Manager is an easy way to access Disk Management and create VHD or VHDX files. Here is how it works:

Step 1.   In Server Manager, select **Tools > Computer Management**.

Step 2.   In Computer Management, under **Storage**, choose **Disk Management**, as shown in Figure 4-3.

Step 3.   Select an active volume and then, from the **Action** menu in Disk Manager, choose **Create VHD** to open the **Create and Attach Virtual Hard Disk** window, as shown in Figure 4-4.

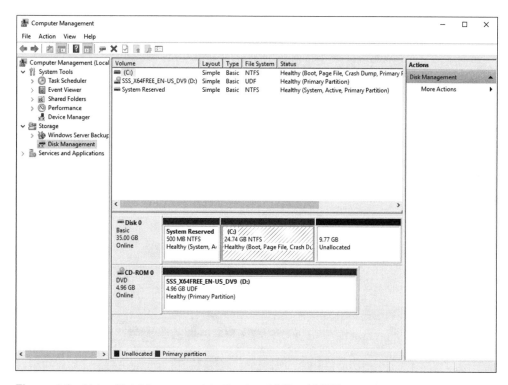

Figure 4-3 Using Disk Management to Create a VHD or VHDX

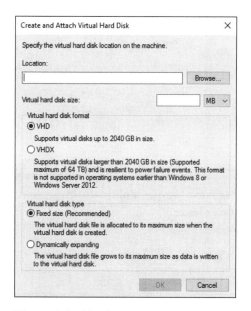

Figure 4-4 The Create and Attach Virtual Hard Disk Window

Step 4.   Specify the location of the VHD or VHDX, the size of the disk, the format of the disk (Gen 1 VHD or Gen 2 VHDX) and whether the VHD is of a fixed size or dynamically expanding.

Step 5.   Confirm that the VHDX appears in Disk Management, as shown in Figure 4-5 (ours is the 1 GB Disk 1).

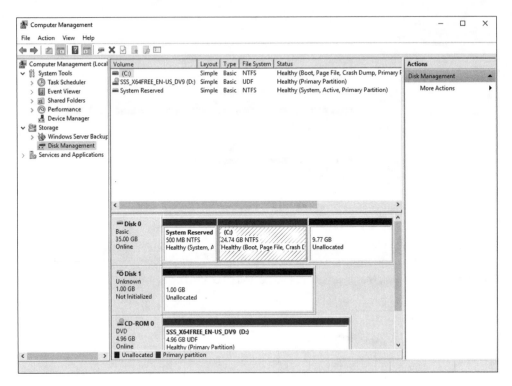

Figure 4-5   The VHDX in Disk Management

Step 6.   Right-click the disk identifier on the left and choose **Initialize Disk,** as shown in Figure 4-6.

Step 7.   Choose the MBR or GPT partition method and click **OK**.

Step 8.   Right-click your VHDX and choose **New Simple Volume** to create and mount your virtual hard disk to a drive letter.

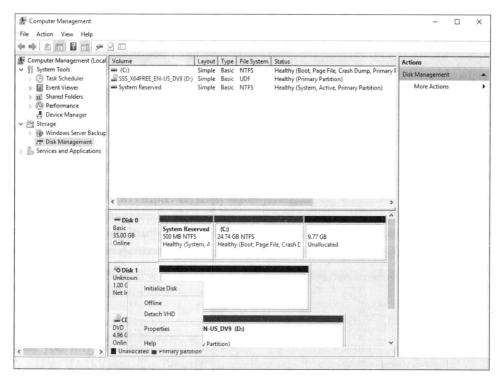

Figure 4-6 Accessing the Initialize Disk Options

Of course, PowerShell offers cmdlets to make these storage manipulations as well. Here are some key cmdlets you should know:

- **New-VHD**: Creates a new VHD or VHDX:

```
New-VHD [-Path] <String[]> [-SizeBytes] <UInt64> [-AsJob]
   [-BlockSizeBytes <UInt32> ] [-CimSession <Microsoft.
   Management.Infrastructure.CimSession[]> ] [-ComputerName
   <String[]> ] [-Credential <System.Management.Automation.
   PSCredential[]> ] [-Dynamic] [-LogicalSectorSizeBytes <UInt32>
   {512 | 4096} ] [-PhysicalSectorSizeBytes <UInt32> {512 | 4096}
   ] [-Confirm] [-WhatIf] [ <CommonParameters>]
```

- **Mount-VHD**: Mounts one or more virtual hard disks:

```
Mount-VHD [-Path] <String[]> [-CimSession <Microsoft.Management.
   Infrastructure.CimSession[]> ] [-ComputerName <String[]> ]
   [-Credential <System.Management.Automation.PSCredential[]> ]
   [-NoDriveLetter] [-Passthru] [-ReadOnly] [-SnapshotId
   <Nullable [System.Guid]> ] [-Confirm] [-WhatIf] [
   <CommonParameters>]
```

- **Get-Disk**: Gets one or more disks visible to the operating system:

```
Get-Disk [[-Number] <UInt32[]> ] [-CimSession <CimSession[]>
] [-ThrottleLimit <Int32> ] [ <CommonParameters>] [
<WorkflowParameters>]
```

- **Initialize-Disk**: Initializes a RAW disk for first time use, enabling the disk to be formatted and used to store data:

```
Initialize-Disk [-Number] <UInt32[]> [-CimSession <CimSession[]>
] [-PartitionStyle <PartitionStyle> {Unknown | MBR | GPT} ]
[-PassThru] [-ThrottleLimit <Int32> ] [-Confirm] [-WhatIf] [
<CommonParameters>] [ <WorkflowParameters>]
```

- **New-Partition**: Creates a new partition on an existing Disk object:

```
New-Partition [-DiskNumber] <UInt32[]> [-Alignment <UInt32> ]
[-AssignDriveLetter] [-CimSession <CimSession[]> ]
[-DriveLetter <Char> ] [-GptType <String> ] [-IsActive]
[-IsHidden] [-MbrType <MbrType> {FAT12 | FAT16 | Extended
| Huge | IFS | FAT32} ] [-Offset <UInt64> ] [-Size
<UInt64> ] [-ThrottleLimit <Int32> ] [-UseMaximumSize] [
<CommonParameters>] [ <WorkflowParameters>]
```

- **Format-Volume**: Formats one or more existing volumes or a new volume on an existing partition:

```
Format-Volume [-DriveLetter] <Char[]> [-AllocationUnitSize
<UInt32> ] [-CimSession <CimSession[]> ] [-Compress]
[-DisableHeatGathering] [-FileSystem <String> {FAT |
FAT32 | exFAT | NTFS | ReFS} ] [-Force] [-Full] [-IsDAX]
[-NewFileSystemLabel <String> ] [-SetIntegrityStreams
<Boolean> ] [-ShortFileNameSupport <Boolean> ]
[-ThrottleLimit <Int32> ] [-UseLargeFRS] [-Confirm] [-WhatIf]
[ <CommonParameters>] [ <WorkflowParameters>]
```

- **Get-Partition**: Returns a list of all partition objects visible on all disks, or optionally a filtered list using specified parameters:

```
Get-Partition [[-DiskNumber] <UInt32[]> ] [[-PartitionNumber]
<UInt32[]> ] [-CimSession <CimSession[]> ] [-ThrottleLimit
<Int32> ] [ <CommonParameters>] [ <WorkflowParameters>]
```

- **Add-PartitionAccessPath**: Adds an access path such as a drive letter or folder to a partition:

```
Add-PartitionAccessPath [-DiskNumber] <UInt32[]>
[-PartitionNumber] <UInt32[]> [[-AccessPath] <String>
] [-AssignDriveLetter] [-CimSession <CimSession[]> ]
[-PassThru] [-ThrottleLimit <Int32> ] [-Confirm] [-WhatIf] [
<CommonParameters>] [ <WorkflowParameters>]
```

- **Dismount-VHD**: Dismounts a virtual hard disk:

```
Dismount-VHD [-DiskNumber] <UInt32> [-CimSession <Microsoft.
  Management.Infrastructure.CimSession[]> ] [-ComputerName
  <String[]> ] [-Credential <System.Management.Automation.
  PSCredential[]> ] [-Passthru] [-Confirm] [-WhatIf] [
  <CommonParameters>]
```

Determining When to Use NTFS and ReFS File Systems

It is interesting that NTFS is no longer the only realistic option for file formats. Microsoft now provides a new and improved version 2 of the Resilient File System (ReFS).

ReFS has some distinct advantages over NTFS that you should be aware of:

- ReFS gives Accelerated VHDX options in Hyper-V; these options permit massive performance increases when creating and extending a virtual hard disk, when merging checkpoints, and when performing backups.

- A block cloning approach is key to excellent checkpoint performance.

- Use of a 64 KB block size allows optimal performance in Hyper-V, with partition alignment handled automatically by Hyper-V.

- When your Storage Spaces pool uses ReFS as the underlying on-disk format, it leverages new features to greatly improve the repair process.

- ReFS v2 uses the concept of cluster "bands" to group multiple chunks of data together for efficient I/O; this really helps with your use of data tiering—specifically in moving data between tiers.

- Automatic integrity checking exists in ReFS.

- ReFS features new data scrubbing techniques.

- ReFS offers better protection against data degradation.

- It features built-in drive recovery and redundancy.

- ReFS supports up to 1 trillion terabytes.

- You can create new volumes faster with ReFS.

There are also some disadvantages to ReFS that you should be aware of:

- It cannot replace NTFS in all scenarios.

- You cannot use it with Clustered Shared Volumes.

- There is no conversion capability between NTFS and ReFS.

- There is no file-based deduplication.

- There are no disk quotas.

- There are no object identifiers.

- There is no encryption support.

- You cannot use named streams.

- There is no transaction support.

- There are no hard links.

- There is no support for external attributes.

- There is no support for 8.3 filenames.

SMB and NFS Shares

Creating and managing SMB or NFS shares for a network can be critical for your Windows Server 2016 requirements. The following sections examine these topics. Remember that SMB shares are used in Windows environments, while NFS shares are found in UNIX environments.

Configuring SMB and NFS Shares Using Server Manager

NFS and SMB shares of various complexity are simple to create directly from within Server Manager. Follow these steps:

Step 1.   Launch Server Manager.

Step 2.   Choose **File and Storage Services** in the left column.

Step 3.   Select **Shares.**

Step 4.   In the Shares area, right-click an empty space and choose **New Share** to launch the **New Share Wizard**, as shown in Figure 4-7.

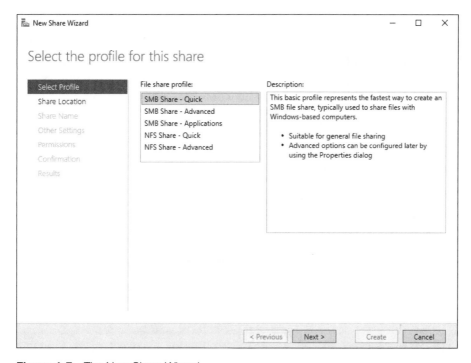

Figure 4-7   The New Share Wizard

Notice that this wizard offers many options for share creation, including the following:

- **SMB Share - Quick**: This choice is for the simple creation of shares for mainly Windows-based computers.

- **SMB Share - Advanced**: This option creates the SMB share with many more advanced options, including the following:

  - **Setting the shares' owners**: This can be critical when users are denied access to the share.

  - **Configuring the default classification of data in the share**: This assists in the creation of management and access policies.

  - **Enabling quotas**: This allows restrictions on the space that users can consume.

- **SMB Share - Applications**: This choice creates SMB shares with settings designed for Hyper-V, certain databases, and other server applications.

- **NFS Share - Quick**: This option provides the fastest method of creating basic shares to be used primarily by UNIX-based systems. To use this option, you must install Server for NFS, found under the File and Storage Services - Files and iSCSI Services node of Roles and Features.

- **NFS Share - Advanced**: This choice creates the NFS share with advanced options. Note that it requires the installation of Server for NFS as well as the File Server Resource Manager. Advanced options include the following:

  - **Setting the shares' owners:** This can be critical when users are denied access to the share.

  - **Configuring the default classification of data in the share:** This can aid in the creation of management and access policies.

  - **Enabling quotas:** This allows restrictions on the space that users can consume.

Configuring SMB and NFS Shares and Server and Client Settings with PowerShell

A robust set of cmdlets exists for SMB and NFS share management, as well as the control of server and client settings for both SMB and NFS.

Table 4-2 details the SMB-related cmdlets you should be aware of.

Table 4-2 SMB PowerShell Cmdlets

PowerShell Cmdlet	Description
Block-SmbShareAccess	Adds a deny ACE for a trustee to the security descriptor of the SMB share
Close-SmbOpenFile	Closes a file that is open by one of the clients of the SMB server
Close-SmbSession	Forcibly ends the SMB session
Disable-SmbDelegation	Disables a constrained delegation authorization for an SMB client and server
Enable-SmbDelegation	Enables a constrained delegation authorization for an SMB client and server
Get-SmbBandwidthLimit	Gets the list of SMB bandwidth caps for each traffic category

PowerShell Cmdlet	Description
Get-SmbClientConfiguration	Retrieves the SMB client configuration
Get-SmbClientNetworkInterface	Retrieves the network interfaces used by the SMB client
Get-SmbConnection	Retrieves the connections established from the SMB client to the SMB servers
Get-SmbDelegation	Gets the constrained delegation authorizations for an SMB client
Get-SmbMapping	Retrieves the SMB client directory mappings created for a server
Get-SmbMultichannelConnection	Retrieves the SMB connections made between the SMB client network interfaces and the SMB server network interfaces
Get-SmbMultichannelConstraint	Retrieves the constraints that define how the SMB client uses network interfaces to connect to the servers
Get-SmbOpenFile	Retrieves basic information about the files that are open on behalf of the clients of the SMB server
Get-SmbServerConfiguration	Retrieves the SMB server configuration
Get-SmbServerNetworkInterface	Retrieves the network interfaces used by the SMB server
Get-SmbSession	Retrieves information about the SMB sessions that are currently established between the SMB server and the associated clients
Get-SmbShare	Retrieves the SMB shares on the computer
Get-SmbShareAccess	Retrieves the ACL of the SMB share
Grant-SmbShareAccess	Adds an allow ACE for a trustee to the security descriptor of the SMB share
New-SmbMapping	Creates an SMB mapping
New-SmbMultichannelConstraint	Creates an SMB multichannel constraint for the specified server
New-SmbShare	Creates an SMB share
Remove-SmbBandwidthLimit	Removes SMB bandwidth caps
Remove-SmbMapping	Removes the SMB mapping to an SMB share
Remove-SmbMultichannelConstraint	Removes SMB multichannel constraints
Remove-SmbShare	Deletes the specified SMB shares

PowerShell Cmdlet	Description
Revoke-SmbShareAccess	Removes all the allow ACEs for a trustee from the security descriptor of the SMB share
Set-SmbBandwidthLimit	Adds an SMB bandwidth cap
Set-SmbClientConfiguration	Sets the SMB client configuration
Set-SmbPathAcl	Sets the ACL for the file system folder to match the ACL used by an SMB share
Set-SmbServerConfiguration	Sets the SMB Service configuration
Set-SmbShare	Modifies the properties of the SMB share
Unblock-SmbShareAccess	Removes all the deny ACEs for the trustee from the security descriptor of the SMB share
Update-SmbMultichannelConnection	Forces the SMB client to update the multichannel-related information

Table 4-3 details the NFS-related cmdlets you should be aware of.

Table 4-3   NFS PowerShell Cmdlets

PowerShell Cmdlet	Description
Disconnect-NfsSession	Disconnects NFS sessions that a client computer established on an NFS server
Get-NfsClientConfiguration	Gets configuration settings for an NFS client
Get-NfsClientgroup	Gets client groups configured on an NFS server
Get-NfsClientLock	Gets file locks that a client computer holds on an NFS server
Get-NfsMappedIdentity	Gets an NFS mapped identity
Get-NfsMappingStore	Gets configuration settings for an identity mapping store
Get-NfsMountedClient	Gets clients that are connected to an NFS server
Get-NfsNetgroup	Gets a netgroup
Get-NfsNetgroupStore	Gets settings for a netgroup store
Get-NfsOpenFile	Gets information about files that are open on an NFS server for a client computer
Get-NfsServerConfiguration	Gets configuration settings for an NFS server
Get-NfsSession	Gets information about which client computers are currently connected to one or more shares on an NFS server

PowerShell Cmdlet	Description
Get-NfsShare	Gets NFS shares on an NFS server
Get-NfsSharePermission	Gets information about permissions that an NFS server grants to exported NFS shares
Get-NfsStatistics	Gets RPC call statistics that an NFS server maintains
Grant-NfsSharePermission	Grants permission to access shares that an NFS server exports
Install-NfsMappingStore	Installs and initializes an AD LDS instance as an identity mapping store
New-NfsClientgroup	Creates a client group on an NFS server
New-NfsMappedIdentity	Creates a new NFS mapped identity
New-NfsNetgroup	Creates a netgroup
New-NfsShare	Creates an NFS file share
Remove-NfsClientgroup	Removes a client group from an NFS server
Remove-NfsMappedIdentity	Removes a mapping between a UNIX account and a Windows account
Remove-NfsNetgroup	Removes a netgroup
Remove-NfsShare	Stops sharing NFS shares
Rename-NfsClientgroup	Renames a client group on an NFS server
Reset-NfsStatistics	Resets RPC call statistics that an NFS server maintains
Resolve-NfsMappedIdentity	Resolves the mapping of a Windows user account or group account to a UNIX identifier
Revoke-NfsClientLock	Releases file locks that a client computer holds on an NFS server
Revoke-NfsMountedClient	Revokes a mounted client from an NFS server
Revoke-NfsOpenFile	Revokes open files on an NFS server for a client computer
Revoke-NfsSharePermission	Revokes permission to access shares that an NFS server exports
Set-NfsClientConfiguration	Changes configuration settings for an NFS client
Set-NfsClientgroup	Adds and removes client computers from a client group
Set-NfsMappedIdentity	Modifies a mapped identity
Set-NfsMappingStore	Modifies configuration settings for an identity mapping store
Set-NfsNetgroup	Modifies a netgroup
Set-NfsNetgroupStore	Modifies netgroup configuration settings

PowerShell Cmdlet	Description
Set-NfsServerConfiguration	Changes configuration settings for an NFS server
Set-NfsShare	Changes configuration settings of an NFS share
Test-NfsMappedIdentity	Verifies that a mapped identity is correctly configured
Test-NfsMappingStore	Verifies that an identity mapping store is configured correctly

File and Folder Permissions

File and folder permissions enable granular security controls over data in a network. This section describes the options available for these files and folders.

Before you read the details of the powerful NTFS file and folder permissions that you should become an expert in, remember that share permissions are also provided in Windows Server 2016. The share permissions include the following:

- Basic share permissions:
  - Read
  - Read/Write

- Advanced share permissions:
  - Full Control
  - Change
  - Read

A weakness of share permissions is that they take effect only when the resource is accessed over a network connection. Local access to the file and folder resources is not changed by share permissions.

For this reason, administrators often "override" share permissions by granting the Everyone group Full Control via the share permissions and then using NTFS file and folder permissions to control access both locally and over the network connection. Another reason administrators often use NTFS permissions over shared permissions is that, as you will soon learn, the NTFS permissions are more varied and granular.

To access the share permissions, use the Sharing tab on the Properties dialog for a folder in the File Explorer.

Use the Security tab on the Properties dialog for a file or folder to set NTFS permissions.

These are the basic NTFS file permissions:

- Full Control
- Modify
- Read & Execute
- Read
- Write

These are the special NTFS file permissions:

- Full Control
- Traverse Folder/Execute File
- List Folder/Read Data
- Read Attributes
- Read Extended Attributes
- Create Files/Write Data
- Create Folders/Append Data
- Write Attributes
- Write Extended Attributes
- Delete
- Read Permissions
- Change Permissions
- Take Ownership

These are the basic NTFS folder permissions:

- Full Control
- Modify
- Read & Execute
- List Folder Contents
- Read
- Write

These are the special NTFS folder permissions:

- Full Control

- Traverse Folder/Execute File

- List Folder/Read Data

- Read Attributes

- Read Extended Attributes

- Create Files/Write Data

- Create Folders/Append Data

- Write Attributes

- Write Extended Attributes

- Delete Subfolders and Files

- Delete

- Read Permissions

- Change Permissions

- Take Ownership

In addition to understanding these options that are available for permissions, it is critical that you understand the following points:

- File permissions always take precedence over folder permissions—that is, if a user can execute a program in a folder, this is possible even if such permissions do not exist at the folder level.

- Permissions are cumulative—that is, users obtain the cumulative effect of different permissions they might obtain through different group memberships.

- Deny permissions always override Allow permissions. Note that this is the one powerful exception to the preceding rule of permissions being cumulative.

- Permissions migrate from the top down in a process known as inheritance. Inheritance allows files and folders created within already existing folders to have a set of permissions automatically assigned to them.

- You enable or disable inheritance in the Advanced Security Settings window, as shown in Figure 4-8.

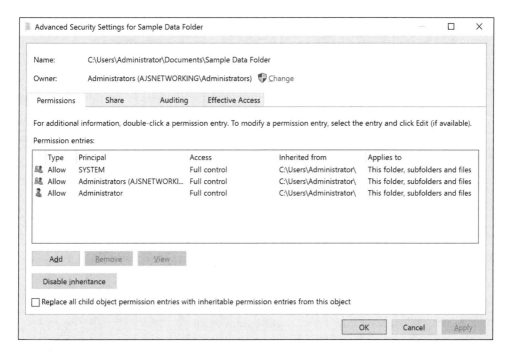

Figure 4-8 The Advanced Security Settings Window

- The specified owner of a file or folder has full control over the file or folder and therefore keeps the ability to change permissions on it, regardless of the effect of other permissions on that file or folder.

- By default, the owner of the file or folder is the object that created it.

- There is a special permission called Take Ownership that an owner can assign to any other user or group; this allows that user or group to assume the role of owner and therefore assign permissions at will.

- The administrator account on a system has the Take Ownership permission by default.

- The Effective Access tab (shown not selected in Figure 4-8) allows you to easily determine the effective permissions for a user, group, or device, given various cumulative and inherited permissions that might exist.

Exam Preparation Tasks

As mentioned in the section "How to Use This Book" in the Introduction, you have a couple choices for exam preparation: the exercises here, Chapter 21, "Final Preparation," and the exam simulation questions in the Pearson Test Prep Software Online.

Review All Key Topics

Review the most important topics in this chapter, noted with the Key Topics icon in the outer margin of the page. Table 4-4 lists these key topics and the page number on which each is found.

Table 4-4   Key Topics for Chapter 4

Key Topic Element	Description	Page Number
List	Standard Format and Advanced Format	61
Steps	Converting an MBR disk to GPT	64
List	PowerShell cmdlets for VHD and VHDX creation	67
List	ReFS advantages over NTFS	69
List	Basic NTFS file permissions	77
List	Basic NTFS folder permissions	77

Complete Tables and Lists from Memory

Print a copy of Appendix B, "Memory Tables" (found on the book website), or at least the section for this chapter, and complete the tables and lists from memory. Appendix C, "Memory Tables Answer Key," also on the website, includes completed tables and lists you can use to check your work.

Define Key Terms

Define the following key terms from this chapter and check your answers against the glossary:

Standard Format Disk, Advanced Format Disk, Master Boot Record (MBR), GUID Partition Table (GPT), VHD or VHDX, NTFS, ReFS, SMB, NFS

Q&A

The answers to these questions appear in Appendix A. For more practice with exam format questions, use the Pearson Test Prep Software Online.

1. Under Computer Management, what tool would you use to create and attach VHDX disks?

2. What option would you choose in Server Manager's New Share Wizard in order to create a share for UNIX systems that would include quotas?

3. What NTFS permission always overrides all other access permissions?

This chapter covers the following subjects:

- **Storage Spaces:** Windows Server 2016 makes it simple to combine multiple physical disks into whatever logical storage scheme you might need. The industry term for this is storage virtualization. Of course, this section details this technology for you.

- **Storage Area Networks:** Windows Server 2016 can integrate very well with Fibre Channel and related Storage Area Network (SAN) technologies. This part of the chapter covers topics like the creation of iSCSI targets and initiators as well as advanced topics like DCB and MPIO.

- **Storage Replica:** A great new feature of Windows Server 2016 is the replication of data between storage locations. This section describes the various options available, and when they are right for your design.

## CHAPTER 5

Server Storage

Microsoft offers many rich storage features in Windows Server 2016. This chapter covers some of the most important ones, including Storage Spaces, Storage Area Network (SAN) features, and Storage Replica capabilities.

"Do I Know This Already?" Quiz

The "Do I Know This Already?" quiz allows you to assess whether you should read the entire chapter. Table 5-1 lists the major headings in this chapter and the "Do I Know This Already?" quiz questions covering the material in those headings so you can assess your knowledge of these specific areas. The answers to the "Do I Know This Already?" quiz appear in Appendix A, "Answers to the 'Do I Know This Already?' Quizzes and Q&A Questions."

Table 5-1 "Do I Know This Already?" Foundation Topics Section-to-Question Mapping

Foundation Topics Section	Questions
Storage Spaces	1, 2
Storage Area Networks	3, 4
Storage Replica	5, 6

CAUTION The goal of self-assessment is to gauge your mastery of the topics in this chapter. If you do not know the answer to a question or are only partially sure of the answer, you should mark your answer as incorrect for purposes of the self-assessment. Giving yourself credit for an answer you correctly guess skews your self-assessment results and might provide you with a false sense of security.

1. What Storage Spaces layout choice is similar to RAID 5?

   a. Simple

   b. Three-way mirror

   c. Parity

   d. Two-way mirror

2. How many disks are needed for three-way mirroring?

   a. Two

   b. Three

   c. Four

   d. Five

3. What SAN technology is critical for lossless connectivity in a converged network?

   a. iSNS

   b. DCB

   c. MPIO

   d. MCS

4. What SAN technology is critical for resiliency for the connectivity of iSCSI targets?

   a. DCB

   b. iSNS

   c. MPIO

   d. FC

5. In what scenarios could Storage Replica be critical? Choose two.

   a. File Server

   b. SYSVOL

   c. SQL Server

   d. Microsoft Exchange

6. What PowerShell cmdlet do you use to configure Storage Replica?

   a. **New-Replica**

   b. **New-SRPartnership**

   c. **New-SReplica**

   d. **New-SReplicaPeer**

Foundation Topics

Storage Spaces

Storage Spaces offers a nice alternative to a potentially expensive and complex Storage Area Network (SAN). Storage Spaces allows you to use multiple physical disks attached to a Windows Server 2016 system and present them to users in a flexible manner. For example, you can pool together physical disks with Storage Spaces and present them to users as one large logical disk.

NOTE   The Datacenter Edition of Windows Server 2016 offers a new feature called Storage Spaces Direct. This feature can use local, unshared storage to create highly available storage for hosting virtual machine files. Chapter 16, "Storage Spaces Direct," discusses this feature.

Configuring Storage Pools and Storage Spaces

Storage Spaces storage virtualization technology in Windows Server 2016 consists of two components:

- **Storage Pools**: A collection of physical disks presented as logical disks (for example, one large logical disk).
- **Storage Spaces**: Virtual disks created from free space in a Storage Pool. These virtual disks are like LUNs (logical unit numbers) in a Storage Area Network (SAN) environment.

Storage management is extremely flexible and offers many options, including the following:

- The Windows Storage Management API (Application Programming Interface) in Windows Management Instrumentation (WMI)
- PowerShell
- The File and Storage Services role in Server Manager

You can format your Storage Spaces virtual disk as either of the following:

- NTFS
- ReFS

Remember, as discussed in Chapter 4, "Disks and Volumes," that various needs often dictate your choice of formatting. For example, data deduplication needs NTFS as the file system technology.

To configure Storage Spaces, you need to consider the following:

- **Disk-sector size**: If you can use only 512 and/or 512e drives, your pool defaults to 512e; remember that the 512e disks use 4096-byte sectors that emulate 512-byte sectors. If there is one or more 4K drives, the pool defaults to 4K. You can define the sector size for Storage Spaces, but remember that it forces you into the type of disks that you can add.

- **Drive allocation**: This dictates how a pool distributes drives; options include automatic by the OS (the default), manual, or hot spare.

- **Provisioning scheme**: Options are thin provisioned or fixed provisioning space.

Implementing Simple, Mirror, and Parity Storage Layout Options for Disks or Enclosures

Storage layout is obviously a critical choice for Storage Spaces. Valid options include the following:

- **Simple**: Simple features striping but no parity for resiliency; remember that striping means segments of data are written across multiple physical disks. Why would you choose Simple? The answer lies in performance improvements.

- **Two-way and three-way mirrors**: These spaces support two- or three-way copies of the data they host; note that mirror spaces also stripe data across multiple physical disks.

- **Parity**: This Storage Spaces technology is like RAID 5: Data is striped, along with parity information, across multiple physical drives; the parity information permits resiliency.

NOTE You can use Storage Spaces with Failover Clustering, as described in Chapter 14, "Failover Clustering."

It is critical to remember these rules regarding the physical disks of your Storage Spaces configuration:

- To create a storage pool, you need at least one physical disk.

- If you want to create a resilient mirror virtual disk, you need a minimum of two physical disks.

- To create a resilient virtual disk with parity, you need a minimum of three physical disks.

- For three-way mirroring resiliency, you need at least five physical disks.

- Your disks must be blank and unformatted, with no volumes on any disk.

- Failover Clustering cannot use SATA, USB, or SCSI disks.

Follow these steps to configure the Storage Spaces functionality in various configurations:

Step 1. In Server Manager, select **File and Storage Services** and then **Storage Pools,** as shown in Figure 5-1.

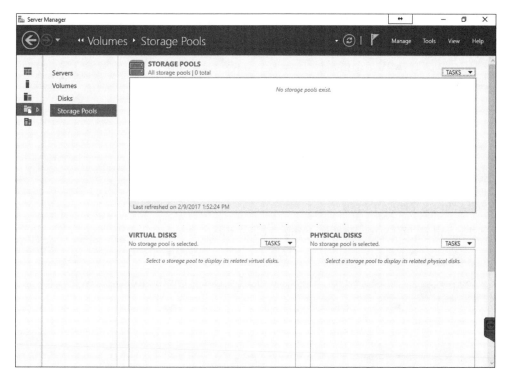

Figure 5-1 Configuring a New Storage Pool

Step 2. Create a new Storage Pool by using the Tasks drop-down menu.

Step 3. Provide values for **Storage Pool Name** and **Available Disk Group**, and choose **Physical Disks** for the pool.

Step 4.   Create a new virtual disk and specify the following values:

- Storage Pool
- Virtual Disk Name
- Enclosure Awareness
- Storage Layout
- Resiliency Settings
- Provisioning Type
- Size of the Virtual Disk

Step 5.   When the virtual disk is created, select **Create a volume when this wizard closes**.

Step 6.   In the **New Volume Wizard**, complete the following:

- Virtual Disk
- Volume Size
- Drive Letter
- File System
- Volume Label

Expanding Storage Pools

Expanding a Storage Pool is simple. Follow these steps:

Step 1.   Add a new virtual disk by navigating to **iSCSI** in Server Manager.

Step 2.   Create a new iSCSI virtual disk by specifying the following values:

- Storage location
- Disk name
- Size
- ISCSI target

Step 3.   In Server Manager, click the **Refresh** button and wait for all the panes to refresh.

Step 4.   In the **STORAGE POOLS** pane, right-click your **Storage Pool** and then add the new physical disk to the Storage Pool.

Step 5.   In the **VIRTUAL DISKS** pane, right-click **Mirrored vDisk** and then extend your virtual disk to the desired size.

Configuring Tiered Storage

Tiered Storage Spaces is an exciting feature in Windows Server 2016. It allows you to mix the types of disks you use in a Storage Space and use them efficiently. For example, you might use slow, large mechanical disks in conjunction with small, fast SSD (solid state drive) disks. Windows Server can dynamically move data based on the frequency of access.

When you add HDDs and SSDs to a Storage Space, Windows Server 2016 registers each type of disk and automatically creates two tiers. By default, each night at 1 a.m., optimization of the disks can occur.

To manually run the optimization, use the following PowerShell command:

```
Get-ScheduledTask -TaskName "Storage Tiers Optimization" |
    Start-ScheduledTask
```

You can pin files to certain tiers by using the PowerShell cmdlet **Set-FileStorageTier**. Here is the complete syntax for this cmdlet:

```
Set-FileStorageTier -DesiredStorageTierFriendlyName <String>
    -FilePath <String> [-CimSession <CimSession[]> ] [-ThrottleLimit
    <Int32> ] [-Confirm] [-WhatIf] [ <CommonParameters>] [
    <WorkflowParameters>]
```

Storage Area Networks

Storage Area Network (SAN) technologies now integrate with Windows Server 2016 more seamlessly than ever before. The sections that follow detail this integration.

Configuring iSCSI Target and Initiator

iSCSI storage provides an inexpensive and simple way to configure a connection to remote disks. An iSCSI SAN implementation typically includes the following:

- **An IP network:** IP is the glue holding the various parts of the datacenter together

- **iSCSI targets**: ISCSI targets advertise storage, just like controllers for hard disk drives of locally attached storage.

- **iSCSI initiators**: iSCSI targets display storage to the iSCSI initiator.

- **iSCSI qualified name (IQN)**: IQNs are unique identifiers that iSCSI uses to address initiators and targets on an iSCSI network.

The iSCSI Target Server role service supports a software-based and hardware-independent iSCSI disk subsystem. You can use the iSCSI Target Server to create iSCSI targets and iSCSI virtual disks, and then you can use Server Manager to manage your iSCSI targets and virtual disks. In Windows Server 2016, the iSCSI Target Server is available as a role service under the File and Storage Services role in Server Manager.

The following Windows PowerShell cmdlets exist for managing the iSCSI Target Server:

```
Install-WindowsFeature FS-iSCSITarget-Server


New-IscsiVirtualDisk [-Path] <String> [-SizeBytes] <UInt64>
   [-BlockSizeBytes <UInt32> ] [-ComputerName <String> ] [-Credential
   <PSCredential> ] [-Description <String> ] [-LogicalSectorSizeBytes
   <UInt32> ] [-PhysicalSectorSizeBytes <UInt32> ] [
   <CommonParameters>]


New-IscsiServerTarget [-TargetName] <String> [-ClusterGroupName
   <String> ] [-ComputerName <String> ] [-Credential <PSCredential> ]
   [-InitiatorIds <InitiatorId[]> ] [ <CommonParameters>]


Add-IscsiVirtualDiskTargetMapping [-TargetName] <String> [-Path]
   <String> [-ComputerName <String> ] [-Credential <PSCredential> ]
   [-Lun <Int32> ] [ <CommonParameters>]
```

Windows Server 2016 installs the iSCSI initiator by default. To connect your computer to an iSCSI target, you only need to start the service and configure it. The following Windows PowerShell cmdlets allow management of the iSCSI initiator:

```
Start-Service msiscsi


Set-Service msiscsi -StartupType "Automatic”


New-IscsiTargetPortal -TargetPortalAddress <String>
   [-AuthenticationType <String> ] [-ChapSecret <String> ]
   [-ChapUsername <String> ] [-CimSession <CimSession[]> ]
   [-InitiatorInstanceName <String> ] [-InitiatorPortalAddress
   <String> ] [-IsDataDigest <Boolean> ] [-IsHeaderDigest <Boolean>
   ] [-TargetPortalPortNumber <UInt16> ] [-ThrottleLimit <Int32> ] [
   <CommonParameters>] [ <WorkflowParameters>]


Connect-IscsiTarget -NodeAddress <String> [-AuthenticationType
   <String> ] [-ChapSecret <String> ] [-ChapUsername <String>
   ] [-CimSession <CimSession[]> ] [-InitiatorInstanceName
   <String> ] [-InitiatorPortalAddress <String> ] [-IsDataDigest
   <Boolean> ] [-IsHeaderDigest <Boolean> ] [-IsMultipathEnabled
   <Boolean> ] [-IsPersistent <Boolean> ] [-ReportToPnP <Boolean>
```

```
] [-TargetPortalAddress <String> ] [-TargetPortalPortNumber
<UInt16> ] [-ThrottleLimit <Int32> ] [ <CommonParameters>] [
<WorkflowParameters>]
```

Configuring iSNS

You use the Internet Storage Name Service (iSNS) protocol for interaction between iSNS servers and iSNS clients. iSNS clients are initiators that are trying to discover targets on an Ethernet network. iSNS eases automated discovery, management, and configuration of iSCSI and Fibre Channel devices (using iFCP gateways) on a TCP/IP network.

NOTE   Windows Server 2016 only supports the discovery of iSCSI devices, not Fibre Channel devices.

Adding iSNS simply installs as a feature in Server 2016, as shown in Figure 5-2.

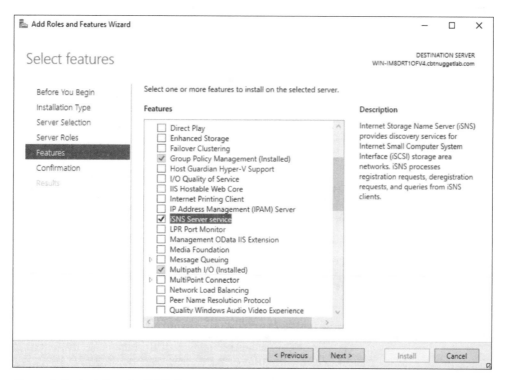

Figure 5-2   Installing the iSNS Feature

Configuring Datacenter Bridging (DCB)

Data Center Bridging (DCB) is a suite of Institute of Electrical and Electronics Engineers (IEEE) standards that enables Converged Fabrics in the data center. This is an environment where storage, data networking, cluster IPC, and management traffic all share the same Ethernet network infrastructure.

DCB offers hardware-based bandwidth allocation to a specific type of traffic and enhances Ethernet transport reliability with the use of priority-based flow control. Hardware-based bandwidth allocation is essential if traffic bypasses the operating system and offloads to a converged network adapter. This adapter might support Internet Small Computer System Interface (iSCSI), Remote Direct Memory Access (RDMA) over Converged Ethernet, or Fiber Channel over Ethernet (FCoE). Priority-based flow control is essential if the upper-layer protocol, such as Fiber Channel, assumes a lossless underlying transport.

You install DCB as a feature in a Windows Server 2016 system as shown in Figure 5-3.

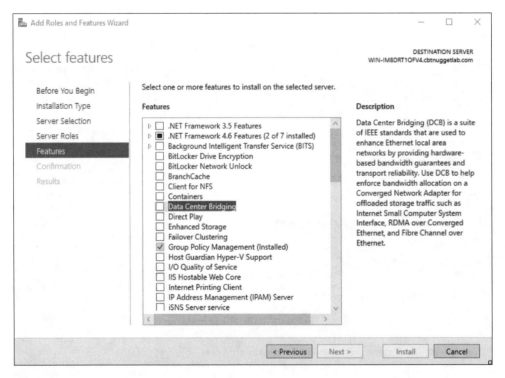

Figure 5-3   Installing DCB

Configuring Multipath IO (MPIO)

Creating a single connection to iSCSI storage makes that storage available. There is an issue, however, because this configuration does not make the storage highly available. If iSCSI loses the connection, the server loses access to its storage. Therefore, you should make most iSCSI storage connections redundant through one of two high-availability technologies—Multiple Connected Session (MCS) and Multipath I/O (MPIO).

MCS is an iSCSI protocol feature that does the following:

- Enables multiple TCP/IP connections from the initiator to the target for the same iSCSI session

- Supports automatic failover

- Needs explicit support by iSCSI SAN devices

MPIO offers redundancy in a different fashion:

- If you have multiple network interface cards in an iSCSI initiator and iSCSI Target Server, you can use MPIO to provide failover redundancy during network outages.

- MPIO needs a device-specific module (DSM) if you want to connect to a third-party SAN device connected to the iSCSI initiator.

- MPIO is widely supported.

- MPIO is more complex to configure and is not as fully automated during failover as MCS.

NOTE Our exam blueprint requires knowledge of the MPIO approach to SAN redundancy. This text presents MCS here for the sake of completeness.

You install MPIO in the Add Roles and Features Wizard, as shown in Figure 5-4.

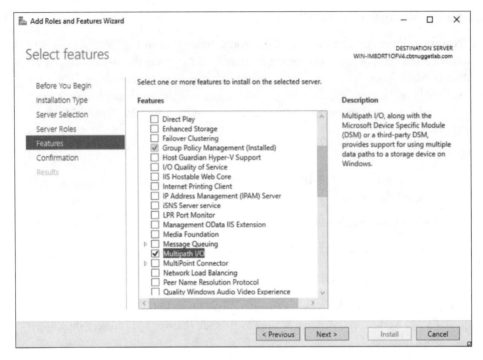

Figure 5-4   Installing MPIO

You can then carry out MPIO policy in the Properties dialog of your storage device (see Figure 5-5).

Figure 5-5   Configuring MPIO Policy

Storage Replica

Another exciting new data storage feature in Windows Server 2016 is Storage Replica. This technology permits storage and agnostic data replication between clusters or servers.

Remember these key points about Storage Replica:

- Synchronous and asynchronous replication choices exist; as the administrator, you can choose based on network latency and geographic distances.

- Storage Replica requires the Datacenter Edition of Windows Server 2016.

- Storage Replica requires GPT initialized disks.

- Supported replication scenarios include Server-to-Server, Cluster-to-Cluster, and Stretch Cluster.

- Only one-to-one replication is supported; a third replica is not an option.

- Storage Replica performs replication at the block level, and therefore you should not consider it for branch office scenarios with slow WAN links.

- Storage Replica can replicate data involving open files.

Determining Usage Scenarios for Storage Replica

While Storage Replica is not application specific, you should note that some replication technologies are better suited for some implementations. Table 5-2 shows appropriate usage scenarios for the Storage Replica feature. Note that this table also helps you determine the appropriate application-specific replication technology.

Table 5-2 Determining Usage Scenarios for Storage Replica

	Virtual Machine	SYSVOL	File Server	Microsoft Exchange	SQL Server
Hyper-V Replica	Yes	Not applicable	Yes (VMs)	No	Yes (VMs)
Storage Replica	Yes	No	Yes	No	Yes
SQL Server AlwaysOn Failover Cluster Instance	No	Not applicable	Not applicable	Not applicable	Yes
SQL Server AlwaysOn Availablity Groups	No	Not applicable	Not applicable	Not applicable	Yes
Microsoft Exchange Database Availability Groups	No	Not applicable	Not applicable	Yes	Not applicable
Distributed File System Replication	No	Yes	Yes	No	No

Implementing Storage Replica for Server-to-Server, Cluster-to-Cluster, and Stretch Cluster Scenarios

As described earlier in this section, there are three scenarios available with Storage Replica:

- Server-to-Server
- Cluster-to-Cluster
- Stretch Cluster

Server-to-Server

You use PowerShell to implement Server-to-Server replication, which involves the following requirements:

- The servers must be participants in a domain.
- Each storage set must have two volumes—one for data and one for logs. The two data volumes must be the same size, and their sector size must also be the same.
- Each file server needs at least a 1 GB connection.
- You need 4 GB of RAM in each server with at least two CPU cores.
- Firewalls must allow ICMP, SMB, and WS-MAN bidirectional traffic.
- You need a network between servers of at least 1 Gbps and 5 ms round-trip latency.
- Both server nodes must have local admin permissions.

Here is sample syntax for a PowerShell configuration:

```
New-SRPartnership -SourceComputerName SVR1 -SourceRGName RepGroup01
  -SourceVolumeName
F: -SourceLogVolumeName G: -DestinationComputerName SVR2
  -DestinationRGName RepGroup02
-DestinationVolumeName F: -DestinationLogVolumeName G:
  -LogSizeInBytes 8GB
```

Here is the complete cmdlet syntax:

```
New-SRPartnership [[-SourceComputerName] <String> ] [-SourceRGName]
  <String> [-DestinationComputerName] <String> [-DestinationRGName]
  <String> [[-ReplicationMode] <ReplicationMode> {Synchronous |
  Asynchronous} ] [[-PreventReplication]] [[-Seeded]] [[-AsyncRPO]
  <UInt32> ] [[-EnableEncryption]] [[-Force]] [-CimSession
  <CimSession[]> ] [-ThrottleLimit <Int32> ] [ <CommonParameters>] [
  <WorkflowParameters>]
```

Cluster-to-Cluster

You use PowerShell to implement Cluster-to-Cluster replication. The requirements for Cluster-to-Cluster replication are identical to those for Server-to-Server.

Here are the steps for PowerShell Cluster-to-Cluster configuration:

Step 1. Grant the first cluster full access to the other cluster by running the **Grant-ClusterAccess** cmdlet on any node in the first cluster or remotely:

```
Grant-SRAccess -ComputerName SRV01 -Cluster SRVCLUSB
```

Step 2. Grant the second cluster full access to the other cluster by running the **Grant-ClusterAccess** cmdlet on any node in the second cluster or remotely:

```
Grant-SRAccess -ComputerName SRV03 -Cluster SRVCLUSA
```

Step 3. Configure the Cluster-to-Cluster replication, specifying the source and destination disks, the source and destination logs, the source and destination cluster names, and the log size. You can perform this command locally on the server or using a remote management computer:

```
New-SRPartnership -SourceComputerName SRVCLUSA -SourceRGName rg01
  -SourceVolumeName c:\ClusterStorage\Volume2
  -SourceLogVolumeName f: -DestinationComputerName SRVCLUSB
  -DestinationRGName rg02 -DestinationVolumeName c:\
ClusterStorage\Volume2 -DestinationLogVolumeName f:
```

Stretch Cluster

Stretch Cluster is a configuration that features one Hyper-V cluster with nodes in two locations and storage in both locations. It allows failover of virtual machines from one cluster to the other. Requirements are identical to those for Server-to-Server and Cluster-to-Cluster.

You configure Stretch Cluster using Failover Cluster Manager or Windows PowerShell. To use the Failover Cluster Manager, follow these steps:

Step 1. Add a source data disk to a role or CSV.

Step 2. Enable replication on that source data disk.

Step 3. Select a destination data disk.

Step 4. Select a source log disk.

Step 5. Select a destination log disk.

To use PowerShell, follow these steps:

Step 1. Add the source data storage only to the cluster as CSV. To get the size, partition, and volume layout of the available disks, use the following commands:

```
Move-ClusterGroup -Name "available storage" -Node sr-srv01


$DiskResources = Get-ClusterResource | Where-Object {
$_.ResourceType -eq 'Physical Disk' -and $_.State -eq 'Online' }
$DiskResources | foreach {
    $resource = $_
    $DiskGuidValue = $resource | Get-ClusterParameter DiskIdGuid


    Get-Disk | where { $_.Guid -eq $DiskGuidValue.Value } |
Get-Partition | Get-Volume |
        Select @{N="Name"; E={$resource.Name}}, @{N="Status";
E={$resource.State}}, DriveLetter, FileSystemLabel, Size,
SizeRemaining
} | FT -AutoSize


Move-ClusterGroup -Name "available storage" -Node sr-srv03


$DiskResources = Get-ClusterResource | Where-Object {
$_.ResourceType -eq 'Physical Disk' -and $_.State -eq 'Online' }
$DiskResources | foreach {
    $resource = $_
    $DiskGuidValue = $resource | Get-ClusterParameter DiskIdGuid


    Get-Disk | where { $_.Guid -eq $DiskGuidValue.Value } | Get-
Partition | Get-Volume |
        Select @{N="Name"; E={$resource.Name}}, @{N="Status";
E={$resource.State}}, DriveLetter, FileSystemLabel, Size,
SizeRemaining
} | FT -AutoSize
```

Step 2. Set the correct disk to CSV:

```
Add-ClusterSharedVolume -Name "Cluster Disk 4"
Get-ClusterSharedVolume
Move-ClusterSharedVolume -Name "Cluster Disk 4" -Node sr-srv01
```

Step 3. Configure the Stretch Cluster, as in this example:

```
New-SRPartnership -SourceComputerName sr-srv01
  -SourceRGName rg01 -SourceVolumeName "C:\ClusterStorage\
  Volume1" -SourceLogVolumeName e: -DestinationComputerName
  sr-srv03 -DestinationRGName rg02 -DestinationVolumeName d:
  -DestinationLogVolumeName e:
```

Exam Preparation Tasks

As mentioned in the section "How to Use This Book" in the Introduction, you have a couple choices for exam preparation: the exercises here, Chapter 21, "Final Preparation," and the exam simulation questions in the Pearson Test Prep Software Online.

Review All Key Topics

Review the most important topics in this chapter, noted with the Key Topics icon in the outer margin of the page. Table 5-3 lists these key topics and the page number on which each is found.

Table 5-3 Key Topics for Chapter 5

Key Topic Element	Description	Page Number
List	Storage layout options	86
Steps	Storage Pool expansion	88
Command	Manually optimizing tiered storage	89
List	PowerShell cmdlets for iSCSI targets	90
List	Storage Replica key points	95

Complete Tables and Lists from Memory

Print a copy of Appendix B, "Memory Tables" (found on the book website), or at least the section for this chapter, and complete the tables and lists from memory. Appendix C, "Memory Tables Answer Key," also on the website, includes completed tables and lists you can use to check your work.

Define Key Terms

Define the following key terms from this chapter and check your answers against the glossary:

Storage Spaces, Storage Pool, Tiered Storage, iSCSI Target, iSCSI Initiator, iSNS, DCB, MPIO, Storage Replica

Q&A

The answers to these questions appear in Appendix A. For more practice with exam format questions, use the Pearson Test Prep Software Online.

1. What two tiers of disk types are used with tiering inside Storage Spaces?

2. What PowerShell command can you use to connect an iSCSI target in a Windows Server 2016 environment?

3. What type of partition system does Storage Replica require on disks? What edition of Windows Server 2016 does it require?

This chapter covers the following subjects:

- **Usage Scenarios for Deduplication:** This section explains when data deduplication is most effective.

- **Implementing Deduplication:** If you wonder how exactly you use data deduplication in Windows Server 2016, this section is for you.

- **Deduplication Monitoring:** You need to ensure that your data deduplication efforts are effective. This section of the chapter ensures that you can successfully monitor such efforts.

## CHAPTER 6

Data Deduplication

Data deduplication is a feature of Windows Server 2016 that helps reduce the impact of redundant data in the storage environment. Obviously, this can help dramatically reduce overall storage costs. Data deduplication optimizes free space on volumes by examining the data on a volume and looking for duplicated portions. Duplicated portions of the volume's dataset are stored once and can even be compressed for added storage and cost savings.

"Do I Know This Already?" Quiz

The "Do I Know This Already?" quiz allows you to assess whether you should read the entire chapter. Table 6-1 lists the major headings in this chapter and the "Do I Know This Already?" quiz questions covering the material in those headings so you can assess your knowledge of these specific areas. The answers to the "Do I Know This Already?" quiz appear in Appendix A, "Answers to the 'Do I Know This Already?' Quizzes and Q&A Questions."

Table 6-1 "Do I Know This Already?" Foundation Topics Section-to-Question Mapping

Foundation Topics Section	Questions
Usage Scenarios for Deduplication	1, 2
Implementing Deduplication	3, 4
Deduplication Monitoring	5, 6

CAUTION The goal of self-assessment is to gauge your mastery of the topics in this chapter. If you do not know the answer to a question or are only partially sure of the answer, you should mark your answer as incorrect for purposes of the self-assessment. Giving yourself credit for an answer you correctly guess skews your self-assessment results and might provide you with a false sense of security.

1. What tool should you use to evaluate your workload for data deduplication?

   a. DeDupEval

   b. ICD

   c. ADK

   d. DDPEval

2. When should you be concerned regarding deduplication and performance?

   a. When you are using HDDs instead of SSDs

   b. When you are using it against a general file server

   c. When you are using it against a VDI

   d. When you are integrating it with backup

3. Which of the following is not a valid usage type in data deduplication?

   a. Default

   b. Backup

   c. Hyper-V

   d. SYSVOL

4. What PowerShell command enables data deduplication?

   a. **Enable-DedupVolume**

   b. **Enable-DataDedup**

   c. **Enable-DDVol**

   d. **Enable-DeDupVol**

5. Which of the following is a powerful PowerShell data deduplication monitoring command?

   a. **Get-DedupStats**

   b. **Get-DedupStatus**

   c. **Get-DedupInfo**

   d. **Get-StrorageStats**

6. Which of the following is a special tag that notifies the file system to pass off I/O to a specified file system filter?

   a. Reparse point

   b. Churn flag

   c. Checkpoint

   d. Pass point

Foundation Topics

Usage Scenarios for Deduplication

The storage space savings that you realize from data deduplication will certainly vary based on workloads. Microsoft provides the following estimates:

- **User documents**: 30% to 50%
- **Deployment shares**: 70% to 80%
- **Virtualization libraries**: 80% to 95%
- **General file shares**: 50% to 60%

Given this information, you should consider data deduplication in the following scenarios:

- **With general-purpose file servers:** There will be plenty of opportunity for data deduplication to work its magic in these environments—often consisting of team shares, user home folders, work folders, and software development shares.

- **With Virtualized Desktop Infrastructure (VDI) deployments:** Many virtual hard disks are practically identical.

- **With backup targets:** So much of the data we store as backups is identical to other data we have backed up!

You should consider the following questions before deploying data deduplication for a workload.

- **Does my workload have enough duplication to benefit from the feature?** Learn how much duplication your workload's dataset has by using the Data Deduplication Savings Evaluation tool, **DDPEval**. After installing this tool, you can find it at C:\Windows\System32\DDPEval.exe. **DDPEval** can evaluate the potential for optimization against directly connected volumes and mapped or unmapped network shares.

- **Will data deduplication affect performance negatively?** Keep in mind that data deduplication is a periodic task that could interrupt the performance requirements of your workload. This is of most concern for workloads stored in traditional HDDs as opposed to SSDs.

- **What are the resource requirements of the workload?** Storage that has "downtime," such as weekends, is often an excellent candidate for data deduplication since this processing can occur during those times.

Implementing Deduplication

The following is an important list of data deduplication terminology you should be familiar with before implementation:

- **Chunk**: A part of a file that Data Deduplication selected by the chunking algorithm as likely to occur in other, similar files

- **Chunk store**: An organized series of container files in the System Volume Information folder that **DDPEval** uses to uniquely store chunks

- **Dedup**: An abbreviation for data deduplication that is commonly used in PowerShell, Windows Server APIs and components, and the Windows Server community

- **File metadata**: Information that describes properties about the file that are not related to the main content of the file

- **File stream**: The main content of the file

- **File system**: The software and on-disk data structure that the operating system uses to store files on storage media

- **File system filter**: A plugin that modifies the default behavior of the file system

- **Optimization**: The process of chunking a file and storing its unique chunks in the chunk store

- **Optimization policy**: A policy which specifies the files that should be considered for data deduplication

- **Reparse point**: A special tag that notifies the file system to pass off I/O to a specified file system filter; in data deduplication, it is the way optimized files are stored (pointers to a chunk map)

- **Volume**: A Windows construct for a logical storage drive that may span multiple physical storage devices across one or more servers

- **Workload**: An application that runs on Windows Server

Windows Server 2016 significantly enhances data deduplication in several ways:

- **Support for larger volumes**: Server 2016 now supports volume sizes up to 64 TB.

- **Support for larger files**: Files up to 1 TB are fully supported.

- **Support for Nano Server**: Data deduplication functions in the Nano Server environment.

- **Simplified backup support**: A new default usage type now supports seamless deployment of data deduplication for virtualized backup applications.

There are three usage types to choose from when implementing data deduplication:

- **Default**: This is the option to choose for general-purpose file servers.

    - Background optimization

    - Default optimization policy: Minimum file age = 3 days; Optimize in-use files = No; Optimize partial files = No

- **Hyper-V**: This is deduplication tuned specifically for VDI servers.

    - Background optimization

    - Default optimization policy: Minimum file age = 3 days; Optimize in-use files = Yes; Optimize partial files = Yes

    - "Under-the-hood" tweaks for Hyper-V interoperability

- **Backup**: This is tuning for virtualized backup applications.

    - Priority optimization

    - Default optimization policy: Minimum file age = 0 days; Optimize in-use files = Yes; Optimize partial files = No

    - "Under-the-hood" tweaks for interop with DPM/DPM-like solutions

You should be familiar with the following jobs that make data deduplication possible:

- **Optimization**: Deduplicates by chunking data on a volume per the volume policy settings, (optionally) compressing those chunks, and storing chunks uniquely in the chunk store

- **Garbage Collection**: Reclaims disk space by removing unnecessary chunks that are no longer being referenced by files that have been recently modified or deleted

- **Integrity Scrubbing**: Identifies corruption in the chunk store due to disk failures or bad sectors

- **Unoptimization**: Undoes the optimization done by deduplication and disables data deduplication for that volume

To install Data Deduplication, follow these steps:

Step 1.   In the Add Roles and Feature Wizard, select **Server Roles** and then select **Data Deduplication**, as shown in Figure 6-1.

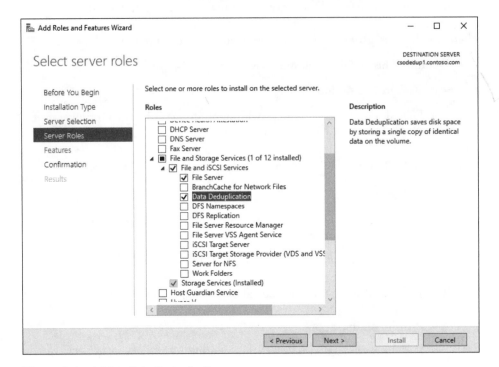

Figure 6-1   Adding Data Deduplication

Step 2.   Click **Next** until the Install button is active, and then click **Install**.

You can also install Data Deduplication by using PowerShell, as shown here:

```
Install-WindowsFeature -Name FS-Data-Deduplication
```

Nano Server is an excellent host for Data Deduplication. To install on this edition, follow these steps:

Step 1.   Create a Nano Server installation with Storage installed.

Step 2.   From a server running Windows Server 2016, execute the following:

```
Install-WindowsFeature -ComputerName <MyNanoServer> -Name
    FS-Data-Deduplication
```

To enable Data Deduplication in Server Manager, follow these steps:

Step 1.   Select **File and Storage Services** in Server Manager.

Step 2.   Select **Volumes** from File and Storage Services.

Step 3.   Right-click the desired volume and select **Configure Data Deduplication,** as shown in Figure 6-2.

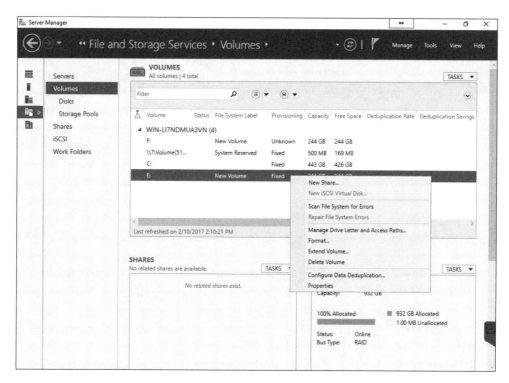

Figure 6-2   Selecting a Volume for Data Deduplication

Step 4.   Select the desired usage type from the drop-down box and click **OK**, as shown in Figure 6-3.

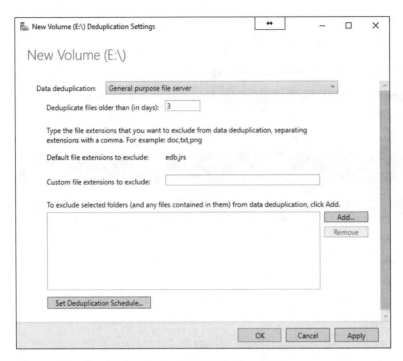

Figure 6-3   Configuring the Data Deduplication Settings

For PowerShell, use the **Enable-DedupVolume** cmdlet, which has the following
syntax:

```
Enable-DedupVolume [-Volume] <String[]> [-CimSession <CimSession[]>
] [-DataAccess] [-ThrottleLimit <Int32> ] [-UsageType <UsageType>
{Default | HyperV | Backup} ] [ <CommonParameters>]
```

Data deduplication jobs can be run manually at any time using the following
PowerShell cmdlets:

- **Start-DedupJob**: Starts a new data deduplication job:

```
Start-DedupJob [-Type] <Type> {Optimization | GarbageCollection
   | Scrubbing | Unoptimization} [[-Volume] <String[]>
   ] [-CimSession <CimSession[]> ] [-Cores <System.
   UInt32> ] [-Full] [-InputOutputThrottle <System.UInt32> ]
   [-InputOutputThrottleLevel <InputOutputThrottleLevel> {None |
   Low | Medium | High | Maximum} ] [-Memory <UInt32> ]
   [-Preempt] [-Priority <Priority> {Low | Normal | High} ]
   [-ReadOnly] [-StopWhenSystemBusy] [-ThrottleLimit <Int32> ]
   [-Timestamp <DateTime> ] [-Wait] [ <CommonParameters>]
```

- **Stop-DedupJob**: Stops a data deduplication job that's already in progress (or removes it from the queue):

```
Stop-DedupJob [-Volume] <String[]> [[-Type] <Type[]> ]
   [-CimSession <CimSession[]> ] [-PassThru] [-ThrottleLimit
   <Int32> ] [ <CommonParameters>]
```

- **Get-DedupJob**: Shows all the active and queued data deduplication jobs:

```
Get-DedupJob [[-Type] <Type[]> ] [[-Volume] <String[]> ]
   [-CimSession <CimSession[]> ] [-ThrottleLimit <Int32> ] [
   <CommonParameters>]
```

To disable date deduplication, run the following:

```
Start-DedupJob -Type Unoptimization -Volume <Desired-Volume>
```

NOTE The Unoptimization job fails if the volume does not have sufficient space to hold the unoptimized data.

Deduplication Monitoring

Obviously, monitoring is a key element of your success with data deduplication.

You can use **Get-DedupStatus** in PowerShell for the most effective monitoring. Keep in mind the following:

- For the Optimization job, look at LastOptimizationResult (0 = success), LastOptimizationResultMessage, and LastOptimizationTime (should be recent)

- For the Garbage Collection job, look at LastGarbageCollectionResult (0 = success), LastGarbageCollectionResultMessage, and LastGarbageCollectionTime (should be recent)

- For the Integrity Scrubbing job, look at LastScrubbingResult (0 = success), LastScrubbingResultMessage, and LastScrubbingTime (should be recent)

An important indicator of Optimization job failure is a downward-trending optimization rate, which might indicate that the Optimization jobs are not keeping up with the rate of changes, or churn. You can check the optimization rate by using the **Get-DedupStatus** PowerShell cmdlet.

Get-DedupStatus has two fields that are relevant to the optimization rate, both of which are important values to track:

- **OptimizedFilesSavingsRate** applies only to the files that are "in-policy" for optimization (space used by optimized files after optimization/logical size of optimized files)

- **SavingsRate** applies to the entire volume (space used by optimized files after optimization/total logical size of the optimization)

Here is the complete syntax for the **Get-DedupStatus** cmdlet:

```
Get-DedupStatus [[-Volume] <String[]> ] [-CimSession <CimSession[]> ]
    [-ThrottleLimit <Int32> ] [ <CommonParameters>]
```

Exam Preparation Tasks

As mentioned in the section "How to Use This Book" in the Introduction, you have a couple choices for exam preparation: the exercises here, Chapter 21, "Final Preparation," and the exam simulation questions in the Pearson Test Prep Software Online.

Review All Key Topics

Review the most important topics in this chapter, noted with the Key Topics icon in the outer margin of the page. Table 6-2 lists these key topics and the page number on which each is found.

Table 6-2 Key Topics for Chapter 6

Key Topic Element	Description	Page Number
List	Scenarios for data deduplication	105
List	Data deduplication terminology	106
Command	PowerShell implementation of data deduplication	110
Command	PowerShell monitoring of data deduplication	111

Complete Tables and Lists from Memory

There are no memory tables in this chapter.

Define Key Terms

Define the following key terms from this chapter and check your answers against the glossary:

Chunk, Chunk Store, Dedup, File Metadata, File Stream, File System, File System Filter, Optimization, Optimization Policy, Reparse Point, Volume, Workload

Q&A

The answers to these questions appear in Appendix A. For more practice with exam format questions, use the Pearson Test Prep Software Online.

1. Name three scenarios that would be ideal for data deduplication.

2. What data deduplication policy specifies that files should be considered for data deduplication?

3. What two fields in **Get-DedupStatus** are relevant to the optimization rate?

This chapter covers the following subjects:

- **Preparing for Installation:** Just as with Server 2016 itself, you must carry out careful planning before you attempt to roll out a Hyper-V deployment. This section ensures that you are aware of the various requirements.

- **Installing Hyper-V:** When it is time to deploy Hyper-V, you should use this section as a guide. It discusses the installation of Hyper-V using the GUI as well as PowerShell.

- **Managing VMs:** There are many options for managing the many VMs you might have in a Hyper-V deployment. This section ensures that you are familiar with these options.

CHAPTER 7

Installing Hyper-V

Hyper-V allows amazing system virtualization and was one of the main areas of focus for Microsoft in revising Server 2012 R2 for the new and improved Server 2016 version. This chapter examines many of these improved capabilities, including nested virtualization.

"Do I Know This Already?" Quiz

The "Do I Know This Already?" quiz allows you to assess whether you should read the entire chapter. Table 7-1 lists the major headings in this chapter and the "Do I Know This Already?" quiz questions covering the material in those headings so you can assess your knowledge of these specific areas. The answers to the "Do I Know This Already?" quiz appear in Appendix A, "Answers to the 'Do I Know This Already?' Quizzes and Q&A Questions."

Table 7-1 "Do I Know This Already?" Foundation Topics Section-to-Question Mapping

Foundation Topics Section	Questions
Preparing for Installation	1, 2
Installing Hyper-V	3, 4
Managing VMs	5, 6

CAUTION The goal of self-assessment is to gauge your mastery of the topics in this chapter. If you do not know the answer to a question or are only partially sure of the answer, you should mark your answer as incorrect for purposes of the self-assessment. Giving yourself credit for an answer you correctly guess skews your self-assessment results and might provide you with a false sense of security.

1. At least how much RAM should you reserve for the host Windows Server 2016 OS in a Hyper-V deployment?

   a. 8 GB

   b. 1 GB

   c. 4 GB

   d. 2 GB

2. What application can you run to test your system for Hyper-V?

   a. TestHyperV.exe

   b. Systeminfo.exe

   c. TestVirtual.exe

   d. CheckVHD.exe

3. What PowerShell cmdlet can you use to install Hyper-V?

   a. **Install-HyperV**

   b. **NewFeature-HyperV**

   c. **Install-WindowsFeature**

   d. **Create-WindowsHyperV**

4. What cmdlet can you use to check for the success of the installation of Hyper-V?

   a. **Get-WindowsFeature**

   b. **Acquire-WindowsFeature**

   c. **Check-HyperV**

   d. **Test-HyperV**

5. Which option can you use if you are not logged on as the admin of your Hyper-V system and you want to manage the remote Hyper-V device?

   a. Delegate to self admin

   b. Connect as admin

   c. Elevate permission

   d. Connect as another user

6. To enable nested virtualization, at least how much RAM should you have?

   a. 2 GB

   b. 4 GB

   c. 8 GB

   d. 16 GB

Foundation Topics

Preparing for Installation

Microsoft certainly understands the importance of its server-based virtualization platform and has added many new features and improvements to the platform. Here are the main new features you should be aware of:

- **Windows Server Hyper-V containers and Docker**: Docker support offers more application isolation than using other container technologies.

- **Host resource protection**: You can protect virtual machines from other VMs that might be trying to use excessive resources.

- **Nested virtualization**: This awesome new feature lets you create virtualization instances inside an existing VM.

- **PowerShell Direct**: This feature allows you to run commands in PowerShell against your virtual machines; this is carried out with special configuration or remoting capabilities.

- **Shielded virtual machines**: You can encrypt virtual machines and force them to run on host guardian server clients only.

- **Virtual Trusted Platform Modules**: You can use Trusted Platform Modules (TPM) in virtual machines.

- **BitLocker Drive Encryption**: You can use BitLocker Drive Encryption with virtual machines.

- **Hot Add/Remove Memory**: While a VM is online, you can now add static memory.

- **Hot Add/Remove Network Adapters**: While a VM is online, you can now add network adapters.

The following features have been greatly improved:

- **Checkpoints**: Windows Server 2016 improves checkpoints with a new production checkpoint feature; production checkpoints are "point in time" images of a virtual machine, which can be restored later in a way that is completely supported for all production workloads; this is achieved through using backup technology inside the VM instead of the more traditional saved state approach.

- **Linux**: Many of the latest versions of Linux can now use Secure Boot.

- **Storage Quality of Server (QoS)**: Windows Server 2016 improves QoS dramatically with support for Scale-Out File Server and centrally managed QoS policies.

The following are some of the Hyper-V Manager improvements:

- **Hyper-V Manager**: This critical management tool now supports alternate credentials.

- **Connections over the Web Services Management Protocol**: Hyper-V Manager can communicate using Kerberos, MT LAN Manager, or Credential Security Support Provider.

- **Previous version support**: The Hyper-V Manager running on Windows Server 2016 can manage earlier versions of Hyper-V (Windows Server 2012, for example).

Installation Prerequisites

It is critical that you supply the proper prerequisites for the installation of Hyper-V:

- x64 processor with Second Level Address Translation (SLAT)

- A minimum of 4 GB of RAM

- At least 1 GB of RAM for the host operating system of Windows Server 2016

- VM Monitor Mode extensions

- Virtualization support enabled in the BIOS or UEFI

- Processors with Intel Virtualization Technology (Intel VT) or AMD Virtualization (AMD-V) technology

- Available and enabled hardware-enforced Data Execution Prevention (DEP); for Intel systems, this is the XD bit (execute disable bit), and for AMD systems, it is the NX bit (no execute bit)

You should not use third-party virtualization apps that rely on the same processor features that Hyper-V needs; examples include VMware Workstation and VirtualBox.

NOTE You can use Systeminfo.exe from a command prompt or Windows Power-Shell to check your system for the requirements. There is a Hyper-V Requirements section in the report.

Remember that certain advanced features in Hyper-V need specific components. Consider the following examples:

- **Discrete device assignment**: The processor must have either Intel's Extended Page Table (EPT) or AMD's Nested Page Table (NPT); the chipset must have interrupt remapping, such as Intel's VT-d with the Interrupt Remapping capability (VT-d2) or any version of AMD I/O Memory Management Unit (I/O MMU); DMA remapping is required, such as Intel's VT-d with Queued Invalidations or any AMD I/O MMU; Access Control Service (ACS) must be available on PCI Express root ports; and devices need GPU or nonvolatile memory express (NVMe).

- **Shielded virtual machines have the following requirements**:

  - **Host requirements**: UEFI 2.3.1c supports secure, measured boot; TPM v2.0 protects platform security assets; IOMMU (Intel VT-D) enables the hypervisor to provide direct memory access (DMA) protection.

  - **Virtual machine requirements**: The VM must be Generation 2, and the guest operating system must be Windows Server 2016, Windows Server 2012 R2, or Windows Server 2012.

Installing Hyper-V

To install Hyper-V using the GUI, follow these steps:

Step 1.   In Server Manager, select **Manage > Add Roles and Features**.

Step 2.   On the **Before You Begin** page, verify that your destination server and network environment are prepared for the role and feature you want to install and click **Next**.

Step 3.   On the **Select Installation Type** page, as shown in Figure 7-1, select **Role-based or feature-based installation** and then click **Next**.

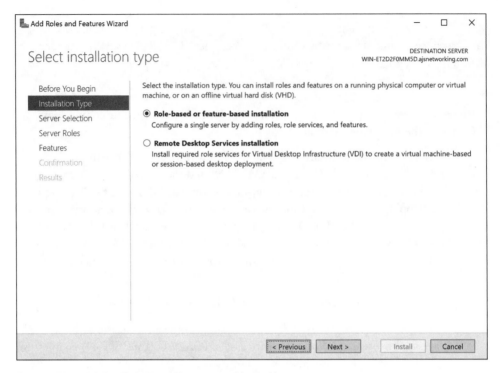

Figure 7-1   Adding Roles and Features to Hyper-V

Step 4.   On the **Select Destination Server** page, select a server from the server pool and then click **Next.**

Step 5.   On the **Select Server Roles** page, select **Hyper-V**, as shown in Figure 7-2.

Step 6.   To add the tools you use to create and manage virtual machines, click **Add Features** on the **Features** page and click **Next**.

Step 7.   On the **Create Virtual Switches** page (see Figure 7-3), the **Virtual Machine Migration** page, and the **Default Stores** page, select the proper options.

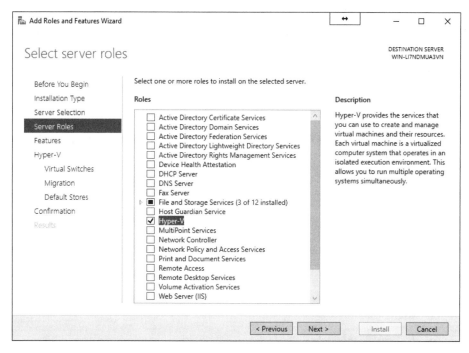

Figure 7-2   Selecting the Hyper-V Role

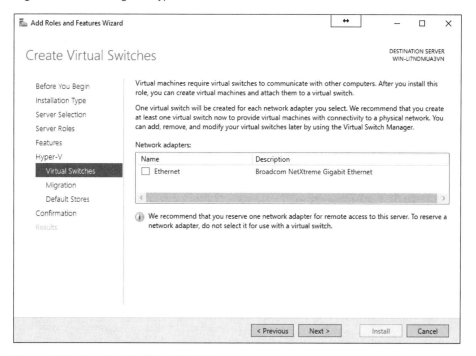

Figure 7-3   Creating the Virtual Switch

Step 8.   On the **Confirm Installation Selections** page, click **Restart to restart** the destination server automatically, if required, and then click **Install**.

To install Hyper-V using the **Install-WindowsFeature** cmdlet, follow these steps:

Step 1.   Launch **Windows PowerShell**, right-click, and choose **Run as Administrator**.

Step 2.   To install Hyper-V on a server you are connected to remotely, run this command:

```
Install-WindowsFeature -Name Hyper-V -ComputerName
  <computer_name> -IncludeManagementTools -Restart
```

NOTE   If you are performing the installation on the local server, run the command without the **-ComputerName** parameter.

Step 3.   After the server restarts, check the success of installation with the following command:

```
Get-WindowsFeature -ComputerName <computer_name>
```

Managing VMs

As described in the following sections, there are more options for managing VMs in your Hyper-V environment than ever before.

Delegating Virtual Machine Management

Your fellow administrators can connect to the Hyper-V host when they are not running on the local computer as a user that is a member of either the Hyper-V Administrators group or a member of the Administrators group of your Hyper-V host. Admins can follow these steps in Hyper-V Manager:

Step 1.   In Server Manager, select **Tools > Hyper-V Manager**.

Step 2.   In the left pane, select **Hyper-V Manager**.

Step 3.   Click **Connect to Server** in the **Actions** pane (see Figure 7-4).

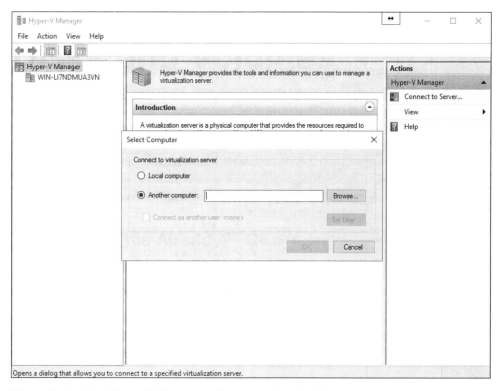

Figure 7-4   Using Hyper-V Manager to Connect to Another Server

> **Step 4.**   Select **Another computer** in the **Select Computer** dialog and then click **Connect as another user**.

> **Step 5.**   Click **Set User**.

You can also use delegation so that an administrator can connect to a system that is outside his or her domain or with no domain at all:

> **Step 1.**   On the Hyper-V host where you want remote management capabilities, open PowerShell as an administrator.

> **Step 2.**   Run the following commands:

```
Set-Item WSMan:\localhost\Client\TrustedHosts -Value
  "fqdn-of-hyper-v-host"


Enable-WSManCredSSP -Role client -DelegateComputer
  "fqdn-of-hyper-v-host"
```

Step 3.   Configure the following group policy:

Computer Configuration > Administrative Templates > System > Credentials Delegation > Allow delegating fresh credentials with NTLM-only server authentication

Then click **Enable** and add wsman/fqdn-of-hyper-v-host. Figure 7-5 shows credentials delegation settings in the Group Policy Editor.

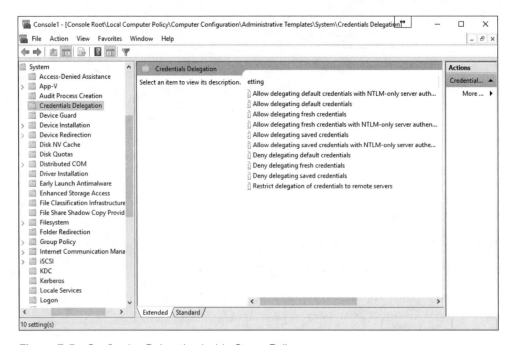

Figure 7-5   Configuring Delegation Inside Group Policy

Step 4.   Open Hyper-V Manager.

Step 5.   Right-click **Hyper-V Manager** in the left pane.

Step 6.   Click **Connect to Server.**

PowerShell Direct

Remember from Chapter 3, "Working with Images," that there are two ways to run PowerShell Direct:

- Create and exit a PowerShell Direct session using **PSSession** cmdlets.
- Run a script or command with the **Invoke-Command** cmdlet.

Nested Virtualization

To enable nested virtualization, you need the following:

- At least 4 GB of RAM

- Windows Server 2016 or Windows 10 Anniversary Update as your operating system

- A virtual machine the same build as the host for the VM that is running Hyper-V

- An Intel processor with VT-x and EPT technology

To configure nested virtualization, follow these steps:

Step 1.   Create a virtual machine.

Step 2.   With the virtual machine in the OFF state, run the following command on the physical Hyper-V host:

```
Set-VMProcessor -VMName <VMName> -ExposeVirtualizationExtensions
    $true
```

Step 3.   Start the virtual machine.

Step 4.   Install Hyper-V on the virtual machine.

Exam Preparation Tasks

As mentioned in the section "How to Use This Book" in the Introduction, you have a couple choices for exam preparation: the exercises here, Chapter 21, "Final Preparation," and the exam simulation questions in the Pearson Test Prep Software Online.

Review All Key Topics

Review the most important topics in this chapter, noted with the Key Topics icon in the outer margin of the page. Table 7-2 lists these key topics and the page number on which each is found.

Table 7-2   Key Topics for Chapter 7

Key Topic Element	Description	Page Number
List	Prerequisites for Hyper-V installation	118
Steps	Installing Hyper-V	119
Steps	Delegating Hyper-V management	123
Steps	Configuring nested virtualization	125

Complete Tables and Lists from Memory

There are no memory tables for this chapter.

Define Key Terms

Define the following key terms from this chapter and check your answers against the glossary:

Docker, PowerShell Direct, Shielded Virtual Machine, Checkpoints, Hyper-V Manager, Nested Virtualization

Q&A

The answers to these questions appear in Appendix A. For more practice with exam format questions, use the Pearson Test Prep Software Online.

1. Name at least three requirements that you must meet in order to run shielded virtual machines.

2. How can you install Hyper-V using the GUI?

3. Name at least two requirements for nested virtualization.

This chapter covers the following subjects:

- **Basic Virtual Machine Deployment:** This section covers rather basic configurations that are nonetheless critical. In fact, this area of the chapter delves into important considerations such as memory and resource metering.

- **Advanced Virtual Machine Deployment:** This part of the chapter details more advanced virtual machine management techniques, including best practices for Linux and FreeBSD environments.

## CHAPTER 8

Working with Virtual Machines

In the heavily virtualized world of information technology, virtual machines play a key role in the datacenter. This chapter focuses on the deployment and management of these various virtual machines, using some important best practices.

"Do I Know This Already?" Quiz

The "Do I Know This Already?" quiz allows you to assess whether you should read the entire chapter. Table 8-1 lists the major headings in this chapter and the "Do I Know This Already?" quiz questions covering the material in those headings so you can assess your knowledge of these specific areas. The answers to the "Do I Know This Already?" quiz appear in Appendix A, "Answers to the 'Do I Know This Already?' Quizzes and Q&A Questions."

Table 8-1 "Do I Know This Already?" Foundation Topics Section-to-Question Mapping

Foundation Topics Section	Questions
Basic Virtual Machine Deployment	1–4
Advanced Virtual Machine Deployment	5–8

CAUTION The goal of self-assessment is to gauge your mastery of the topics in this chapter. If you do not know the answer to a question or are only partially sure of the answer, you should mark your answer as incorrect for purposes of the self-assessment. Giving yourself credit for an answer you correctly guess skews your self-assessment results and might provide you with a false sense of security.

1. Which is not an Add Hardware option for a VM in Hyper-V?

   a. SCSI controller

   b. Virtual Fibre Channel adapter

   c. Legacy network adapter

   d. Smart paging file location

2. What cmdlet do you use to update a VM version?

   a. **Update-VMVersion**

   b. **Update-VMType**

   c. **Upgrade-VM**

   d. **Upgrade-VersionVM**

3. What dynamic memory setting allows you to specify how to prioritize the availability of memory for this virtual machine compared to other virtual machines on the host?

   a. Resource metering

   b. Memory weight

   c. Memory buffer

   d. Maximum RAM

4. What cmdlet enables resource metering?

   a. **Enable-VMMetering**

   b. **Enable-RMVM**

   c. **Enable-VMResourceMetering**

   d. **Enable-VMRM**

5. What mode allows you to resize the VMConnect window?

   a. DDA Mode

   b. KVM Mode

   c. Enhanced Session Mode

   d. Virtual Machine Compatibility Mode

6. Which of the following is a false statement about LIS and BIS?

    a. FreeBSD 10.0 contains BIS.

    b. They provide drivers and services for improved integration.

    c. They are never present in distributions.

    d. LIS 4.0 ships with two scripts: Install.SH and Upgrade.SH.

7. Which OS is not enabled for Secure Boot?

    a. CentOS 6.0 and later

    b. RHEL 7 and later

    c. Ubuntu 14.04 and later

    d. SUSE Linux Enterprise Server 12 and later

8. Which of the following is not an option when moving a VM?

    a. Moving all the VM's data to a single location

    b. Moving the VM's data to different locations

    c. Moving the VM's virtual hard disks

    d. Moving just the VM configuration file

Foundation Topics

Basic Virtual Machine Deployment

One of the key first decisions with virtual machines in the Hyper-V environment of Windows Server 2016 is the use of Generation 1 versus Generation 2 VMs. The section "Planning for Windows Server Virtualization" in Chapter 3, "Working with Images," discusses this key topic at length. Be sure to refresh your memory on this information if required. Here is a brief recap of the advantages of Generation 2 VMs:

- PXE boot
- SCSI boot
- Boot volume size
- VHDX boot volume resizing
- Software-based peripherals
- Enhanced Session Mode

- Shielded Virtual Machines
- Storage Spaces Direct

> **NOTE** Shielded Virtual Machines ensure that the disk and the system state are encrypted and accessible only by authorized administrators; Virtual Machine Connection inside of Hyper-V Manager cannot be used to connect to these machines.

An Overview of Virtual Machine Settings

Settings for virtual machines are stored in *.vmcx* and *.vmrs* files. A *.vmcx file* is for VM configuration settings, while a *.vmrs file* is for runtime data.

Remember that virtual machines use simulated (virtual) hardware. This abstraction layer manages access to the actual physical hardware of the host. Note that Generation 1 virtual machines have the following hardware by default:

- BIOS
- Memory
- Processor
- IDE controller
- SCSI controller
- Hyper-V-specific network adapter
- COM port
- Disk drive

The following options are available with the Add Hardware option in the Properties dialog of a virtual machine:

- SCSI controller
- Legacy network adapter
- Virtual Fibre Channel adapter
- Microsoft RemoteFX 3D video adapter

> **NOTE** To start a VM from the network, we use a Gen 2 VM or a Gen 1 VM with the legacy network adapter.

Available management settings include the following:

- Name
- Integration services
- Checkpoint file location
- Smart paging file location

- Automatic start action
- Automatic stop action

Virtual Machine Configuration Versions

Configuration versions represent a virtual machine's compatibility settings for its configuration, *saved stateseckpoint files*. In earlier versions of Hyper-V, virtual machines upgraded as soon as they moved to the upgraded host. With Windows Server 2016, a virtual machine's configuration version does not upgrade automatically. The process of upgrading the VM version is now "manual" with Hyper-V in Windows Server 2016.

This is an important change because, with rolling upgrades, it is highly likely that a Hyper-V failover cluster might have both Windows Server 2012 R2 and Windows Server 2016. Windows Server 2012 R2 version 5.0 runs on both Windows Server 2012 R2 and Windows Server 2016 hosts. This allows administrators to leave virtual machines unchanged until the upgrade of all failover cluster nodes is complete. After you upgrade all hosts or when you believe you will not need to move your virtual machines to legacy hosts, you can shut down a virtual machine and upgrade the configuration version when needed.

To check a virtual machine's configuration number, run the following command in an elevated PowerShell command prompt:

```
Get-VM * | Format-Table Name, Version
```

Here is the complete syntax of the **Get-VM** cmdlet:

```
Get-VM [[-Name] <String[]>] [-CimSession <CimSession[]>]
  [-ComputerName <String[]>] [-Credential <PSCredential[]>]
  [<CommonParameters>]
```

To update the version of a single virtual machine, run the following command from an elevated PowerSheld prompt:

```
Update-VMVersion -Name VM1304
```

Here is the complete syntax of the **Update-VMVersion** cmdlet:

```
Update-VMVersion [-CimSession <CimSession[]>] [-ComputerName
  <String[]>] [-Credential <PSCredential[]>] [-Name]
  <String[]> [-Force] [-AsJob] [-Passthru] [-WhatIf] [-Confirm]
  [<CommonParameters>]
```

To update all of the virtual machines' versions on all cluster nodes, run the following command sequence from an elevated PowerShell command prompt:

```
Get-VM -ComputerName (Get-Clusternode) | Stop-VM
Get-VM -ComputerName (Get-Clusternode) | Update-Version -confirm
  $false
Get-VM -ComputerName (Get-Clusternode) | Start-VM
```

Remember that you cannot take advantage of new Windows Server 2016 Hyper-V features (for example, adding or removing memory from a running virtual machine) until the upgrade has taken place.

Creating a Virtual Machine

Follow these steps to create a new virtual machine in Windows Server 2016 Hyper-V:

Step 1. Launch the Hyper-V Manager by selecting **Tools** > **Hyper-V Manager**. (This step assumes that you have installed Hyper-V and its management tools properly, as described in Chapter 7, "Installing Hyper-V.")

Step 2. Ensure that your Hyper-V host is selected in the left pane and choose **Action** > **New** > **Virtual Machine,** as shown in Figure 8-1.

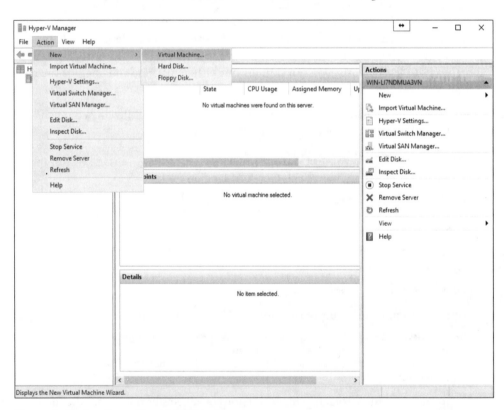

Figure 8-1   Creating a New Virtual Machine

Step 3.   Click **Next** in the **New Virtual Machine Wizard - Before You Begin** page.

Step 4.   Provide a name for your virtual machine and select a location on the **Specify Name and Location page**, as shown in Figure 8-2. Click **Next** when you are done.

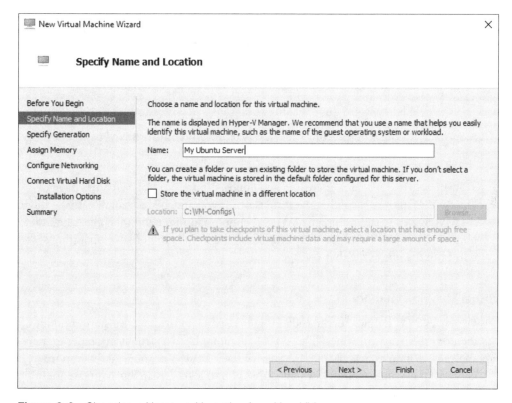

Figure 8-2   Choosing a Name and Location for a New VM

Step 5.   On the **Specify Generation** page, choose a **Generation 1** or **Generation 2** virtual machine. Remember that this choice cannot be changed once the VM is created. Click **Next**.

Step 6.   Assign memory and decide on the usage of dynamic memory for your virtual machine on the **Assign Memory** page. Click **Next**.

Step 7. Select your network adapter on the **Configure Networking** page and click **Next**.

Step 8. Select your virtual hard disk settings on the **Connect Virtual Hard Disk** page. Click **Next**.

Step 9. On the Installation Options page, choose from one of three options:

- **Install an operating system later**

- **Install an operating system from a bootable image file**

- **Install an operating system from a network-based installation server**

When you are done making selections, click **Next**.

Step 10. On the **Completing the New Virtual Machine Wizard** page, click **Finish**.

Your new virtual machine is created and appears in the Virtual Machines page of Hyper-V Manager. Note that the state is off. If you attached a bootable image file to the VM in step 9, right-click the VM and choose **Connect** and then click the **Start** button on the toolbar of the VM. This starts the installation of your operating system from the image file that you specified.

Virtual Machine Memory

Way back in Windows Server 2008 Hyper-V, you had to allocate a static amount of memory to virtual machines. This was challenging from a virtualization design perspective. Windows Server 2008 R2 Service Pack 1 (SP1) introduced the important concept of dynamic memory, which allows you to let the virtual machine request more memory as needed, up to a certain limit.

Figure 8-3 shows the robust options available for the configuration of dynamic memory available in Windows Server 2016.

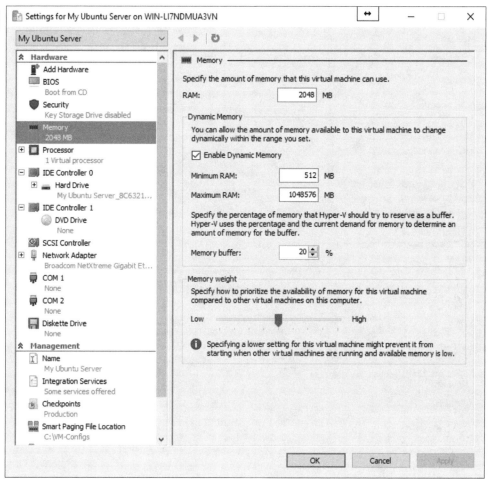

Figure 8-3   Configuring Dynamic Memory for a VM

Non-uniform memory access (NUMA) support continues to exist in Windows Server 2016. NUMA is a computer memory design in which the memory access time depends on the memory location relative to the processor. Under NUMA, a processor can access its own local memory faster than non-local memory (memory local to another processor or memory shared between processors). The benefits of NUMA are limited to certain workloads, notably on servers where the data are often associated strongly with certain tasks or users. Figure 8.4 shows the NUMA configurations possible in Server 2016 for a VM.

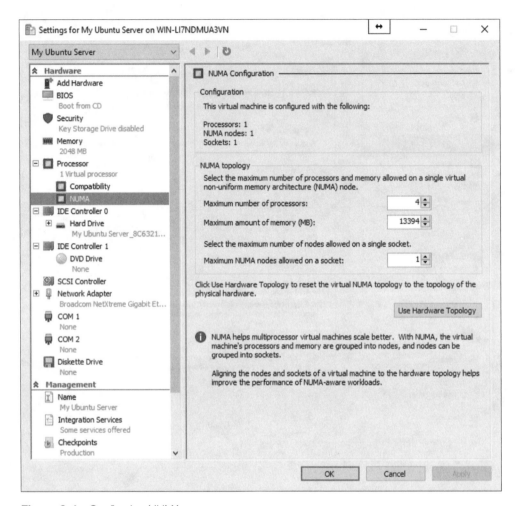

Figure 8-4   Configuring NUMA

While it is rare to manipulate the NUMA settings for a virtual machine, you might need to do so in a scenario where you plan to live migrate a VM to a server that supports a different (smaller) NUMA topology. Using the NUMA settings for both servers of the smaller of the two servers guards against VM problems.

Windows Server 2016 includes the first version of Hyper-V that allows a running virtual machine that has been configured for a static amount of memory to have memory "hot added" to the VM. Notice in Figure 8-5 that the options for altering the virtual memory of the running VM are available, while those that are not configurable for the running VM are grayed out.

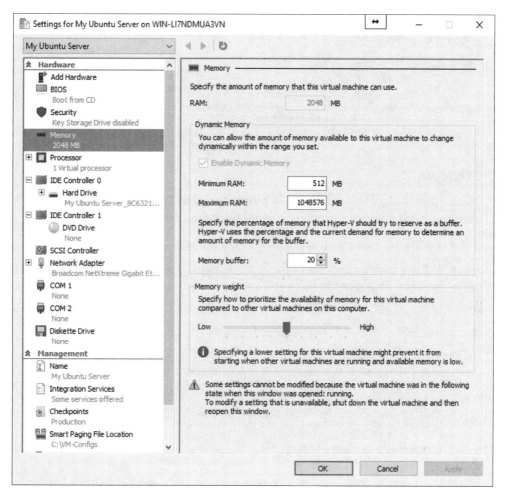

Figure 8-5   Hot Adding or Removal of VM Memory

Hyper-V also supports smart paging, which eliminates the need to provide more memory than is needed to run the VM just because VM startup might temporarily require more memory. Smart paging uses disk paging for more temporary memory when additional memory beyond the minimum allocation is required to start a virtual machine. This does have one major disadvantage, however, smart paging VMs suffer in restart performance compared to their VM peers.

You can configure VM memory in the GUI or by using the **Set-VMMemory** cmdlet in PowerShell. Here is the complete syntax:

```
Set-VMMemory [-CimSession <CimSession[]>] [-ComputerName <String[]>]
   [-Credential <PSCredential[]>] [-VMName] <String[]> [-Buffer
   <Int32>] [-DynamicMemoryEnabled <Boolean>] [-MaximumBytes <Int64>]
   [-StartupBytes <Int64>] [-MinimumBytes <Int64>] [-Priority <Int32>]
   [-MaximumAmountPerNumaNodeBytes <Int64>] [-ResourcePoolName
   <String>] [-Passthru] [-WhatIf] [-Confirm] [<CommonParameters>]
```

Checkpoints

Checkpoints allow for "snapshots" of a virtual machine at certain points in time. It is critical that you keep these points in mind regarding checkpoints in Hyper-V:

- Each VM can have a maximum of 50 checkpoints.

- When creating checkpoints for multiple virtual machines that have dependencies, you should create them at the same time to ensure synchronization of items such as computer account passwords.

- Checkpoints do not replace backups.

- With a standard checkpoint, Hyper-V creates an *.avhd* file that stores the data that differentiates the checkpoint from either the previous checkpoint or the parent virtual hard disk.

- With a production checkpoint, Hyper-V uses Volume Shadow Copy Service (VSS) or File System Freeze for Linux; note that production checkpoints are much closer to a state backup.

Creating a checkpoint is simple. As shown in Figure 8-6, you right-click a virtual machine in Hyper-V Manager and select **Checkpoint**.

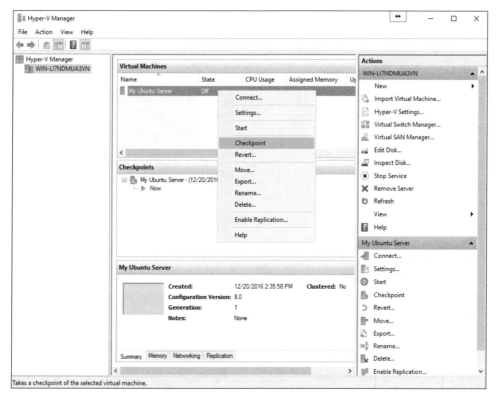

Figure 8-6 Creating a New Checkpoint

Resource Metering

Resource metering was added to Hyper-V in Windows Server 2012. Resource metering allows the tracking of total and average resource utilizations of a virtual machine, which you can view at any time. This metering information persists even if the virtual machine moves between Hyper-V nodes. You can gain access to this resource metering data by using PowerShell or WMI.

To enable resource metering for a VM, use this PowerShell command:

```
Enable-VMResourceMetering -VMName <VM name>
```

Here is the complete syntax:

```
Enable-VMResourceMetering [-CimSession <CimSession[]>] [-ComputerName
    <String[]>] [-Credential <PSCredential[]>] [-VMName] <String[]>
    [<CommonParameters>]
```

To view this valuable data in a detailed list format, use the following command:

```
Measure-VM -Name <VM name>
```

Here is the complete syntax:

```
Measure-VM [-CimSession <CimSession[]>] [-ComputerName
   <String[]>] [-Credential <PSCredential[]>] [-Name] <String[]>
   [<CommonParameters>]
```

Keep in mind that these metrics never reset unless you disable resource metering or perform a manual reset with the following command:

```
Reset-VMResourceMetering -VMName <VM name>
```

Here is the complete syntax:

```
Reset-VMResourceMetering [-CimSession <CimSession[]>] [-ComputerName
   <String[]>] [-Credential <PSCredential[]>] [-VMName] <String[]>
   [<CommonParameters>]
```

To disable resource metering, use this command:

```
Disable-VMResourceMetering -VMName <VM name>
```

Here is the complete syntax:

```
Disable-VMResourceMetering [-CimSession <CimSession[]>]
   [-ComputerName <String[]>] [-Credential <PSCredential[]>] [-VMName]
   <String[]> [<CommonParameters>]
```

You can also check to see which of your VMs have resource metering enabled by using this command:

```
Get-VM | Format-Table Name, ResourceMeteringEnable
```

Managing Integration Services

A number of services improve the integration between the host server and the operating system in the virtual machine. Integration services that are available through the settings of the VM with Windows Server 2016 include the following:

- **Operating system shutdown**: This permits the "graceful" shutdown of the OS in the VM, using the controls in Hyper-V for shutdown; you can also use the **Stop-VM** cmdlet in PowerShell.

- **Time synchronization**: This permits the synchronization of time in the guest OS with that of the host.

- **Data exchange**: Also known as key-value pairs (KVP), data exchange permits the sharing of information between the host and the virtual machine; access to this data from the host is only available using WMI scripts.

- **Heartbeat**: The heartbeat service monitors the state of running virtual machines by reporting a heartbeat at regular intervals; you can check the heartbeat status of a virtual machine on the Summary tab of the virtual machine's details page, or you can use the **Get-VMIntegrationSerivce** cmdlet:

```
Get-VMIntegrationService [-CimSession <CimSession[]>]
   [-ComputerName <String[]>] [-Credential <PSCredential[]>]
   [-VMName] <String[]> [[-Name] <String[]>] [<CommonParameters>]
```

- **Backup (volume snapshot)**: The backup service enables consistent backup of the virtual machines from backup software running on the host. The backup service allows for a virtual machine to be backed up while it is running without any interruption to the virtual machine or the services running in the virtual machine.

- **Guest services**: You can copy files to a running virtual machine without using a network connection. To copy a file to a virtual machine, you need to use the **Copy-VMFile** PowerShell cmdlet:

```
Copy-VMFile [-CimSession <CimSession[]>] [-ComputerName
   <String[]>] [-Credential <PSCredential[]>] [-Name] <String[]>
   [-SourcePath] <String> [-DestinationPath] <String> -FileSource
   <CopyFileSourceType> [-CreateFullPath] [-Force] [-AsJob]
   [-WhatIf] [-Confirm] [<CommonParameters>]
```

Advanced Virtual Machine Deployment

This section covers more advanced manipulations of virtual machines.

Enhanced Session Mode

Enhanced Session Mode permits use of VMConnect to use a computer's local resources within a VM. Maybe you want to use a removable flash drive or printer of the host. Enhanced Session Mode also lets you resize the VMConnect window.

You set Enhanced Session Mode through the settings for the Hyper-V machine itself in the Hyper-V Manager, as shown in Figure 8-7.

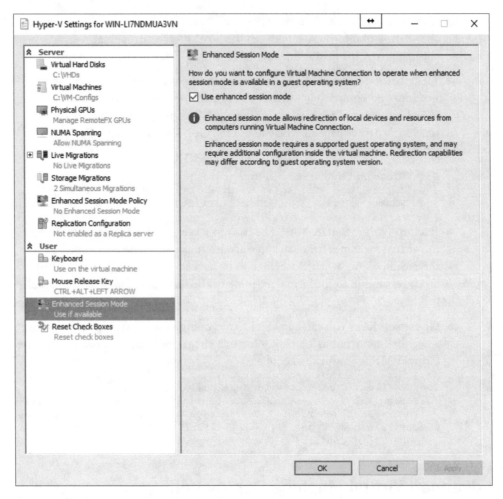

Figure 8-7   Setting Enhanced Session Mode

Linux Integration Services (LIS) and FreeBSD Integration Services (BIS)

Linux Integration Services provides drivers and services for improved Linux integration in Hyper-V environments. Once Linux Integration Services are deployed, virtual machines running Linux distributions can use features like the following:

- Live migration
- Jumbo frames
- VLAN tagging and trunking
- Support for symmetric multiprocessing (SMP)
- Static IP injection

- VHDX resizing
- Virtual Fibre Channel
- Live virtual machine backup
- Hot adding and removal of memory using the Dynamic Memory feature

> **NOTE** Some Linux distributions require that you add LIS, while others come with it already installed.

LIS 4.0 ships with two scripts: Install.SH and Upgrade.SH. In earlier versions of LIS, you had to switch to the correct Linux distribution directory before you could install/upgrade LIS on a Linux virtual machine. Now with Hyper-V LIS 4.0, you need to execute only one script to either install (Install.SH) or upgrade (Upgrade. SH) on a Linux distribution.

Follow these steps if your Linux distribution shipped with LIS installed:

Step 1. Edit the modules file located in /etc/initramfs-tools, using this command:

```
sudo vi /etc/initramfs-tools/modules
```

Step 2. In the vi editor, navigate to the last line in the file and use the insert (**I**) command to append and enter the following lines:

```
hv_vmbus
hv_storvsc
hv_blkvsc
hv_netvsc
```

Step 3. Save the file by pressing the Esc key and then issue the : **x** command.

Step 4. Run the following command to re-initialize the modules file:

```
sudo update-initramfs -u
```

Step 5. Reboot the virtual machine by executing the following command:

```
sudo shutdown -r now
```

If your Linux distro does not ship with LIS installed, follow these steps:

Step 1. Attach the LinuxICv35.ISO file to a Linux virtual machine.

Step 2. As a root user, execute this command to mount the ISO file:

```
mount /dev/cdrom /media
```

Step 3. Run the script provided with the LIS ISO to install LIS:

```
./install.sh
```

Step 4. Type **reboot** and press **Enter**.

Microsoft has given upgrade scripts to update the Hyper-V LIS drivers for Linux distributions. Follow the preceding steps to mount the ISO file, switch to the directory relevant to your Linux distribution, and execute the Upgrade.sh script.

Once the script has finished installing LIS drivers and services, reboot the virtual machine so that the Hyper-V LIS drivers and services are registered with the Linux kernel.

For older FreeBSD releases (before 10.0), Microsoft offers ports that hold the installable BIS drivers and corresponding daemons for FreeBSD virtual machines. For newer FreeBSD releases, BIS is built in to the FreeBSD operating system, and no separate download or installation is required except that a KVP ports download is needed for FreeBSD 10.0.

Secure Boot

Linux operating systems running on Generation 2 virtual machines can now boot with the Secure Boot option enabled. The following operating systems are enabled for Secure Boot on hosts that run Server 2016:

- Ubuntu 14.04 and later

- SUSE Linux Enterprise Server 12 and later

- Red Hat Enterprise Linux 7.0 and later

- CentOS 7.0 and later

Before you boot the virtual machine for the first time, you must configure it to use the Microsoft UEFI Certificate Authority. You can do this from Hyper-V Manager, Virtual Machine Manager, or an elevated Windows PowerShell session.

With PowerShell, run this command:

```
Set-VMFirmware -VMName SAMPLEVM -SecureBootTemplate
  MicrosoftUEFICertificateAuthority
```

The full syntax is as follows:

```
Set-VMFirmware [-CimSession <CimSession[]>] [-ComputerName
<String[]>] [-Credential <PSCredential[]>] [-VMName]
<String[]> [-BootOrder <VMComponentObject[]>] [-FirstBootDevice
<VMComponentObject>] [-EnableSecureBoot <OnOffState>]
[-SecureBootTemplate <String>] [-SecureBootTemplateId <Guid>]
[-PreferredNetworkBootProtocol <IPProtocolPreference>] [-ConsoleMode
<ConsoleModeType>] [-PauseAfterBootFailure <OnOffState>] [-Passthru]
[-WhatIf] [-Confirm] [<CommonParameters>]
```

Importing, Exporting, and Moving Virtual Machines

Simple export and import capabilities in Hyper-V enable the easy transfer of virtual machines between physical hosts or virtual hosts (as is the case in nested virtualization). This functionality also enables you to create point-in-time backups of virtual machines.

Import functionality is much improved in Windows Server 2016, and the Hyper-V Manager is able to detect such problems as missing virtual hard disks or virtual switches. Server 2016 also supports the import of virtual machines from copies of virtual machine configurations, checkpoints, or virtual hard disk files. This is critical in recovery situations where the guest OS has failed but the virtual machine files are fine.

To import a virtual machine in Hyper-V Manager, follow these simple steps:

Step 1. In the **Actions** pane of the console, click **Import Virtual Machine.**

Step 2. On the **Before You Begin** page, click **Next.**

Step 3. On the **Locate Folder** page, specify the folder that hosts the virtual machine files and click **Next** (see Figure 8-8).

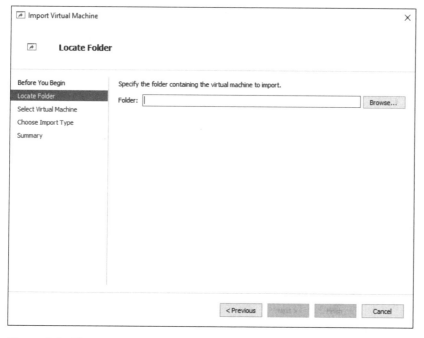

Figure 8-8 The Import Virtual Machine Wizard

Step 4.   On the Select Virtual Machine page, choose the virtual machine you want to import and then click **Next.**

Step 5.   On the **Choose Import Type** page, choose one of the following:

- **Register the virtual machine in-place (use the existing unique ID)**
- **Restore the virtual machine (use the existing unique ID)**
- **Copy the virtual machine (create a new unique ID)**

You can also import virtual machines by using the **Import-VM** cmdlet in PowerShell.

When performing an export, you have a choice of two options:

- **Export a checkpoint**: Right-click the checkpoint in Hyper-V Manager and click **Export.**
- **Export the virtual machine with a checkpoint**: Click the virtual machine and then click **Export** to export the virtual machine and all associated checkpoints it might have.

    Exporting a virtual machine does not affect the existing virtual machine. Understand, however, that you cannot import the virtual machine again unless you use the **Copy the Virtual Machine** option, which creates a new unique ID.

> **NOTE**   Beginning with Windows Server 2012 R2, you do not have to stop or pause the virtual machine in order to export it.

There are two ways to move a virtual machine. There is the live migration and then there is the option of a move of the actual virtual machine. Live migration must be enabled and occurs when you move a VM from one host to another while keeping the virtual machine online and available to clients. This is a Failover Clustering capability.

The move of the actual machine offers these options:

- Move all the virtual machine's data to a single location.
- Move the virtual machine's data to different locations.
- Move the virtual machine's virtual hard disks.

In Hyper-V Manager, moving a VM is a simple matter of right-clicking the VM and selecting **Move** from the shortcut menu.

The **Move-VM** cmdlet of PowerShell is an alternative to GUI-based VM moves. The full syntax for this PowerShell cmdlet is as follows:

```
Move-VM [-ComputerName <String[]>] [-Credential <PSCredential[]>]
   [-Name] <String> [-DestinationHost] <String>
   [-DestinationCredential <PSCredential>] [-IncludeStorage]
   [-DestinationStoragePath <String>] [-ResourcePoolName <String>]
   [-RetainVhdCopiesOnSource] [-RemoveSourceUnmanagedVhds] [-AsJob]
   [-Passthru] [-WhatIf] [-Confirm] [<CommonParameters>]
```

Discrete Device Assignment (DDA)

Windows Server 2012 introduced support for technology termed SR-IOV, which permits compatible network adapters that connect via PCI Express to bypass the Hyper-V virtual switch completely and be mapped directly to a VM. This, of course, gives very low-latency connectivity.

Discrete Device Assignment (DDA) in Windows Server 2016 enables PCI Express–connected devices to connect more directly to VMs. This is very useful in scenarios where hardware is not functioning properly because of unrecognized drivers. DDA allows the use of the hardware's IHV drivers instead of generic virtual device drivers. This can be critical with certain storage and graphical adapters.

Note that DDA drops the sharing of hardware with the host or with other VMs. Also, live migration is not possible since the VM is bound to hardware in a specific host.

Best Practices for VM Deployment

Here are some best practices to keep in mind for VM deployments:

- Use dynamic memory. The only exception is if you are hosting applications that would continue to request more memory if available.

- Set the minimum and maximum memory for VMs.

- Avoid using differencing disks. Using them may reduce disk space, but they can dramatically reduce performance.

- Use multiple Hyper-V-specific network adapters connected to different external virtual switches to provide redundancy in the networking configuration.

- Store virtual machine files on their own volumes if you are not using shared storage. Doing this will minimize the impact of a single virtual machine's hard disk growth on other VMs.

Exam Preparation Tasks

As mentioned in the section "How to Use This Book" in the Introduction, you have a couple choices for exam preparation: the exercises here, Chapter 21, "Final Preparation," and the exam simulation questions in the Pearson Test Prep Software Online.

Review All Key Topics

Review the most important topics in this chapter, noted with the Key Topics icon in the outer margin of the page. Table 8-2 lists these key topics and the page number on which each is found.

Table 8-2   Key Topics for Chapter 8

Key Topic Element	Description	Page Number
Command	Updating the version of a VM	133
Steps	Creating a VM	134
Figure 8-3	Configuring dynamic memory for a VM	137
Command	Enabling resource metering	141
List	Integration services	142
Command	Enabling secure boot	146
List	Best practices for VM deployment	149

Complete Tables and Lists from Memory

There are no memory tables in this chapter.

Define Key Terms

Define the following key terms from this chapter and check your answers against the glossary:

Configuration Version, NUMA, Smart Paging, Checkpoint, Resource Metering, Enhanced Session Mode, LIS/BIS, DDA

Q&A

The answers to these questions appear in Appendix A. For more practice with exam format questions, use the Pearson Test Prep Software Online.

1. Name at least two Add Hardware options for a Generation 1 VM.

2. What change has been made in Windows Server 2016 regarding VM versions?

3. What three options exist when creating a VM for an OS install?

4. What are three options you can use for importing a VM?

5. What two options are available when exporting a VM?

6. Name at least three best practices for VM deployment.

This chapter covers the following subjects:

- **Creating VHD, VHDX, and VHDS Virtual Hard Disks:** This section provides information about each type of virtual hard disk in use today. It also discusses the creation and manipulation of virtual hard disks in Windows Server 2016.

- **Checkpoints:** This section builds on the introduction to checkpoints in Chapter 8, "Working with Virtual Machines." It provides details on the two types of checkpoints that are now possible and discusses checkpoint management tasks.

- **Storage Quality of Service:** This section details the new storage quality of service (QoS) capabilities introduced in Windows Server 2016. It also provides information on configuration and monitoring of this feature.

## CHAPTER 9

Hyper-V Storage

You will be thrilled to know that you have many different storage options when it comes to Hyper-V virtual machines in Windows Server 2016. This chapter is your go-to guide and reference for these options for your production workloads. It also provides the facts you need to recall in the certification exam from Microsoft.

"Do I Know This Already?" Quiz

The "Do I Know This Already?" quiz allows you to assess whether you should read the entire chapter. Table 9-1 lists the major headings in this chapter and the "Do I Know This Already?" quiz questions covering the material in those headings so you can assess your knowledge of these specific areas. The answers to the "Do I Know This Already?" quiz appear in Appendix A, "Answers to the 'Do I Know This Already?' Quizzes and Q&A Questions."

Table 9-1 "Do I Know This Already?" Foundation Topics Section-to-Question Mapping

Foundation Topics Section	Questions
Creating VHD, VHDX, and VHDS Virtual Hard Disks	1–3
Checkpoints	4
Storage Quality of Service	5, 6

CAUTION The goal of self-assessment is to gauge your mastery of the topics in this chapter. If you do not know the answer to a question or are only partially sure of the answer, you should mark your answer as incorrect for purposes of the self-assessment. Giving yourself credit for an answer you correctly guess skews your self-assessment results and might provide you with a false sense of security.

1. Which of the following is not a tool that you can use to create a virtual hard disk?

   a. diskpart

   b. SAN Manager

   c. Disk Management

   d. PowerShell

2. How much space does a VHDX support?

   a. 8 TB

   b. 2 TB

   c. 64 TB

   d. 1 TB

3. What cmdlet creates a new differencing disk?

   a. **New-DiffDisk**

   b. **New-VHD**

   c. **New-Diff**

   d. **New-VHDDiff**

4. What type of checkpoint is the default for Windows Server 2016?

   a. Standard

   b. General

   c. Production

   d. Lab

5. What deployment scenarios does storage QoS support? Choose two.

   a. Hyper-V using a Scale-Out File Server

   b. Hyper-V using Generation 2 VMs

   c. Hyper-V using virtual Fibre Channel

   d. Hyper-V using Clustered Shared Volumes

6. In what type of storage QoS policy are the MinimumIOPS and the MaximumIOPS and Bandwidth shared among all flows assigned to the policy?

    a. Shared

    b. Dedicated

    c. Grouped

    d. Aggregated

Foundation Topics

Creating VHD, VHDX, and VHDS Virtual Hard Disks

Virtual hard disks are extremely flexible storage containers that act just like physical hard drives in many ways. As with an actual hard drive, you can use a VHD or VHDX to store data, or you can use one to host an operating system on either a physical or virtual machine.

Just like with physical disks, there are many ways to create and manipulate virtual hard disks. Here are just some:

- The Hyper-V Manager
- The Disk Management Console
- The **diskpart** command-line tool
- The **New-VHD** Windows PowerShell cmdlet

A "classic" virtual hard disk has a .VHD extension. A new and improved virtual hard disk appeared in Windows Server 2012. This improved VHDX virtual hard disk features the following benefits:

- Because disk sizes may increase dramatically, a VHDX supports 64 TB, whereas the older VHD supports only 2 TB.
- The disk structure is improved to reduce the chances of problems when a host server suffers a power outage.
- The VHDX features much better storage alignment when used with large sector sizes.
- The VHDX allows a larger block size for dynamically expanding and differencing disks, which provides better performance for these workloads.

Windows Server 2016 provides an Edit Disk tool that permits the conversion of VHD to VHDX and vice versa.

Windows Server 2016 also introduces a new VHD format: VHDS. These shared virtual hard disks can be shared by multiple virtual machines.

There are many types of virtual hard disks that you can create for specific purposes and workloads, including the following:

- Fixed size
- Dynamically expanding
- Pass-through
- Differencing

Fixed-Size VHD

A fixed-size virtual hard disk can offer some performance advantages. For example, a fixed-size disk should experience less fragmentation than other styles. Of course, the issue is that you might not allocate enough space (or you might allocate too much space) for what your VM actually needs. The virtual hard disk does not engage in thin provisioning and must consume the fixed amount of space you assigned on the actual physical storage. You can use a dynamically expanding virtual hard disk to avoid this issue.

NOTE   Disk fragmentation is less of an issue when virtual hard disks are hosted on RAID volumes or on SSDs. Recent Hyper-V improvements also minimize the performance differences between dynamically expanding and fixed-size virtual hard disks.

To create a fixed-size virtual hard disk, follow these steps:

Step 1.   In **Server Manager**, select **Tools** > **Hyper-V Manager**.

Step 2.   In the **Actions** pane, click **New** > **Hard Disk**.

Step 3.   On the **Before You Begin** page of the **New Virtual Hard Disk Wizard**, click **Next**.

Step 4.   On the **Choose Disk Format** page, select **VHD** or **VHDX** or **VHD Set** and then click **Next** (see Figure 9-1).

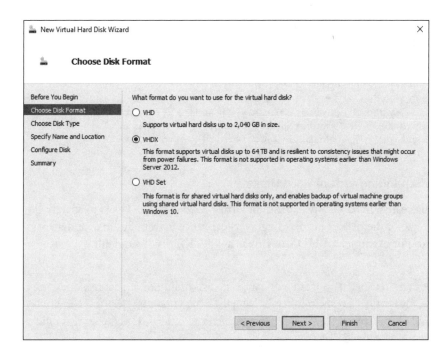

Figure 9-1   Choosing a Disk Format in the New Virtual Hard Disk Wizard

Step 5.   On the **Choose Disk Type** page, choose **Fixed size** and then click **Next**.

Step 6.   On the **Specify Name and Location** page, enter a name for the virtual hard disk, specify a folder to host the virtual hard disk file, and click **Next**.

Step 7.   On the **Configure Disk** page, select one of the following options:

- **Create a new blank virtual hard disk of the specified size:** Select this option for a new disk of any size and any purpose. Of course, the disk is empty of contents.

- **Copy the contents of a specified physical disk:** Select this option to replicate an existing physical disk on the server as a virtual hard disk. The fixed-size hard disk will be the same size as the disk that you have replicated. Replicating an existing physical hard disk does not alter data on the existing disk.

- **Copy the contents of a specified virtual hard disk:** Select this option to create a new fixed-size hard disk based on the contents of an existing virtual hard disk.

You can create a new fixed-size hard disk by using the **New-VHD** PowerShell cmdlet and the **-Fixed** parameter. Here is the complete syntax for the **New-VHD** cmdlet:

```
New-VHD [-Path] <String[]> [-SizeBytes] <UInt64> [-Dynamic]
   [-BlockSizeBytes <UInt32>] [-LogicalSectorSizeBytes <UInt32>]
   [-PhysicalSectorSizeBytes <UInt32>] [-AsJob] [-CimSession
   <CimSession[]>] [-ComputerName <String[]>] [-Credential
   <PSCredential[]>] [-WhatIf] [-Confirm] [<CommonParameters>]
```

Dynamically Expanding Virtual Hard Disks

When you create a dynamically expanding virtual hard disk, the key is to specify the maximum size of the disk. This disk begins its existence extremely small and grows as required. For example, a VHDX begins as a 4096 KB disk by default.

> **NOTE**   When you remove data from a dynamically expanding disk, the disk does not automatically shrink. To shrink the virtual hard disk, you must perform a manual operation. The Optimize-VHD cmdlet permits such operations. Of course, this cmdlet does not work with fixed disks.

To create a dynamically expanding virtual hard disk, follow the preceding steps for creating a fixed-size virtual hard disk. During step 5, however, on the **Choose Disk Type** page, choose **Dynamically expanding size**.

You can also create a new dynamically expanding virtual hard disk by using the **New-VHD** PowerShell cmdlet with the **-Dynamic** parameter.

Pass-Through Disks

A pass-through disk permits a virtual machine to access the actual hard disk of the host directly rather than using a virtual hard disk. For example, you might use a pass-through disk setup in order to have a virtual machine access an iSCSI LUN or a directly attached physical hard disk. Keep in mind the following requirements related to pass-through disks:

- The virtual machine must have exclusive access to the disk.

- Use the host's Disk Management utility to take the target disk offline.

- Once the target disk is offline, you can connect it to one of the virtual machine's disk controllers.

Keeping in mind these requirements, follow these steps to create a pass-through disk:

Step 1.   Ensure that the target hard disk is offline.

Step 2.   Use the **Hyper-V Manager** to edit the existing virtual machine's properties.

Step 3.   Click an **IDE** or **SCSI** controller, click **Add**, and then click **Hard Drive,** as shown in Figure 9-2.

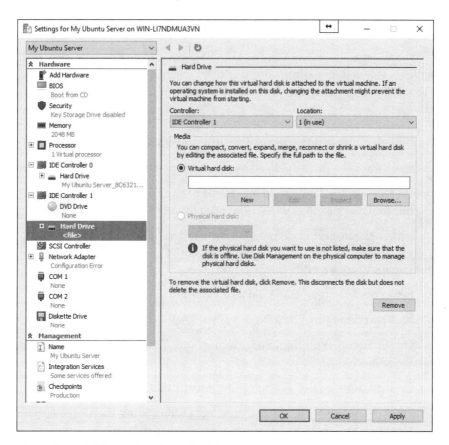

Figure 9-2   Adding a Pass-through Disk

Step 4.   In the **Hard Drive** dialog box, select **Physical Hard Disk**. In the drop-down list box, select the disk that you want to use as the pass-through disk.

NOTE You do not have to shut down a virtual machine if you connect the pass-through disk to the virtual machine's SCSI controller. However, if you want to connect to a virtual machine's IDE controller, it is necessary to shut down the virtual machine.

Differencing Disks

Differencing disks record changes made to a parent disk. Remember that you can use the differencing disk approach to save on hard disk space consumed by virtual machines, but differencing disks negatively affect performance.

You should consider using differencing disks in SSD environments where disks tend to be smaller but so high in performance that they can compensate for performance hits due to differencing disk usage.

Remember these facts about differencing disks:

- You can link multiple differencing disks to a single parent disk.

- When you modify a parent disk, all linked differencing disks fail.

- You can reconnect a differencing disk to the parent by using the Inspect Disk tool; this tool is available in the Actions pane of the Hyper-V Manager.

- You can use the Inspect Disk tool to locate a differencing disk's parent disk.

Follow these steps to create a differencing disk:

Step 1.   In **Server Manager**, select **Tools > Hyper-V Manager**.

Step 2.   In the **Actions** pane, click **New > Hard Disk**.

Step 3.   On the **Before You Begin** page of the **New Virtual Hard Disk Wizard**, click **Next**.

Step 4.   On the **Choose Disk Format** page, select **VHD** and then click **Next**.

Step 5.   On the **Choose Disk Type** page, select **Differencing** and then click **Next** (see Figure 9-3).

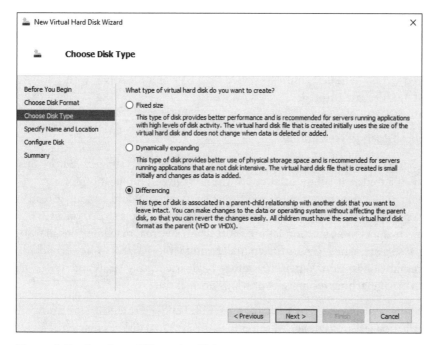

Figure 9-3 Creating a Differencing Disk

Step 6.   On the Specify Name and Location page, provide the location of the parent hard disk and then click **Finish**.

You can also create a differencing disk by using the **New-VHD** PowerShell cmdlet. Here is an example:

```
New-VHD c:\mydiffdisk.vhd -ParentPath c:\myparent.vhd
```

Shared Virtual Hard Disks

Remember that a shared virtual hard disk is used by more than one virtual machine. A perfect use case could be a volume that hosts the database files in a Hyper-V guest failover cluster for Microsoft SQL Server.

Remember these properties of shared virtual disks:

- Both Generation 1 and Generation 2 virtual machines can use shared virtual disks.

- Virtual machines running Windows Server 2012 and newer operating systems have native support for using shared virtual hard disks as shared storage.

- Virtual machines that run Windows Server 2012 support using shared virtual hard disks as shared storage if Windows Server 2012 R2 or Windows Server 2016 integration services are installed.

- Shared virtual hard disks must be stored on CSVs or a file server with SMB 3.0 file-based storage.

Virtual Machine Storage Resiliency

Windows Server 2016 has introduced virtual machine storage resiliency. Before this technology, if a transient failure occurred to the storage communication for a virtual machine, the VM would go into an off state as soon as it could no longer read or write to storage. With Server 2016, when a virtual hard disk is stored on a CSV or SMB share, if a communication failure is detected, a virtual machine goes in to a critical pause state, which causes the compute and memory states to freeze and all I/O communication to stop. When the storage begins accepting reads and writes again, the virtual machine resumes its previous normal state.

When running a virtual machine with a shared VHD and guest cluster, the new storage resiliency feature is designed to remove the attached disk if one virtual machine cannot see the shared disk. This allows the failover cluster to detect the storage failure and take action according to the failover cluster configuration.

This new storage resiliency feature is enabled by default. To disable it, use the following PowerShell cmdlet:

```
Set-VM –AutomaticCriticalErrorAction <None | Pause>
```

You can change the default amount of time that a virtual machine stays in a critical paused state before going into an off state by using the following PowerShell cmdlet:

```
Set-VM –AutomaticCriticalErrorActionTimeout <value in minutes>
```

The complete syntax for the **Set-VM** PowerShell cmdlet is as follows:

```
Set-VM [-CimSession <CimSession[]>] [-ComputerName
  <String[]>] [-Credential <PSCredential[]>] [-Name] <String[]>
  [-GuestControlledCacheTypes <Boolean>] [-LowMemoryMappedIoSpace
  <UInt32>] [-HighMemoryMappedIoSpace <UInt64>]
  [-ProcessorCount <Int64>] [-DynamicMemory] [-StaticMemory]
  [-MemoryMinimumBytes <Int64>] [-MemoryMaximumBytes <Int64>]
  [-MemoryStartupBytes <Int64>] [-AutomaticStartAction <StartAction>]
  [-AutomaticStopAction <StopAction>] [-AutomaticStartDelay
  <Int32>] [-AutomaticCriticalErrorAction <CriticalErrorAction>]
  [-AutomaticCriticalErrorActionTimeout <Int32>] [-LockOnDisconnect
  <OnOffState>] [-Notes <String>] [-NewVMName <String>]
  [-SnapshotFileLocation <String>] [-SmartPagingFilePath
  <String>] [-CheckpointType <CheckpointType>] [-Passthru]
  [-AllowUnverifiedPaths] [-WhatIf] [-Confirm] [<CommonParameters>]
```

Converting and Resizing Virtual Hard Disks

Sometimes you need to perform maintenance tasks such as the following:

- Convert a disk from fixed size to dynamically expanding
- Convert a disk from dynamically expanding to fixed size
- Convert a virtual hard disk from VHD format to VHDX format
- Convert a virtual hard disk from VHDX format to VHD format

When you convert a virtual hard disk, the contents of the existing virtual hard disk are copied to a new virtual hard disk that has the properties you require.

Follow these steps to perform a conversion of a virtual hard disk:

Step 1.   In **Server Manager**, select **Tools > Hyper-V Manager**.

Step 2.   In the **Actions** pane, click **Edit Disk**.

Step 3.   On the **Local Virtual Hard Disk** page, click **Browse**. Select the virtual hard disk you want to convert, as shown in Figure 9-4.

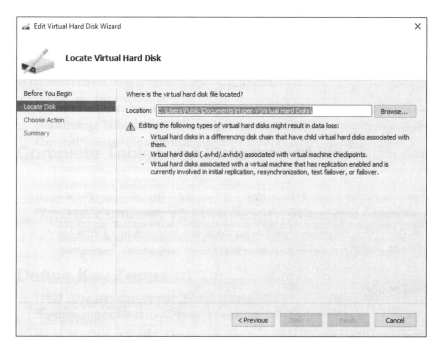

Figure 9-4   Converting a Virtual Hard Disk

Step 4.   On the **Choose Action** page, select **Convert** and then click **Next**.

Step 5.   On the **Convert Virtual Hard Disk** page, select the **VHD** or **VHDX** format. By default, the current disk format is selected. Click **Next**.

Step 6.   If you want to convert the disk from fixed size to dynamically expanding or dynamically expanding to fixed size, on the **Convert Virtual Hard Disk** page, select **Fixed Size** or **Dynamically Expanding**. If you want to convert the hard disk type, choose the appropriate type. Click **Next**.

Step 7.   On the **Configure Disk** page, select the destination location for the disk, click **Next**, and then click **Finish**.

You can shrink a dynamically expanding virtual hard disk that is no longer requiring the space it once needed. To do so, choose the **Compact** option in the Edit Virtual Hard Disk Wizard.

You cannot shrink a fixed-size virtual hard disk. Instead, you need to convert the disk to a dynamically expanding virtual hard disk and then perform the shrink operation.

You can use the **resize-partition** and **resize-VHD** cmdlets in PowerShell to shrink disks as well.

You can also expand both fixed-size and dynamically expanding virtual hard disks. You use the **Edit Virtual Hard Disk Wizard** for this task as well.

If you need to resize a virtual hard disk that is currently being used by a running virtual machine, remember the following prerequisites:

- You can resize a virtual hard disk only if the virtual hard disk is in *.vhdx* format and is connected to a virtual SCSI controller.

- You can resize a shared virtual disk only if the virtual machine is running Windows Server 2016.

- You cannot shrink a virtual hard disk beyond the size of the current volumes that are hosted on the virtual hard disk. Before attempting to shrink such a virtual hard disk, use Disk Manager in the guest VM operating system to reduce the size of the volumes that are hosted on the virtual hard disk.

Fibre Channel Support

Remember that Windows Server 2016 supports Hyper-V virtual Fibre Channel. This is a virtual hardware component that you can add to a virtual machine in order to provide that VM with access Fibre Channel storage in a Storage Area Network (SAN).

Remember these important points related to virtual Fibre Channel:

- You must configure the Hyper-V host with a Fibre Channel host bus adapter (HBA).

- The Fibre Channel HBA must have a driver that supports virtual Fibre Channel.

- The virtual machine must support virtual machine extensions.

- You can deploy up to four virtual Fibre Channel adapters on each virtual machine.

- Virtual Fibre Channel adapters support port virtualization by exposing HBA ports in the guest operating system; this allows the virtual machine to access the SAN by using a standard World Wide Name (WWN) that is associated with the virtual machine.

Location Considerations for Virtual Hard Disks

It is important to consider placement of virtual hard disks so that they do not become VM performance bottlenecks. Consider these factors:

- Ensure that there is a high-performance connection to storage. Avoid remote storage if there is high latency.

- Consider redundant storage and ensure that the volume storing your virtual hard disks is highly fault tolerant.

- Consider high-performance storage such as SSDs whenever possible.

- Ensure that there is adequate growth space.

Checkpoints

As initially discussed in Chapter 8, checkpoints have been enhanced in Windows Server 2016. You now have a choice of standard or production checkpoints:

NOTE The default is production checkpoints for new virtual machines in Windows Server 2016.

- **Production checkpoint**: This is a "point in time" image of the virtual machine. A production checkpoint can be restored later in a way that is supported by all workloads. A production checkpoint uses a backup technology inside the guest VM to create the checkpoint; note that this is an alternative to saved state technology.

- **Standard checkpoint**: This is a checkpoint that captures the state, data, and hardware configuration of a running virtual machine. Standard checkpoints are intended for use in development and testing scenarios; for example, you might use a standard checkpoint to re-create a specific state of a virtual machine so that you can further troubleshoot a scenario.

Follow these steps to change checkpoints to production or standard checkpoints:

Step 1. In **Server Manager**, select **Tools > Hyper-V Manager**.

Step 2. In Hyper-V Manager, right-click the virtual machine and choose **Settings**.

Step 3. Select either **Production checkpoints** or **Standard checkpoints** (see Figure 9-5). Note that if you choose **Production checkpoints**, you can also specify whether the host should take a standard checkpoint if a production checkpoint is not possible. If you clear this option, there is a risk that no checkpoint is taken.

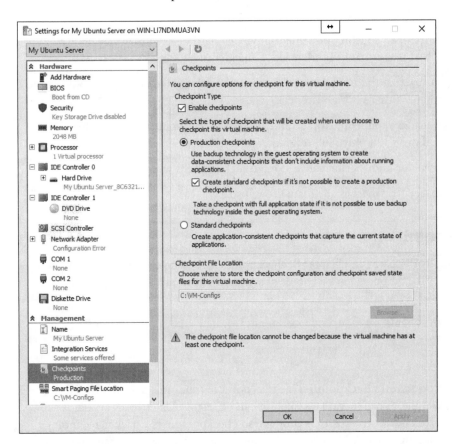

Figure 9-5   Creating a New Checkpoint

Step 4.   If you need to store the checkpoint configuration files in a different location, change this location in the Checkpoint File Location section.

Step 5.   Click **Apply** to save your changes and click **OK** to close the dialog box.

You can also choose to enable or disable checkpoints for each virtual machine. To do so, follow these steps:

Step 1.   In **Server Manager**, select **Tools** > **Hyper-V Manager**.

Step 2.   In **Hyper-V Manager**, right-click the virtual machine and choose **Settings**.

Step 3.   Under the **Management** section, select **Checkpoints**.

Step 4.   To allow checkpoints to be taken, ensure that **Enable checkpoints** is selected. To disable checkpoints, simply clear this check box.

Step 5.   Click **Apply** to save your changes, and click **OK** to close the dialog box.

Storage Quality of Service

Storage QoS in Windows Server 2016 provides central monitoring and management of storage performance for virtual machines using Hyper-V and Scale-Out File Server roles.

Consider the following about storage QoS:

- It permits fairness improvements between VMs using the same file cluster.

- It allows policy-based minimum and maximum performance goals to be configured in units of normalized IOPs.

- It prevents single virtual machines from consuming all storage resources.

- You can view performance details of all running virtual machines and the configuration of the Scale-Out File Server cluster from a single location.

- It provides consistent performance to virtual machines, even in dense and overprovisioned environments.

Storage QoS supports two deployment scenarios:

- Hyper-V using Scale-Out File Server

- Hyper-V using Clustered Shared Volumes

Scale-Out File Server uses the SMB3 protocol. A new Policy Manager assists the file server cluster. This Policy Manager provides central storage performance monitoring. It communicates the storage QoS policy and limits or reservations back to the Hyper-V server. The Hyper-V server controls the performance of VMs.

Table 9-2 lists terms associated with storage QoS that you should know.

Table 9-2 Storage QoS Terms

Storage QoS Term	Definition
Normalized IOPs	A count of the storage input/output operations per second
Flow	Each file opened by a Hyper-V server to a virtual hard disk
InitiatorName	The name of the virtual machine that is reported to Scale-Out File Server for each flow
InitiatorID	An identifier that matches the virtual machine ID
Policy	A QoS object stored in the cluster database that has the following properties: PolicyId, MinimumIOPS, MaximumIOPS, ParentPolicy, and PolicyType
PolicyId	A unique identifier for a policy
MinimumIOPS	The minimum normalized IOPs that will be provided by a policy; a reservation
MaximumIOPS	The maximum normalized IOPS that will be limited by a policy; a limit
Aggregated	A policy type in which the specified MinimumIOPS and MaximumIOPS and Bandwidth are shared among all flows assigned to the policy
Dedicated	A policy type in which the specified MinimumIOPs and MaximumIOPs and Bandwidth are managed for individual VHD/VHDX

If you have configured a new failover cluster and configured Cluster Shared Volume on Windows Server 2016, then the storage QoS feature is set up automatically.

After you have created a failover cluster and configured a CSV disk, the storage QoS resource is displayed as a cluster core resource and is visible in both Failover Cluster Manager and Windows PowerShell. To view the status in PowerShell, use the following cmdlet:

```
Get-ClusterResource -Name "Storage Qos Resource"
```

The complete syntax for the **Get-ClusterResource** PowerShell cmdlet is as follows:

```
Get-ClusterResource [-InputObject <psobject>] [[-Name]
   <StringCollection>] [-Cluster <string>] [<CommonParameters>]
```

You can manage storage QoS policies and monitor flows from compute hosts by using the Remote Server Administration tools.

The **Get-StorageQosFlow** cmdlet shows all current flows initiated by Hyper-V servers. All data is collected by the Scale-Out File Server cluster, so this cmdlet can be used on any node in the Scale-Out File Server cluster or against a remote server using the **-CimSession** parameter.

Storage performance metrics are also collected on a per–storage volume level, in addition to the per–flow performance metrics. This makes it easy to see the average total use in normalized IOPs, latency, and aggregate limits and reservations applied to a volume. To get this information, use the following PowerShell cmdlet:

```
Get-StorageQosVolume | Format-List
```

The complete syntax for the **Get-StorageQosVolume** PowerShell cmdlet is as follows:

```
Get-StorageQosVolume [-VolumeId <Guid[]>] [-Mountpoint <String[]>]
   [-Status <Status[]>] [-CimSession <CimSession[]>] [-ThrottleLimit
   <Int32>] [-AsJob] [<CommonParameters>]
```

To create storage policies, use the following PowerShell cmdlet:

```
New-StorageQosPolicy
```

The full syntax for the **New-StorageQosPolicy** PowerShell cmdlet is as follows:

```
New-StorageQosPolicy [[-PolicyId] <Guid>] [[-Name] <String>]
   [[-MaximumIops] <UInt64>] [[-MinimumIops] <UInt64>]
   [[-MaximumIOBandwidth] <UInt64>] [[-ParentPolicy] <CimInstance>]
   [[-PolicyType] <PolicyType>] [-AsJob] [-CimSession <CimSession>]
   [-ThrottleLimit <Int32>] [-WhatIf] [-Confirm] [<CommonParameters>]
```

You then apply these storage policies by using the **-QoSPolicyID** option in **Set-VMHardDiskDrive**.

You can easily confirm that policies are applied by using the following cmdlet:

```
Get-StorageQosFlow
```

The full syntax for the **Get-StorageQosFlow** PowerShell cmdlet is as follows:

```
Get-StorageQoSFlow [[-FlowId] <Guid>] [[-InitiatorId] <String>]
   [[-FilePath] <String>] [[-VolumeId] <String>] [[-InitiatorName]
   <String>] [[-InitiatorNodeName] <String>] [[-StorageNodeName]
   <String>] [[-Status] <Status>] [-IncludeHidden] [-AsJob]
   [-CimSession <CimSession>] [-ThrottleLimit <Int32>]
   [<CommonParameters>]
```

On the Hyper-V server, you can also use the script **Get-VMHardDiskDrivePolicy.ps1** to see what policy is applied to a virtual hard disk drive.

You can use aggregated policies if you want multiple virtual hard disks to share a single pool of IOPs and bandwidth. Aside from the PolicyType that is specified, there is no difference between creating dedicated and aggregated policies.

It is also easy to remove a storage QoS policy, as shown in this example:

```
PS C:\> Get-VM -Name WinOltp1 | Get-VMHardDiskDrive |
   Set-VMHardDiskDrive -QoSPolicyID $null
```

Exam Preparation Tasks

As mentioned in the section "How to Use This Book" in the Introduction, you have a couple choices for exam preparation: the exercises here, Chapter 21, "Final Preparation," and the exam simulation questions in the Pearson Test Prep Software Online.

Review All Key Topics

Review the most important topics in this chapter, noted with the Key Topics icon in the outer margin of the page. Table 9-3 lists these key topics and the page number on which each is found.

Table 9-3   Key Topics for Chapter 9

Key Topic Element	Description	Page Number
List	VHDX improvements	155
Steps	Creating a fixed-size VHD	156
Steps	Creating a pass-through disk	159
List	Facts about differencing disks	160
List	Differences between standard and production checkpoints	165
List	Storage QoS capabilities	167

Complete Tables and Lists from Memory

Print a copy of Appendix B, "Memory Tables" (found on the book website), or at least the section for this chapter, and complete the tables and lists from memory. Appendix C, "Memory Tables Answer Key," also on the website, includes completed tables and lists you can use to check your work.

Define Key Terms

Define the following key terms from this chapter and check your answers against the glossary:

Pass-through disk, Differencing disk, Shared virtual hard disk, Storage Quality of Service

Q&A

The answers to these questions appear in Appendix A. For more practice with exam format questions, use the Pearson Test Prep Software Online.

1. What option do you choose from the Actions pane in Hyper-V Manager to convert a VHD?

2. What type of checkpoint is designed for testing and development environments?

3. What cmdlet creates a new storage QoS policy?

This chapter covers the following subjects:

- **Network Interface Cards:** The first key ingredient in a virtual network is a NIC. This section provides an overview of new virtual networking features in Windows Server 2016 and then describes these critical network components.

- **Virtual Switches:** The second major part in a virtual network is the virtual switch to which a virtual machine and its NIC connect. This section of the chapter details these powerful structures.

- **Virtual Network Performance:** The final section of this chapter deals with how to improve the performance of a virtual network, using a wide range of techniques. This section also offers some powerful best practices to keep in mind as you are planning and deploying a virtual datacenter.

## CHAPTER 10

Hyper-V Networking

Modern virtualized data centers involve many networking components. This chapter examines virtual NICs and virtual switches, as well as the optimization of virtual networks.

"Do I Know This Already?" Quiz

The "Do I Know This Already?" quiz allows you to assess whether you should read the entire chapter. Table 10-1 lists the major headings in this chapter and the "Do I Know This Already?" quiz questions covering the material in those headings so you can assess your knowledge of these specific areas. The answers to the "Do I Know This Already?" quiz appear in Appendix A, "Answers to the 'Do I Know This Already?' Quizzes and Q&A Questions."

Table 10-1 "Do I Know This Already?" Foundation Topics Section-to-Question Mapping

Foundation Topics Section	Questions
Network Interface Cards	1, 2
Virtual Switches	3, 4
Virtual Network Performance	5, 6

CAUTION The goal of self-assessment is to gauge your mastery of the topics in this chapter. If you do not know the answer to a question or are only partially sure of the answer, you should mark your answer as incorrect for purposes of the self-assessment. Giving yourself credit for an answer you correctly guess skews your self-assessment results and might provide you with a false sense of security.

1. To add a virtual NIC in the Hyper-V Manager, what shortcut menu option would you choose after selecting your virtual machine?

   a. Add Hardware

   b. Settings

   c. Properties

   d. Hardware

2. If you enable bandwidth management for a vNIC, what options exist? Choose two.

   a. Load

   b. Minimum bandwidth

   c. VLAN distribution

   d. Maximum bandwidth

3. Which virtual switch type permits communication between the VMs on the host and between the VMs and the host itself?

   a. Internal

   b. Private

   c. Firewall

   d. Shielded

4. Which of the following is not an option for a virtual switch in Windows Server 2016?

   a. Internal

   b. Private

   c. External

   d. Firewall

5. What technology delivers packets from an outside virtual machine network directly to a virtualized host operating system?

   a. SET

   b. RDMA

   c. VMQ

   d. FIFO

6. Which technology is SET not compatible with?

   a. 802.1X

   b. RDMA

   c. SR-IOV

   d. DCB

Foundation Topics

Network Interface Cards

An increasing number of datacenter networking components are capable of virtualization, enabling the creation of *software-defined networks*. When a networking device is virtualized, you have the luxury of managing it through Hyper-V Manager or Windows PowerShell.

Windows Server 2016 introduces new, powerful virtual networking features, including the following:

- Features that were once only available in physical appliances are now possible, thanks to improved virtualization in Windows Server 2016. This includes functions like load balancing, network address translation, datacenter firewalls, and Remote Access Service gateways.

- "Container-aware" virtual network features like NAT are available.

- A network controller device allows easy management, troubleshooting, and configuration of both physical and virtual network environments.

- Switch Embedded Teaming (SET) is a new NIC teaming option that you can use for Hyper-V networks. SET features integrated functionality with Hyper-V that offers faster performance and better fault tolerance than traditional teaming.

- Remote Direct Memory Access (RDMA) with Hyper-V permits RDMA services to use Hyper-V switches. You can enable this feature with or without SET.

- Virtual machine multi queues distribute multiple hardware queues for each virtual machine, thereby improving throughput compared to Windows Server 2012 R2.

- Converged network adapters support using a single network adapter or a team of network adapters to handle multiple forms of traffic, management, RDMA, and virtual machine traffic. This reduces the number of specialized adapters you need on each host.

Adding and Removing Virtual Network Interface Cards (vNICs) and Legacy Network Adapters

Remember from Chapter 8, "Working with Virtual Machines," that you create a virtual NIC when you create a virtual machine by using a wizard.

To add or remove a virtual network interface card (vNIC) to or from a virtual machine, follow these steps:

Step 1.   In **Server Manager**, choose **Tools > Hyper-V Manager**.

Step 2.   Right-click your virtual machine on the **Virtual Machines** page and choose **Settings**.

Step 3.   From the **Add Hardware** screen, choose **Network Adapter** and click **Add** (see Figure 10-1). Notice that you can also choose **Legacy Network Adapter** from this dialog. You should use a legacy network adapter only when absolutely needed, such as when you are performing a network-based installation of the operating system. Performance from virtual NICs is superior.

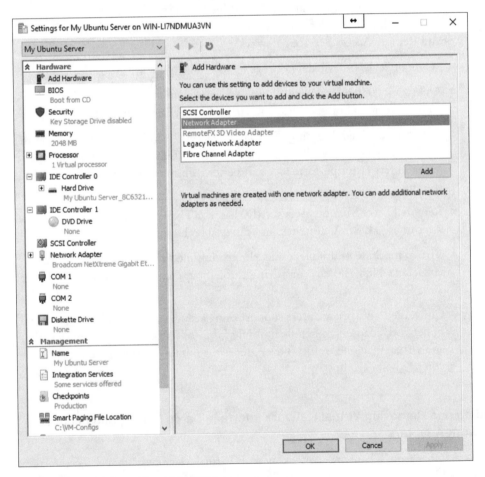

Figure 10-1   Adding a New Virtual NIC

Step 4. Complete the Network Adapter window as follows (see Figure 10-2):

- Select the virtual switch for the network adapter.

- Specify an optional VLAN ID.

- Configure bandwidth management.

- Click **Remove**. (Note that you can easily click this button from the properties of an existing virtual NIC to remove it from the virtual machine.)

Step 5. Click **Apply** when you are finished and click **OK** to close the window.

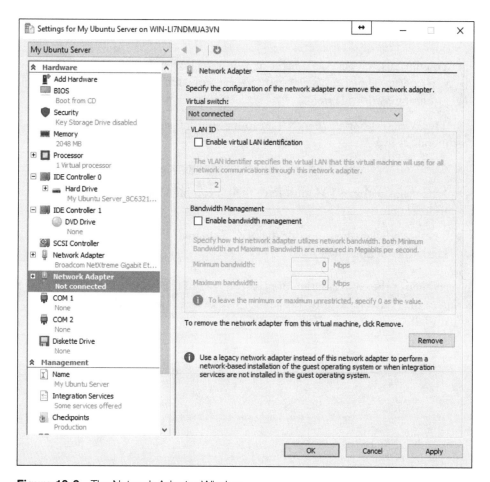

Figure 10-2   The Network Adapter Window

Configuring NIC Teaming in Virtual Machines

 (Remember these important points regarding NIC teaming in VMs in Windows Server 2016:)

- A computer running Hyper-V must have two or more physical network adapters to perform load balancing or failover. A NIC team that holds only one network adapter can use NIC teaming for separation of network traffic with virtual local area networks (VLANs).

- If the network adapters connect to multiple physical switches, the physical switches must be on the same Layer 2 subnet.

- The virtual network adapters you plan to team must connect to an external Hyper-V switch only; teaming is not supported with private or internal virtual switches.

- You must use Hyper-V Manager or Windows PowerShell commands to create two external Hyper-V virtual switches, each of which connects to a different physical network adapter.

- The Windows Server 2016 NIC teaming solution supports teams with two members in VMs.

- A VM's networking interfaces must have configurations that allow teaming.

- NIC teams within a VM must have their Teaming mode configured as Switch Independent.

- The Load Balancing mode for the NIC team in a VM must use the Address Hash distribution mode.

You accomplish the configuration of NIC teaming in the Advanced Features section of the Network Adapter properties accessible in the Settings dialog (see Figure 10-3).

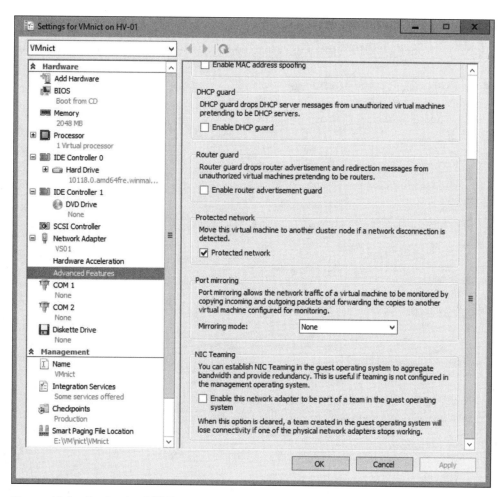

Figure 10-3 Configuring NIC Teaming

Configuring MAC Addresses

Notice from Figure 10-4 that it is easy to control MAC addressing for a virtual NIC.

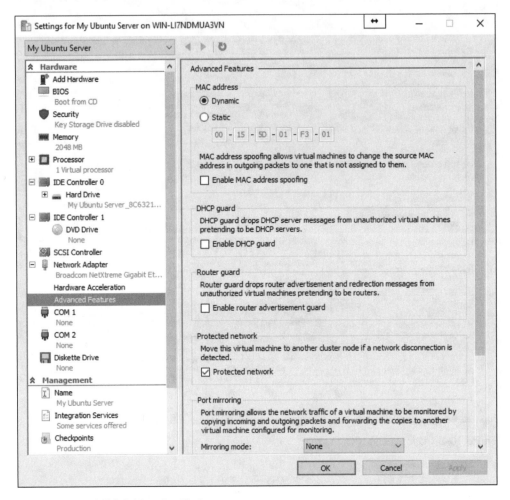

Figure 10-4 MAC Addressing Options

The options include the following:

- Dynamic MAC address assignment

- Static MAC address assignment

- MAC address spoofing, which allows the changing of source MAC addresses in outgoing packets

NOTE   When you configure a NIC team in Switch Independent mode with hash load distribution, the packets from a single source simultaneously distribute across multiple team members. To prevent the switches from getting confused and to prevent MAC flapping alarms, Server 2016 replaces the source MAC address with a different MAC address on the frames transmitted on team members other than the primary team member.

Because of this, each team member uses a different MAC address, and MAC address conflicts are prevented unless a failure occurs. When Server 2016 detects a failure on the primary NIC, the NIC teaming software starts using the primary team member's MAC address on the team member that is chosen to serve as the temporary primary team member.

This change only applies to traffic that was going to be sent on the primary team member with the primary team member's MAC address as its source MAC address. Other traffic continues to be sent with whatever source MAC address it would have used prior to the failure.

Virtual Switches

Remember that virtual switches control how network traffic flows between virtual machines that are hosted on a Hyper-V server, in addition to how network traffic flows between virtual machines and the rest of the network.

There are three supported virtual switch types in Windows Server 2016, as shown in Table 10-2.

Table 10-2   Virtual Switch Types

Virtual Switch Type	Description
External virtual switch	This virtual switch maps a network to a specific network adapter or network adapter team. You can map an external network to a wireless network adapter if you have installed the wireless LAN service on the host Hyper-V server and if the Hyper-V server has a compatible network adapter.
Internal virtual switch	This virtual switch permits communication between the virtual machines on a Hyper-V host and permits communication between the virtual machines and the Hyper-V host itself.
Private virtual switch	Private virtual switches permit communication between virtual machines on a Hyper-V host. You cannot use private switches to communicate between the virtual machines and the Hyper-V host.

When configuring a virtual network, you can configure a virtual LAN (VLAN) ID to associate with the network. You can use this ID to extend existing VLANs on an external network to VLANs within the Hyper-V host's network switch. Remember that VLANs partition network traffic. VLANs function as separate logical networks. Traffic can pass only from one VLAN to another if it passes through a router.

You can configure the following extensions for each virtual switch type:

- **Microsoft Network Driver Interface Specification (NDIS) Capture**: This extension allows the capture of data that travels across a virtual switch.

- **Microsoft Windows Filtering Platform**: This extension allows filtering of data that travels across a virtual switch.

To create and configure new virtual switches, use the Virtual Switch Manager, or use the New-VMSwitch and Set-VMSwitch cmdlets, which are available from the Actions pane of Hyper-V Manager. Figure 10-5 shows this interface.

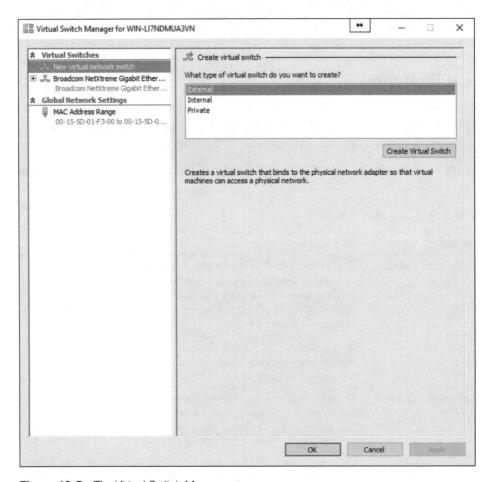

Figure 10-5   The Virtual Switch Manager

Virtual Network Performance

You can use virtual networking in Windows Server 2016 to isolate virtual machines from different organizations even if they are connected to the same physical network. You can also use network virtualization to separate development and production of virtual machines. For example, say that you are offering infrastructure as a service (IaaS) to competing businesses. You can use network virtualization to go beyond assigning these virtual machines to separate VLANs as a way of isolating network traffic.

Network virtualization is a technology that you deploy primarily in scenarios where you use Hyper-V to host virtual machines for non-Microsoft organizations. Network virtualization has the advantage of allowing you to configure all network isolation on the Hyper-V host. With VLANs, it is also necessary to configure switches with the correct VLAN IDs.

When you configure network virtualization, each guest virtual machine has two IP addresses, which function as follows:

- **Customer IP address**: The customer assigns this IP address to the virtual machine. You can configure this IP address so that communication with the customer's internal network can occur even though the virtual machine might be hosted on a Hyper-V server that is connected to a separate public IP network. Using the **ipconfig** command on the virtual machine shows the customer IP address.

- **Provider IP address**: The physical network assigns this IP address, which is visible to the hosting provider and to other hosts on the physical network. This IP address is not visible from the virtual machine.

You can use network virtualization to host multiple virtual machines that use the same customer IP address, such as 192.168.15.101, on the same Hyper-V host. When you do this, the virtual machines are assigned different IP addresses by the hosting provider; however, this address is not apparent from within the virtual machine.

You manage network virtualization by using Windows PowerShell cmdlets or System Center Virtual Machine Manager (SCVMM). All network virtualization cmdlets are in the NetWNV module for Windows PowerShell. Tenants gain access to virtual machines that take advantage of network virtualization through routing and remote access. They make a tunneled connection from their network to the virtualized network on the Hyper-V server.

Virtual Machine Queue

Virtual Machine Queue (VMQ) is a type of hardware packet filtering that delivers packets from an outside virtual machine network directly to a virtualized host operating system. VMQ functions by allowing a NIC to transfer incoming frames directly to the NIC's receive buffer, using Direct Memory Access (DMA). VMQ reduces plenty of overhead in this process.

Rather than one processor handling all the network data exchanges, with VMQ, different processors can process packets for different virtual machines.

You configure VMQ by using the **set-netadaptervmq** cmdlet in Windows PowerShell or the Hardware Acceleration node in your Network Adapter properties inside Hyper-V. Here is the complete syntax for the cmdlet:

```
Set-NetAdapterVmq [-Name] <String[]> [-IncludeHidden]
  [-BaseProcessorGroup <UInt16>]
 [-BaseProcessorNumber <Byte>] [-MaxProcessors <UInt32>]
   [-MaxProcessorNumber <Byte>] [-NumaNode <UInt16>]
 [-Enabled <Boolean>] [-NoRestart] [-CimSession <CimSession[]>]
   [-ThrottleLimit <Int32>] [-AsJob] [-PassThru]
 [-WhatIf] [-Confirm] [<CommonParameters>]
```

Remote Direct Memory Access (RDMA) and Switch Embedded Teaming (SET)

Before Windows Server 2016, it was not possible to configure Remote Direct Memory Access (RDMA) on network adapters that were bound to a NIC team or a Hyper-V virtual switch. This is no longer the case, and you can enable RDMA on network adapters that are bound to a Hyper-V virtual switch with or without Switch Embedded Teaming (SET).

The following steps show how to enable Data Center Bridging (DCB), create a Hyper-V virtual switch with an RDMA virtual NIC, and create a Hyper-V virtual switch with SET and RDMA vNICs:

Step 1. Use the following sample script to enable and configure DCB for SMB Direct:

```
#
# Turn on DCB
Install-WindowsFeature Data-Center-Bridging
#
# Set a policy for SMB-Direct
New-NetQosPolicy "SMB" -NetDirectPortMatchCondition 445
  -PriorityValue8021Action 3
#
# Turn on Flow Control for SMB
```

```
Enable-NetQosFlowControl   -Priority 3
#
# Make sure flow control is off for other traffic
Disable-NetQosFlowControl   -Priority 0,1,2,4,5,6,7
#
# Apply policy to the target adapters
Enable-NetAdapterQos  -Name "SLOT 2"
#
# Give SMB Direct 30% of the bandwidth minimum
New-NetQosTrafficClass "SMB"  -Priority 3  -BandwidthPercentage
  30  -Algorithm ETS
```

Step 2. If SET is not required in your environment, use the following Power-Shell script to create a Hyper-V virtual switch with an RDMA vNIC:

```
#
# Create a vmSwitch without SET
#
New-VMSwitch -Name RDMAswitch -NetAdapterName "SLOT 2"
#
# Add host vNICs and make them RDMA capable
#
Add-VMNetworkAdapter -SwitchName RDMAswitch -Name SMB_1
Enable-NetAdapterRDMA "vEthernet (SMB_1)"
#
# Verify RDMA capabilities
#
Get-NetAdapterRdma
```

Step 3. To make use of RDMA capabilities on your Hyper-V host vNICs, use the following PowerShell script:

```
#
# Create a vmSwitch with SET
#
New-VMSwitch -Name SETswitch -NetAdapterName "SLOT 2","SLOT 3"
  -EnableEmbeddedTeaming $true
#
# Add host vNICs and make them RDMA capable
#
Add-VMNetworkAdapter -SwitchName SETswitch -Name SMB_1
  -managementOS
Add-VMNetworkAdapter -SwitchName SETswitch -Name SMB_2
  -managementOS
Enable-NetAdapterRDMA "vEthernet (SMB_1)","vEthernet (SMB_2)"
```

```
#
# Verify RDMA capabilities; ensure that the capabilities are
  non-zero
#
Get-NetAdapterRdma | fl *
#
# Many switches won't pass traffic class information on untagged
  VLAN traffic,
# so make sure host adapters for RDMA are on VLANs. (This example
  assigns the two SMB_*
# host virtual adapters to VLAN 42.)
#
Set-VMNetworkAdapterIsolation -ManagementOS -VMNetworkAdapterName
  SMB_1  -IsolationMode VLAN -DefaultIsolationID 42
Set-VMNetworkAdapterIsolation -ManagementOS -VMNetworkAdapterName
  SMB_2  -IsolationMode VLAN -DefaultIsolationID 42
```

Table 10-3 outlines the networking technologies that SET is and is not compatible with in Windows Server 2016.

Table 10-3 Networking Technologies Compatible and Not Compatible with SET in Windows Server 2016

Compatible	Not Compatible
Data Center Bridging (DCB)	802.1X authentication
Hyper-V network virtualization; NV-GRE and VXLAN are both supported in Windows Server 2016	IPsec Task Offload (IPsecTO)
Receive-side checksum offloads (IPv4, IPv6, TCP); these are supported if any of the SET team members support them	QoS in host or native operating systems
Remote Direct Memory Access (RDMA)	Receive Segment Coalescing (RSC)
SDN quality of service	Receive Side Scaling (RSS)
Transmit-side checksum offloads (IPv4, IPv6, TCP); these are supported if all the SET team members support them	TCP Chimney Offload
Virtual Machine Queues (VMQ)	Virtual machine QoS (VM-QoS)
Virtual Receive Side Scaling (RSS)	

Virtual Networking Best Practices

Keep in mind the following best practices when you are designing and deploying virtual networks:

- Bandwidth is key. Be sure to provision enough bandwidth so that the bottle-neck of your design is not the network itself.

- Consider using NIC teaming whenever possible.

- Use bandwidth management to give maximum and minimum bandwidth for each virtual network adapter.

- Provision a Hyper-V host with an adapter that supports VMQ. VMQ uses hardware packet filtering to deliver network traffic directly to a virtual machine, which improves performance because the packet does not need to be copied from the host operating system to the virtual machine.

- If you are hosting a large number of virtual machines and need to isolate them, use network virtualization rather than VLANs.

Exam Preparation Tasks

As mentioned in the section "How to Use This Book" in the Introduction, you have a couple choices for exam preparation: the exercises here, Chapter 21, "Final Preparation," and the exam simulation questions in the Pearson Test Prep Software Online.

Review All Key Topics

Review the most important topics in this chapter, noted with the Key Topics icon in the outer margin of the page. Table 10-4 lists these key topics and the page number on which each is found.

Table 10-4 Key Topics for Chapter 10

Key Topic Element	Description	Page Number
Steps	Virtual NIC creation	167
List	NIC teaming	178
Steps	RDMA and SET	184
List	Virtual network best practices	186

Complete Tables and Lists from Memory

Print a copy of Appendix B, "Memory Tables" (found on the book website), or at least the section for this chapter, and complete the tables and lists from memory. Appendix C, "Memory Tables Answer Key," also on the website, includes completed tables and lists to check your work.

Define Key Terms

Define the following key terms from this chapter and check your answers against the glossary:

SET, RDMA, vNIC, Virtual Machine Queues

Q&A

The answers to these questions appear in Appendix A. For more practice with exam format questions, use the Pearson Test Prep Software Online.

1. Name at least three new virtual networking features in Windows Server 2016.

2. What is the main GUI for virtual switch management and creation that is launched from Hyper-V Manager?

3. Name at least two virtual networking best practices.

This chapter covers the following subjects:

- **An Overview of Containers:** This section presents an overview of containers and discusses appropriate usage scenarios for Windows.

- **Docker:** This part of the chapter covers the installation of Docker and the configuration of its startup options.

- **Host Installation:** This area details the installation of a Windows Server container host, in both physical and virtual environments.

- **Container Deployment**: This section covers the actual deployment of containers.

## CHAPTER 11

Deploying Containers

Anyone who has heard anything about Windows Server 2016 will marvel at the support for containers that is now integrated into the operating system. This is one of two chapters dedicated to this important topic. This chapter deals with deployment issues, and Chapter 12, "Managing Containers," covers management topics.

"Do I Know This Already?" Quiz

The "Do I Know This Already?" quiz allows you to assess whether you should read the entire chapter. Table 11-1 lists the major headings in this chapter and the "Do I Know This Already?" quiz questions covering the material in those headings so you can assess your knowledge of these specific areas. The answers to the "Do I Know This Already?" quiz appear in Appendix A, "Answers to the 'Do I Know This Already?' Quizzes and Q&A Questions."

Table 11-1 "Do I Know This Already?" Foundation Topics Section-to-Question Mapping

Foundation Topics Section	Questions
An Overview of Containers	1, 2
Docker	3, 4
Host Installation	5, 6
Container Deployment	7, 8

CAUTION The goal of self-assessment is to gauge your mastery of the topics in this chapter. If you do not know the answer to a question or are only partially sure of the answer, you should mark your answer as incorrect for purposes of the self-assessment. Giving yourself credit for an answer you correctly guess skews your self-assessment results and might provide you with a false sense of security.

1. What types of containers can you create in Windows Server 2016? Choose two.

   a. Windows Server

   b. Linux

   c. Legacy Windows

   d. Hyper-V

2. What layer captures all actions after a container has started?

   a. Sandbox

   b. Service abstraction

   c. API layer

   d. VM machine layer

3. Docker is a requirement for working with which type of container in Windows Server 2016?

   a. Windows Server

   b. Hyper-V

   c. Legacy Windows

   d. Linux

4. What file includes startup parameter information for Docker?

   a. init.ini

   b. config.ini

   c. daemon.json

   d. start.ini

5. What do you install before working with containers?

   a. Base image

   b. Defender

   c. Server Core

   d. Nano Server

6. What command installs the Nano Server base image?

   a. **get-nanoserver**

   b. **get-docker-install nanoserver**

   c. **docker pull microsoft/nanoserver**

   d. **docker install nanoserver**

7. What do you use to manage the Nano Server if it is your container host?

   a. PowerShell

   b. Computer management

   c. Command prompt

   d. bash

8. What command deploys a container?

   a. **deploy container**

   b. **install image**

   c. **docker run**

   d. **docker container install**

Foundation Topics

An Overview of Containers

The new Windows containers feature is described in many different creative ways. Ultimately, you just need to understand that Windows containers enable many isolated applications to run on one computer system. The applications "spin up" remarkably fast—much faster than a full VM (which boasts great boot speed to begin with). Containers are also highly scalable and portable. Portability is such an incredible feature, allowing you to easily move a workload using a very small file footprint—incredibly smaller than a VM.

NOTE Although containers in Windows Server 2016 are the most exciting new feature for many of us, remember that this technology is not a focus in your MCSA certification exam. It is not surprising to see just one or two questions total regarding this new virtualization feature addition to Windows Server.

Two different types of container runtimes are included with Server 2016, each with a different degree of application isolation:

- **Windows Server containers, which achieve isolation through namespace and process isolation**: A Windows Server container shares a kernel with the container host and all containers running on the host. Windows Server containers isolate applications on the same container host. Each container has its own view of the host system, including the kernel, processes, file systems, the registry, and other components. They work between the user mode level and the kernel mode level.

- **Hyper-V containers, which encapsulate each container in a lightweight virtual machine**: These containers expand on the isolation given by Windows Server containers by running each container in a highly optimized virtual machine. In this configuration, the kernel of the container host is not shared with the Hyper-V containers. Hyper-V containers are based on a container technology that is rooted in hardware-assisted virtualization. With hardware-assisted virtualization, Hyper-V containers' applications are provided a highly isolated environment in which to operate, and the host operating system cannot be affected in any way by any running container.

You should also be aware of the following added features introduced with Windows containers:

- Nano Server is an ideal host for both Windows Server and Hyper-V containers.

- Container data management capabilities are enhanced with container shared folders.

- You can implement container resource restrictions.

From the container application's perspective, a container seems to be an isolated Windows operating system, with its own file system, devices, and configuration.

Containers can be very confusing at first; when you are working with them, they may seem identical to virtual machines. A container runs an operating system, has a file system, and can be accessed over a network just as if it were a physical or virtual computer system. Keep in mind, however, that the technology and concepts behind containers are very different from those of virtual machines.

Table 11-2 gives some key concepts you should be aware of before working with containers.

Table 11-2 Container Concepts

Concept	Description
Container host	A container host is a physical or virtual computer system configured with the Windows Container feature; it runs one or more Windows containers.
Container image	The container image shows the state of the virtual container, including such things as registry or file system changes; you can discard a container image or use it as a base image for new containers.
Sandbox	After a container has started, all write actions such as file system modifications, registry modifications, or software installations are captured in the sandbox layer.
Container OS image	The container OS image is the first layer of potentially many image layers that make up a container; this image provides the operating system environment and cannot be modified.
Container repository	Each time you create a container image, the container image and its dependencies are stored in a local repository.
Container management technology	You can manage Windows containers by using both Windows PowerShell and Docker.
Containers for IT professionals	IT professionals can use containers to give standardized environments for their development, QA, and production teams.
Containers for developers	When you containerize an app, only the app and the components needed to run it are combined into an image; you can use containers to start up lightweight and portable app components—or micro-services—for distributed apps and quickly scale each service separately.

Before installing Windows containers, first, be sure of your operating system requirements:

- The Windows container feature is only available on Windows Server 2016 (Core and with Desktop Experience), Nano Server, and Windows 10 Professional and Enterprise (Anniversary Edition or later).

- The Hyper-V role must be installed.

- Windows Server container hosts must have Windows installed to c:, although this restriction does not apply if only Hyper-V containers are deployed.

If a Windows container host is to run from a Hyper-V virtual machine, nested virtualization needs to be enabled. Nested virtualization has the following requirements:

- At least 4 GB RAM must be available for the virtualized Hyper-V host.

- Windows Server 2016 or Windows 10 must be running on the host system, and Windows Server (Full, Core) or Nano Server must be running on the virtual machine.

- The processor must have Intel VT-x. (Containers are currently available only for Intel processors.)

- The container host VM needs at least two virtual processors.

Windows containers are offered with two container base images, Windows Server Core and Nano Server. Not all configurations support both OS images. Table 11-3 details the supported configurations.

Table 11-3   Supported Base Images

Host OS	Windows Server Container	Hyper-V Container
Server 2016 with Desktop	Server Core/Nano Server	Server Core/Nano Server
Server 2016 Core	Server Core/Nano Server	Server Core/Nano Server
Nano Server	Nano Server	Server Core/Nano Server
Windows 10 Pro/Enterprise	Not available	Server Core/Nano Server

Because Windows Server containers and the underlying host share a single kernel, the container's base image must match that of the host. If the versions are different, the container may start, but full functionally is not guaranteed.

The Windows operating system has four levels of versioning: Major, Minor, Build, and Revision (for example, 10.0.14393.0). The build number changes only when new versions of the OS are published. The revision number is updated as Windows updates are applied. Windows Server containers are blocked from starting when the build number is different.

To check what version a Windows host has installed, you can query HKEY_LOCAL_MACHINE\Software\Microsoft\Windows NT\CurrentVersion. To check what version your base image is using, you can review the tags on the Docker hub or the image hash table provided in the image description.

Unlike Windows Server containers, each Hyper-V container uses its own instance of the Windows kernel. You can therefore mismatch the container host and container image versions.

Docker

It is nearly impossible for datacenter engineers who were working with containers before the advent of Windows Server 2016 to not immediately think of Docker. Docker is the premier container creation and management tool enjoyed by Unix engineers for quite some time. Many are thrilled to see this functionality arrive in Windows Server 2016.

Installing Docker on Windows Server and Nano Server

This section looks at the steps for installing Docker for a Windows container host on either Windows Server 2016 or Windows Server Core 2016. This system might be a physical system or a virtual system.

Docker is a requirement for working with Windows containers. Note that Docker consists of two components: the Docker Engine and the Docker Client.

The following instructions for installing Docker are identical if you are installing Docker in a Windows Server 2016 Core or in a Nano Server environment:

Step 1.   Launch an elevated PowerShell session by right-clicking the PowerShell shortcut and choosing **Run as Administrator.**

Step 2.   Install the OneGet PowerShell module by using the following syntax and, if prompted to install the NuGet provider, respond with **Y**:

```
Install-Module -Name DockerMsftProvider -Repository PSGallery
    -Force
```

Step 3.   Use OneGet to install the latest version of Docker, using the following syntax and, if prompted that the source is not trusted, respond with **Y**:

```
Install-Package -Name docker -ProviderName DockerMsftProvider
```

Step 4.   Following successful installation, reboot your system using the following syntax:

```
Restart-Computer -Force
```

Configuring Docker Daemon Startup Options

The Docker Engine can accept many custom configurations, including the following:

- Configuring how the daemon accepts incoming requests

- Configuring default networking options

- Configuring debug and/or log settings

On Windows, these configurations can be specified in a configuration file or by using Windows Service Control Manager.

The preferred method for configuring the Docker Engine in Windows is using a configuration file, which is at **c:\ProgramData\docker\config\daemon.json**. You can create this file if it does not already exist.

NOTE Not every available Docker configuration option is applicable to Docker on Windows. The example that follows shows the configuration options that are Windows applicable. Only the desired configuration changes need to be added to the configuration file.

```json
{
    "authorization-plugins": [],
    "dns": [],
    "dns-opts": [],
    "dns-search": [],
    "exec-opts": [],
    "storage-driver": "",
    "storage-opts": [],
    "labels": [],
    "log-driver": "",
    "mtu": 0,
    "pidfile": "",
    "graph": "",
    "cluster-store": "",
    "cluster-advertise": "",
    "debug": true,
    "hosts": [],
    "log-level": "",
    "tlsverify": true,
    "tlscacert": "",
    "tlscert": "",
    "tlskey": "",
    "group": "",
    "default-ulimits": {},
    "bridge": "",
    "fixed-cidr": "",
    "raw-logs": false,
    "registry-mirrors": [],
    "insecure-registries": [],
    "disable-legacy-registry": false
}
```

For example, you might configure Docker to accept incoming connections on port 2375 by using the following configuration file settings:

```
{
    "hosts": ["tcp://0.0.0.0:2375"]
}
```

You can also configure the Docker Engine by modifying the Docker service, using **sc config**. Using this method, Docker Engine flags are set directly on the Docker service. For example, you can run the following command in an elevated command prompt to have Docker accept incoming connections on port 2375:

```
sc config docker binpath= "\"C:\Program Files\docker\dockerd.exe\"
   --run-service -H tcp://0.0.0.0:2375"
```

Host Installation

This section details how to deploy a Windows container host to either Windows Server 2016 or Windows Server Core 2016 on a physical system or a virtual system.

Before working with Windows containers, a base image needs to be installed. Base images are available with either Windows Server Core or Nano Server as the underlying operating system.

To install the Windows Server Core base image, run the following from an elevated PowerShell prompt:

```
docker pull microsoft/windowsservercore
```

To install the Nano Server base image, run the following from an elevated PowerShell prompt:

```
docker pull microsoft/nanoserver
```

To run Hyper-V containers, the Hyper-V role is required. If the Windows container host is itself a Hyper-V virtual machine, nested virtualization needs to be enabled before you install the Hyper-V role.

The following script configures nested virtualization for the container host:

```
#replace with the virtual machine name
$vm = "<virtual-machine>"

#configure virtual processor
Set-VMProcessor -VMName $vm -ExposeVirtualizationExtensions $true
   -Count 2
```

```
#disable dynamic memory
Set-VMMemory $vm -DynamicMemoryEnabled $false

#enable mac spoofing
Get-VMNetworkAdapter -VMName $vm | Set-VMNetworkAdapter
  -MacAddressSpoofing On
```

This script runs on the parent Hyper-V machine. Ensure that the container host virtual machine is turned off when running this script.

To enable the Hyper-V feature using PowerShell, run the following command in an elevated PowerShell session:

Install-WindowsFeature hyper-v

For Nano Server with Windows containers, install the base container images following the instructions previously provided.

For best results, manage Docker on Nano Server from a remote system. To manage a remote Docker server, follow these steps:

Step 1. Create a firewall rule on the container host for the Docker connection. This will be port 2375 for an unsecure connection or port 2376 for a secure connection. Use the following syntax in an elevated command prompt:

```
netsh advfirewall firewall add rule name="Docker daemon " dir=in
   action=allow protocol=TCP localport=2375
```

Step 2. To configure the Docker Engine to accept incoming connections over TCP, create a daemon.json file at **c:\ProgramData\docker\config\ daemon.json** on the Nano Server host, using the following syntax in an elevated PowerShell session:

```
new-item -Type File c:\ProgramData\docker\config\daemon.json
```

Step 3. Run the following command to add a connection configuration to the daemon.json file:

```
Add-Content 'c:\programdata\docker\config\daemon.json' '{
   "hosts": ["tcp://0.0.0.0:2375", "npipe://"] }'
```

This configures the Docker Engine to accept incoming connections over TCP port 2375. This is an unsecure connection and is not advised but can be used for isolated testing.

Step 4. Restart the Docker service by using the following command:

```
Restart-Service docker
```

Step 5.   On the remote system where you will be working, download the Docker client by using the following syntax:

```
Invoke-WebRequest "https://download.docker.com/components/engine/
    windows-server/cs-1.12/docker.zip" -OutFile "$env:TEMP\docker.
    zip" -UseBasicParsing
```

Step 6.   Extract the compressed package by using the following syntax:

```
Expand-Archive -Path "$env:TEMP\docker.zip" -DestinationPath
    $env:ProgramFiles
```

Step 7.   Run the following two commands to add the Docker directory to the system path:

```
# For quick use, does not require shell to be restarted.
$env:path += ";c:\program files\docker"


# For persistent use, will apply even after a reboot.
[Environment]::SetEnvironmentVariable("Path", $env:Path + ";C:\
    Program Files\Docker", [EnvironmentVariableTarget]::Machine)
```

Step 8.   To access the remote Docker host, use the **docker -H** parameter, like this:

```
docker -H tcp://<IPADDRESS>:2375 run -it microsoft/nanoserver cmd
```

Step 9.   Create an environmental variable **DOCKER_HOST** to remove the **-H** parameter requirement. You can use the following PowerShell command for this:

```
$env:DOCKER_HOST = "tcp://<ipaddress of server>:2375"
```

To deploy Hyper-V containers, the Hyper-V role is required on the container host. If the Windows container host is itself a Hyper-V virtual machine, nested virtualization needs to be enabled. Follow these steps to add the Hyper-V role:

Step 1.   Install the Hyper-V role on the Nano Server container host:

```
Install-NanoServerPackage Microsoft-NanoServer-Compute-Package
```

Step 2.   Reboot the Nano Server host after the Hyper-V role has been installed:

```
Restart-Computer
```

Container Deployment

If you are using Nano Server as a container host, consider that because Nano Server does not have interactive logon capabilities, all management must be completed from a remote system, using PowerShell. Follow these steps to deploy a container:

Step 1.   Add the Nano Server system to trusted hosts of the remote system. Replace the IP address with the IP address of the Nano Server, like this:

```
Set-Item WSMan:\localhost\Client\TrustedHosts 192.168.1.50 -Force
```

Step 2.   Create the remote PowerShell session, using the following syntax:

```
Enter-PSSession -ComputerName 192.168.1.50 -Credential ~\
Administrator
```

When you complete these steps, you are in a remote PowerShell session with the Nano Server system.

To deploy your first container, you download a pre-created .NET sample image from the Docker Hub registry and deploy a simple container running a .Net Hello World application. To do so, you use **docker run** to deploy the .Net container and download the container image, which may take a few minutes. Use this syntax:

```
docker run microsoft/dotnet-samples:dotnetapp-nanoserver
```

The container starts, prints the hello world message, and then exits.

Exam Preparation Tasks

As mentioned in the section "How to Use This Book" in the Introduction, you have a couple choices for exam preparation: the exercises here, Chapter 21, "Final Preparation," and the exam simulation questions in the Pearson Test Prep Software Online.

Review All Key Topics

Review the most important topics in this chapter, noted with the Key Topics icon in the outer margin of the page. Table 11-4 lists these key topics and the page number on which each is found.

Table 11-4   Key Topics for Chapter 11

Key Topic Element	Description	Page Number
List	Types of containers	194
List	Installation requirements	195
Steps	Installing Docker	197

Complete Tables and Lists from Memory

Print a copy of Appendix B, "Memory Tables" (found on the book website), or at least the section for this chapter, and complete the tables and lists from memory. Appendix C, "Memory Tables Answer Key," also on the website, includes completed tables and lists you can use to check your work.

Define Key Terms

Define the following key terms from this chapter and check your answers against the glossary:

Windows Server Container, Hyper-V Container, Docker

Q&A

The answers to these questions appear in Appendix A. For more practice with exam format questions, use the Pearson Test Prep Software Online.

1. Nano Server is ideal for hosting what type of containers?

2. How many virtual processors does a container host need?

3. What container types can Windows Server 2016 Core host?

4. What are two options for managing Docker startup parameters?

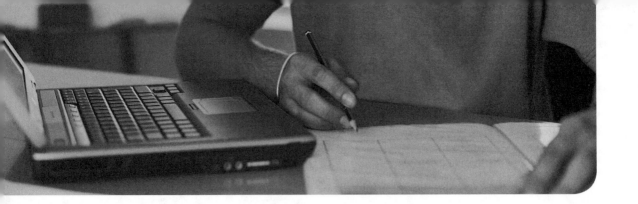

This chapter covers the following subjects:

- **Docker Daemon and Windows PowerShell:** This section examines two powerful options for container management: the Docker daemon and Windows PowerShell.

- **Windows Container Networking:** Applications in a Windows container certainly need networking connectivity, just like their non-container peers. This section details how this works.

- **Other Management Topics:** This final area of this chapter covers other important container management topics, such as the management of container data volumes, resource control, and the creation and management of new container images with tools such as **dockerfile** and public clouds.

## CHAPTER 12

Managing Containers

There are many options for managing containers in the Windows Server 2016 environment. This chapter discusses many powerful management features and platforms.

"Do I Know This Already?" Quiz

The "Do I Know This Already?" quiz allows you to assess whether you should read the entire chapter. Table 12-1 lists the major headings in this chapter and the "Do I Know This Already?" quiz questions covering the material in those headings so you can assess your knowledge of these specific areas. The answers to the "Do I Know This Already?" quiz appear in Appendix A, "Answers to the 'Do I Know This Already?' Quizzes and Q&A Questions."

Table 12-1 "Do I Know This Already?" Foundation Topics Section-to-Question Mapping

Foundation Topics Section	Questions
Docker Daemon and Windows PowerShell	1, 2
Windows Container Networking	3, 4
Other Management Topics	5, 6

CAUTION The goal of self-assessment is to gauge your mastery of the topics in this chapter. If you do not know the answer to a question or are only partially sure of the answer, you should mark your answer as incorrect for purposes of the self-assessment. Giving yourself credit for an answer you correctly guess skews your self-assessment results and might provide you with a false sense of security.

1. What does the **-it** switch do with the **docker run** command?

    a. It exports the container.

    b. It runs the container with resource management settings.

    c. It runs the container in the context of an IT administrator.

    (d.) It allocates a pseudo TTY connected to the container.

2. What PowerShell command deletes a container?

    a. **Delete-Container**

    (b.) **Remove-Container**

    c. **Erase-Container**

    d. **Scrub-Container**

3. Which of the following is not an option for a container network driver?

    a. NAT

    b. L2 Tunnel

    c. Transparent

    (d.) L2 NAT

4. What does the following PowerShell cmdlet accomplish?

    ```
    Get-VMNetworkAdapter - VMName ContainerHostVM |
      Set-VMNetworkAdapter - MacAddressSpoofing On
    ```

    (a.) It permits DHCP IP address assignment by enabling MAC address spoofing.

    b. It permits firewalling by enabling MAC address spoofing.

    c. It permits NAT by enabling MAC address spoofing.

    d. It permits virtual networking by enabling MAC address spoofing.

5. You delete a container that is using a volume on the container host. Which statement is true?

    a. You cannot delete the container if it has a linked volume.

    b. The volume is also deleted if it is empty.

    (c.) The volume is not deleted.

    d. The volume is always deleted.

6. Which resource control switch specifies the nodes on a NUMA host that a container can use?

    a. -cpu-shares

    b. -cpuset-mems

    c. -cpuset-cpus

    d. -c

Foundation Topics

If you are excited about containers, this chapter should be very exciting for you. It examines container management in detail.

Docker Daemon and Windows PowerShell

Managing containers is simple, thanks to powerful commands you can use with the Docker daemon and PowerShell.

Docker Daemon

Table 12-2 lists the powerful Docker daemon commands you should know for container management.

Table 12-2 Docker Daemon Container Management Commands

Command	Example	Description
docker run -it	docker run --name test -it debian	Runs a container named test; **-it** instructs Docker to allocate a pseudo TTY connected to the container
docker ps	docker ps -a	Display a list of all the running containers on the host
docker start	docker start dbf9674d14b9	Starts a stopped container
docker stop	docker stop dbf9674d14b9	Stops a running container
docker attach	docker attach dbf9674d14b9	Connects to a session on a running container
docker commit	docker commit dbf9674d14b9 samples/awesome:1.1	Creates a new image
docker rm	docker rm dbf9674d14b9	Removes a container completely

Windows PowerShell

Table 12-3 lists the Windows PowerShell commands you should know for container management.

Table 12-3   PowerShell Container Management Commands

Command	Example	Description
Get-Container	**get-container**	Displays a list of all containers on the host
Start-Container	**start-container dbf9674d14b9**	Starts a stopped container
Stop-Container	**stop-container dbf9674d14b9**	Stops a running container
Enter-ContainerSession, aliased to **Attach-Container**	**enter-containersession dbf9674d14b9**	Connects to a session on a running container
ConvertTo-ContainerImage, aliased to **Commit-Container**	**convertto-containerimage -containeridorname dbf9674d14b9 -repository samples/awesome -tag 1.1**	Creates a new image
Remove-Container	**remove-container dbf9674d14b9**	Removes a container

Windows Container Networking

Applications running in a Windows container certainly need network access like their non-container peers. This brings up many questions, including the following:

- What does the network stack look like for a Windows container?
- How do you assign an IP address to a container?
- How do you attach a container endpoint to a network?
- How do you apply advanced network policy, such as maximum bandwidth restrictions or access control list (ACL) rules?

Figure 12-1 shows the Windows container network stack.

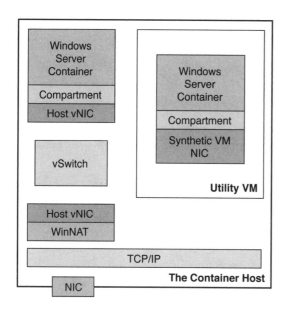

Figure 12-1   The Windows Container Network Stack

Notice that the container host has a physical NIC that it extends to the containers
by using a Hyper-V virtual switch. This is carried out using a host vNIC in the case
of a Windows Server container or a synthetic VM NIC in the case of a Hyper-V
container.

NOTE   Linux containers function much differently than Windows containers. They
use a bridge device and veth pairs to offer basic Layer 2 connectivity to the containers
themselves. This distinction is worth pointing out because the entire container concept stems from Linux.

The Docker client and Docker engine's RESTful API allows the configuration of
container networking.

Windows containers support four different networking drivers or modes: Network
Address Translation (NAT), Transparent, L2 Bridge, and L2 Tunnel.

The Docker engine creates a NAT network by default when the **dockerd** service
first runs. The default internal IP prefix created is 172.16.0.0/12. Container endpoints are automatically attached to this default network and assigned an IP address
from the internal prefix.

You create other networks for a container and dictate connectivity by your networking driver choice, as follows:

- **Network Address Translation**: Each container receives an IP address from an internal, private IP prefix (such as 172.16.0.0/12); this supports port forwarding/mapping from the container host to container endpoints.

- **Transparent**: Each container endpoint connects directly to the physical network. You can assign IPs from the physical network statically or dynamically, using an external DHCP server.

- **L2 Bridge**: Each container endpoint is in the same subnet as the container host. IP addresses must be assigned statically from the same prefix as the container host; all container endpoints on the host have the same MAC address due to Layer 2 address translation.

- **L2 Tunnel**: Microsoft reserves this mode for Microsoft Cloud Stack.

If you want to create a Docker NAT network using a specific prefix, you can change one or two options in the Docker daemon.json file:

- Use the **fixed-cidr**:*<IP Prefix>/Mask* option, which creates the default NAT network with the IP prefix and match specified.

- Use the **bridge:none** option, which does not create a default network; you create a user-defined network with any driver by using the Docker **network create -d** command.

Before performing any of the configuration options in this section, stop the Docker service and delete any preexisting NAT networks. The following code sample demonstrates how to do this:

```
PS C:\> Stop-Service docker
PS C:\> Get-ContainerNetwork | Remove-ContainerNetwork
PS C:\> Start-Service docker
```

If the **fixed-cidr** option is added to the daemon.json file, the Docker engine creates a user-defined NAT network with the custom IP prefix and mask specified. If instead the **bridge:none** option is added, the network needs to be created manually.

```
C:\> docker network create -d nat --subnet=192.168.1.0/24
   --gateway=192.168.1.1 MyNatNetwork
```

By default, container endpoints are connected to the default NAT network. If the NAT network was not created (because **bridge:none** was specified in daemon.json) or access to a different, user-defined network is required, users can specify the **--network** parameter with the **docker run** command:

```
C:\> docker run -it --network=MyNatNetwork <image> <cmd>
```

Before you can access applications running in the container in the NAT network, you need to create port mappings between the container host and the container endpoint. Here is an example:

```
docker run -it -p 8082:80 windowsservercore cmd
```

To use the Transparent networking mode, use this syntax:

```
c:\> docker network create -d transparent MyTransNetwork
```

If the container host is virtualized, and you wish to use DHCP for IP assignment, you must enable **MACAddressSpoofing** on the virtual machine's network adapter:

```
PS C:\> Get-VMNetworkAdapter -VMName ContainerHostVM |
  Set-VMNetworkAdapter -MacAddressSpoofing On
```

To use the L2 Bridge networking mode, you create a container network with driver name **l2bridge**:

```
C:\> docker network create -d l2bridge --subnet=192.168.1.0/24
  --gateway=192.168.1.1 MyBridgeNetwork
```

Other Management Topics

The following sections cover other important miscellaneous container management topics, including managing container data volumes, managing resource control, creating new container images by using **dockerfile**, and managing container images using Microsoft Azure.

Managing Container Data Volumes

You can create data volumes on a container that correspond to a folder on the container host. Keep in mind that if you delete a container, the data volume remains on the container host.

Here is an example of creating a data volume:

```
docker run -it -v c:\datafolder microsoft/windowsservercore
  powershell
```

This example creates a folder named **datafolder** in a new container.

To reuse a data volume, you can specify both the source and destination folders with the **docker run** command, as in the following example:

```
docker run -it -v c:\olddatafolder:c:\datafolder microsoft/
  windowsservercore powershell
```

By default, Docker creates data volumes in read/write mode. To create a read-only data volume, you can add **:ro** to the container folder name, as in the following example:

```
docker run -it -v c:\datafolder:ro microsoft/windowsservercore
   powershell
```

To add a data volume to an existing container, follow these steps:

Step 1.   Use **docker commit** to save to a new image any changes to the existing container.

Step 2.   Use **docker run** to create a new container from the new image.

Step 3.   Use the **-v** switch to add the data volume.

Manage Resource Control

It is an excellent idea to use switches with **docker run** to control resource usage. This is really critical when your host provides resources for many different containers. Table 12-4 shows memory switch parameters you can use.

Table 12-4   Memory Parameters with **docker run**

Parameter	Description
-m or **--memory**	Specifies the amount of memory the container can use; values are an integer and the unit identifier **b**, **k**, **m**, or **g** (for bytes, kilobytes, megabytes, or gigabytes)
-memory-swap	Specifies the total amount of memory plus virtual memory that the container can use
-kernel-memory	Specifies the amount of the memory limit set using the **-m** switch that can be used for kernel memory
-oom-kill-disable	Prevents the kernel from killing container processes when an out-of-memory error occurs

Table 12-5 shows the parameters you can use to set CPU resource controls.

Table 12-5   CPU Parameters with **docker run**

Parameter	Description
-c or **--cpu-shares**	Specifies a value from 0 to 1024 that specifies the weight of the container in contention for the CPU cycles
-cpuset-cpus	Specifies which CPUs in a multiprocessor host system the container can use
-cpuset-mems	Specifies which nodes on a NUMA host the container can use

Creating New Container Images Using dockerfile

The recommended method for creating container images is to build them from
scratch by using a script. You can use the script **dockerfile**, which is a plain text file.
Once a container image is created, you use the **docker build** command to execute it
and create a new file.

The **dockerfile** script consists of instructions and a statement for each instruction.
You insert remarks into the script by preceding them with the pound (**#**) character.
The following is an example of a **dockerfile** script:

```
#install DHCP server
FROM microsoft/windowsservercore
RUN powershell -command install-windowsfeature dhcp
  -includemanagementtools
RUN powershell -configurationname microsoft.powershell -command
  add-dhcpserverv4scope
-state active -activatepolicies $true -name mysample -startrange
  10.10.10.100 -endrange
10.10.10.200 -subnetmask 255.255.255.0
RUN md boot
COPY ./bootfile.wim c:/boot/
CMD powershell
```

Here is an example of using **docker build** to create the new image:

```
docker build -t dhcp .
Manage Container Images Using DockerHub Repository for Public and
  Private Scenarios
```

DockerHub provides a public repository for storing and distributing container
images. Docker Pull and Docker Push move containers to and from the repository.

Register for DockerHub at http://hub.docker.com. Your username becomes the
name of your repository, as shown in this example:

```
asequeira/server10
```

Once you're established on DockerHub, you use the following commands to inter-
act with it:

- **docker login**: Permits login from the command line to DockerHub

- **docker search microsoft --no-trunc**: Permits searching DockerHub from
  the command line

- **docker push asequeira/server10**: Initiates an upload to DockerHub

Managing Container Images by Using Microsoft Azure

It is no surprise that Microsoft's cloud platform, Azure, supports containers. Microsoft Azure is a cloud computing service created by Microsoft for building, deploying, and managing applications and services through a global network of Microsoft-managed data centers. It provides software as a service (SaaS), platform as a service (PaaS), and infrastructure as a service (IaaS). It supports many different programming languages, tools, and frameworks, including both Microsoft-specific and third-party software and systems.

Two main technologies in Azure relate directly to containers:

- You can create a Windows Server 2016 virtual machine in Azure for the creation and management of containers.

- You can use the Azure Container Service (ACS) for creating, configuring, and managing a cluster of virtual machines for running container-based applications.

Exam Preparation Tasks

As mentioned in the section "How to Use This Book" in the Introduction, you have a couple choices for exam preparation: the exercises here, Chapter 21, "Final Preparation," and the exam simulation questions in the Pearson Test Prep Software Online.

Review All Key Topics

Review the most important topics in this chapter, noted with the Key Topics icon in the outer margin of the page. Table 12-6 lists these key topics and the page number on which each is found.

Table 12-6 Key Topics for Chapter 12

Key Topic Element	Description	Page Number
List	Networking options	210
Command	Container data volume creation	211
Command	Using Docker Build to create a new image	213

Complete Tables and Lists from Memory

Print a copy of Appendix B, "Memory Tables" (found on the book website), or at least the section for this chapter, and complete the tables and lists from memory. Appendix C, "Memory Tables Answer Key," also on the website, includes completed tables and lists to check your work.

Define Key Terms

Define the following key terms from this chapter and check your answers against the glossary:

Docker Daemon, Windows Container Stack, Dockerfile, DockerHub, Azure Container Services (ACS)

Q&A

The answers to these questions appear in Appendix A. For more practice with exam format questions, use the Pearson Test Prep Software Online.

1. What Docker daemon command permits you to see a list of all the running containers on a host?

2. What type of container networking configuration permits the container endpoint to connect directly to the physical network and permits static or dynamic IP address assignment?

3. What memory parameter used with **docker run** permits you to specify the memory a container can use?

This chapter covers the following subjects:

- **Hyper-V Replica:** The replication of virtual machines from one host to another is a key part of a disaster recovery configuration. This section details the components and prerequisites, as well as the configuration of Hyper-V Replica.

- **Live Migration:** Moving virtual machines from one host to another is simple, thanks to live migrations. This section covers live migration considerations and implementation. This section also details shared-nothing live migrations.

- **Storage Migration:** Moving just the storage of a virtual machine is a storage migration. This part of the chapter details this process.

## CHAPTER 13

High Availability in Hyper-V

Microsoft makes it very clear just how important high availability is in the modern datacenter. Microsoft also makes it very clear just how important this topic is in the exam environment: It is the largest section of questions you will face!

NOTE For the detailed breakdown on exam topic coverage, visit the Skills Measured section at https://www.microsoft.com/en-us/learning/exam-70-740.aspx.

"Do I Know This Already?" Quiz

The "Do I Know This Already?" quiz allows you to assess whether you should read the entire chapter. Table 13-1 lists the major headings in this chapter and the "Do I Know This Already?" quiz questions covering the material in those headings so you can assess your knowledge of these specific areas. The answers to the "Do I Know This Already?" quiz appear in Appendix A, "Answers to the 'Do I Know This Already?' Quizzes and Q&A Questions."

Table 13-1 "Do I Know This Already?" Foundation Topics Section-to-Question Mapping

Foundation Topics Section	Questions
Hyper-V Replica	1–3
Live Migration	4–6
Storage Migration	7, 8

CAUTION The goal of self-assessment is to gauge your mastery of the topics in this chapter. If you do not know the answer to a question or are only partially sure of the answer, you should mark your answer as incorrect for purposes of the self-assessment. Giving yourself credit for an answer you correctly guess skews your self-assessment results and might provide you with a false sense of security.

1. What is the term for replicating to a third host in Hyper-V Replica?

    a. Extended (chained) replication

    b. Advanced replication

    c. Forest-trust replication

    d. Three-way replication

2. What options exist for authentication in Hyper-V Replica? Choose two.

    a. Kerberos

    b. Token-based

    c. Certificate-based

    d. SCP

3. What options for failover exist in Hyper-V Replica? Choose three.

    a. Production

    b. Test

    c. Planned

    d. Unplanned

4. You can perform a live migration between Windows Server 2016 and Windows Server 2012 R2 if the virtual machine is at least what version?

    a. 2

    b. 3

    c. 4

    d. 5

5. What live migration authentication option forces the configuration of constrained delegation?

    a. SCP

    b. Certificate-based

    c. Kerberos

    d. Token-based

6. What PowerShell cmdlet allows you to configure performance options for live migrations?

   a. **Enable-VMMigration**

   b. **Set-VMMigrationOptions**

   c. **Set-VMHost**

   d. **Set-VMMigrationNetwork**

7. Which of the following is not an example of a component moved in storage migration?

   a. Configuration files

   b. Virtual machine state

   c. Checkpoints

   d. Smart paging files

8. What dramatically simplifies the storage migration process?

   a. Ensuring that the move location is within the same geographic location

   b. Ensuring that the source VM is stopped

   c. Ensuring that the source is not a VHD file

   d. Ensuring the use of pass-through disks

Foundation Topics

Hyper-V Replica

You can implement a large part of disaster recovery thanks to Hyper-V Replica. Hyper-V Replica allows the replication of virtual machines from one host to another. Server 2016 makes this possible by creating a copy of a live virtual machine and setting it as an offline virtual machine copy.

Consider the following regarding Hyper-V Replica:

- **Hyper-V hosts:** You can physically co-locate primary and secondary host servers or use separate geographic locations with replication over a WAN link. Hyper-V hosts can be standalone, clustered, or a mixture of both. There is no Active Directory dependency between the servers, and they do not need to be domain members.

- **Replication and change tracking:** When you enable Hyper-V Replica for a specific virtual machine, initial replication creates an identical replica virtual machine on a secondary host server. Hyper-V Replica then uses change tracking and creates and maintains a log file that captures changes on a virtual machine VHD. The log file plays in reverse order to the replica VHD, based on replication frequency settings; thus, the latest changes store and replicate asynchronously. Replication is over HTTP or HTTPS.

- **Extended (chained) replication:** This type of replication allows the replication of a virtual machine from a primary host to a secondary host and then the replication of the secondary host to a third host. You cannot replicate from the primary host directly to the second and the third. This feature makes Hyper-V Replica more robust for disaster recovery because if an outage occurs, you can recover with both the primary and extended replicas. You can also fail over to the extended replica if your primary and secondary locations fail. You should note that the extended replica does not support application-consistent replication and must use the same VHDs that the secondary replica uses.

- **Failover:** If an outage occurs in your primary location (or secondary, in the case of extended replication), you can manually start a test, planned or unplanned failover.

- **Recovery points:** When you configure replication settings for a virtual machine, you specify the recovery points you want to store from the virtual machine. A recovery point is a snapshot in time from which you can recover a virtual machine. You lose less data if you recover from a very recent recovery point. You can access recovery points up to 24 hours in the past.

Hyper-V Replica Prerequisites

Keep these important prerequisites in mind regarding Hyper-V Replica:

- **Decide which VHDs to replicate**: To conserve network bandwidth, you should exclude VHDs that hold rapidly changing data and data not used by the replica server after failover (for example, page file disks).

- **Determine the synchronization schedule**: The data on the replica server synchronizes per the replication frequency you configure. Options might be

30 seconds, 5 minutes, or 15 minutes. As you choose the frequency, consider the following points:

- Are the virtual machines running critical data with a low recovery point objective (RPO)? The RPO is the maximum targeted period in which data might be lost from an IT service due to a major incident.

- What are your bandwidth considerations?

- Are your VMs highly critical? Highly critical virtual machines need more frequent replication.

- **Decide how to recover data**: By default, Hyper-V Replica stores only a single recovery point. This is the latest replication sent from the primary server to the secondary server. However, if you want the choice to recover data to an earlier point in time, you can specify that more recovery points be stored (to a maximum of 24 hourly points). Having additional recovery points requires more overhead on processing and storage resources.

- **Determine workloads to replicate**: Remember that standard Hyper-V Replica replication maintains state for a VM after failover, but it does not maintain the state of applications running inside that VM. For this type of recovery of your workload state, you create app-consistent recovery points. Note that app-consistent recovery is not available on the extended replica site if you are using extended (chained) replication.

- **Determine the initial replication of virtual machine data**: Replication starts by transferring the current state of the virtual machines. This first state is transmitted directly over the existing network, and this occurs either at once or a later time that you configure. You can also use a preexisting restored virtual machine as the initial copy. Or you can save network bandwidth by copying the initial copy to external media and then physically delivering the media to the replica site. If you want to use a preexisting virtual machine, delete all previous snapshots associated with it.

Implementing Replica

Follow these steps to implement Hyper-V Replica:

Step 1.   In the Hyper-V settings for the server to which you replicate virtual machines, under **Replication Configuration**, select **Enable this computer as a Replica server**, as shown in Figure 13-1.

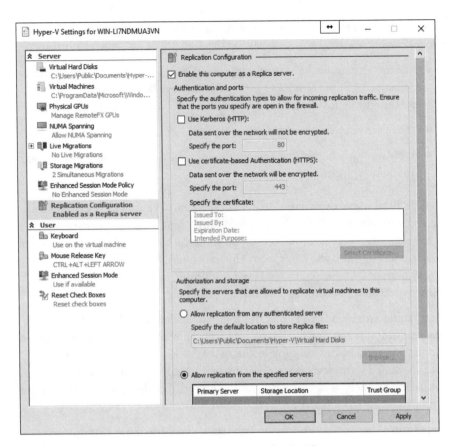

Figure 13-1   Enabling Your Hyper-V Server as a Replica Server

Step 2.   For authentication, Select **Use Kerberos (HTTP)** or **Use certificate-based Authentication (HTTPS).**

Step 3.   For authorization, select **Allow replication from any authenticated server** to allow the replica server to accept virtual machine replication traffic from any primary server that authenticates successfully or select **Allow replication from the specified servers** to accept traffic only from the primary servers you specifically select.

Step 4.   Click **OK.**

Step 5.   To allow replication between the primary and secondary servers, allow traffic through the Windows firewall:

- To enable the rules on a standalone host server, open **Windows Firewall with Advanced Security** and click **Inbound Rules**; to enable HTTP (Kerberos) authentication, right-click **Hyper-V Replica HTTP Listener (TCP-In) >Enable Rule**; to enable HTTPS certificate-based authentication, right-click **Hyper-V Replica HTTPS Listener (TCP-In) > Enable Rule**. Figure 13-2 shows this tool.

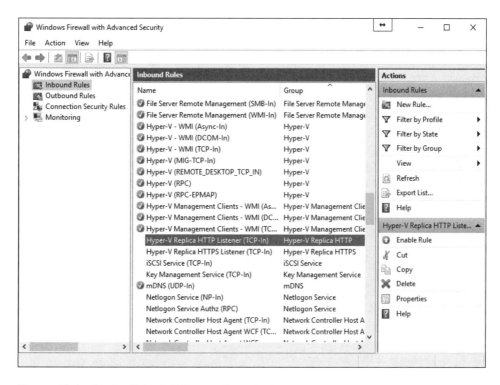

Figure 13-2   Setting Rules in Windows Firewall with Advanced Security

- To enable the rules on a Hyper-V cluster, use the following command from an elevated PowerShell prompt for HTTP:

```
get-clusternode | ForEach-Object {Invoke-command
  -computername $_.name -scriptblock {Enable-Netfirewallrule
  -displayname "Hyper-V Replica HTTP Listener (TCP-In)"}}
```

- To enable the rules on a Hyper-V cluster, use the following command from an elevated PowerShell prompt for HTTPS:

```
get-clusternode | ForEach-Object {Invoke-command
  -computername $_.name -scriptblock {Enable-Netfirewallrule
  -displayname "Hyper-V Replica HTTPS Listener (TCP-In)"}}
```

Step 6. In the **Details** pane of Hyper-V Manager, select a virtual machine by clicking it.

Step 7. Right-click the selected virtual machine and click **Enable Replication** to open the **Enable Replication Wizard**.

Step 8. On the **Before you Begin** page, click **Next.**

Step 9. On the **Specify Replica Server** page, in the **Replica server** box, enter either the NetBIOS or FQDN of the replica server; if the replica server is part of a failover cluster, enter the name of the Hyper-V Replica Broker and click **Next,** as shown in Figure 13-3.

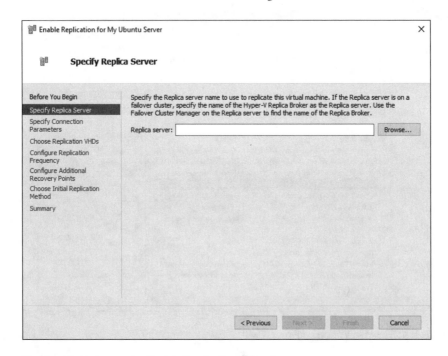

Figure 13-3   Using the Enable Replication Wizard

Step 10. On the **Specify Connection Parameters** page, if Hyper-V Replica has not automatically retrieved the authentication and port settings you configured for the replica server, type in the settings manually.

Step 11. On the **Choose Replication VHDs** page, make sure the VHDs you want to replicate are selected and clear the check boxes for any VHDs that you want to exclude from replication; click **Next**.

Step 12. On the **Configure Replication Frequency** page, specify how often changes should be synchronized from primary to secondary and click **Next**.

Step 13. On the **Configure Additional Recovery Points** page, select whether you want to maintain only the latest recovery point or to create additional points. If you want to consistently recover applications and workloads that have their own VSS writers, select **Volume Shadow Copy Service (VSS) frequency** and specify how often to create app-consistent snapshots. Click **Next**.

Step 14. On the **Choose Initial Replication** page, select the initial replication method to use and click **Next**.

Step 15. On the **Completing the Enable Replication** page, review the information in the summary and then click **Finish**.

Step 16. If you want to configure extended (chained) replication, open the replica server, right-click the virtual machine you want to replicate, select **Replication > Extend Replication,** and specify the replication settings.

After you follow these deployment steps, your replicated environment is complete, and you can run the following failovers, as needed:

- **Test failover**: If you want to run a test failover, right-click the primary virtual machine and select **Replication > Test Failover**. Pick the latest or another recovery point, if configured. A new test virtual machine is created and started on the secondary site. After you have finished testing, select **Stop Test Failover** on the replica virtual machine. Note that for a virtual machine, you can only run one test failover at a time.

- **Planned failover**: To run a planned failover, right-click the primary virtual machine and select **Replication > Planned Failover**. Planned failover performs prerequisite checks to ensure zero data loss. It involves checking that the primary virtual machine is shut down before beginning the failover. After the virtual machine is failed over, the failover process starts replicating the changes back to the primary site when it is available. Note that for this to work, the primary server should be configured to receive replication from the secondary server or from the Hyper-V Replica Broker, in the case of a primary cluster. Planned failover sends the last set of tracked changes.

- **Unplanned failover**: To run an unplanned failover, right-click on the replica virtual machine and select **Replication > Unplanned Failover** from Hyper-V Manager or Failover Clustering Manager. You can recover from the latest recovery point or from previous recovery points if this option is enabled. After failover, check that everything is working as expected on the failed-over virtual machine and then click **Complete** on the replica virtual machine.

Live Migration

Hyper-V live migration involves moving running virtual machines from one physical server to another, with no impact on the availability of virtual machines to users. The following sections present important information related to live migration.

Live Migration Requirements

Remember these important requirements for non-clustered hosts and live migration:

- **A user account with permission to perform the various steps:** Membership in the local Hyper-V Administrators group or the Administrators group on both the source and destination computers meets this need, unless you are configuring constrained delegation. Membership in the Domain Administrators group is required to configure constrained delegation.

- **The Hyper-V role in Windows Server 2016 installed on the source and destination servers:** You can do a live migration between hosts running Windows Server 2016 and Windows Server 2012 R2 if the virtual machine is at least version 5. The systems must be connected to the same virtual switch, and these systems must have the same brand of processor.

- **Source and destination computers:** These computers must either belong to the same Active Directory domain or belong to domains that trust each other.

- **Hyper-V management tools:** The Hyper-V management tools must be installed on a computer running Windows Server 2016 or Windows 10, unless the tools are installed on the source or destination servers and you plan to run the tools from the server.

Live Migration Considerations

You should consider carefully how you want to set up the following parameters:

- **Authentication**: Here your options include:

  - **Kerberos**: This lets you avoid signing in to the server, but you must configure constrained delegation (described in the next section).

  - **CredSSP**: This eliminates the need for constrained delegation but requires a sign-in on the source server; you can do this through a local console session, a Remote Desktop session, or a remote Windows PowerShell session.

- **Performance**: You can set various performance options, as discussed later in this chapter.

- **Network preference**: Here you determine if live migration traffic can use any available network. As a security best practice, consider constraining to trusted, private networks; remember that live migration traffic is not encrypted.

Configuring Constrained Delegation

To configure constrained delegation, follow these steps, using an account that is a member of the Domain Administrators group:

Step 1.   Open the **Active Directory Users and Computers** snap-in; from **Server Manager**, select the server and select **Tools > Active Directory Users and Computers.**

Step 2.   From the **Navigation** pane in **Active Directory Users and Computers**, select the domain and double-click the **Computers** folder.

Step 3.   From the **Computers** folder, right-click the computer account of the source server and then click **Properties.**

Step 4.   From **Properties**, click the **Delegation** tab, as shown in Figure 13-4.

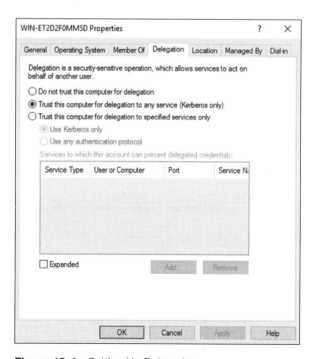

Figure 13-4   Setting Up Delegation

Step 5.   On the Delegation tab, select **Trust this computer for delegation to the specified services only** and then select **Use Kerberos only.**

Step 6.   Click **Add.**

Step 7.   From **Add Services**, click **Users or Computers.**

Step 8.   From **Select Users or Computers**, type the name of the destination server, click **Check Names** to verify it, and then click **OK.**

Step 9.   From **Add Services**, in the list of available services, do the following:

- To move virtual machine storage, select **cifs.**

- To move virtual machines, select **Microsoft Virtual System Migration Service.**

Then click **OK.**

Step 10.   On the **Delegation** tab of the **Properties** dialog box, verify that the services you selected in step 9 are listed as the services to which the destination computer can present delegated credentials and click **OK.**

Step 11.   From the **Computers** folder, select the computer account of the destination server and repeat the process; in the **Select Users or Computers** dialog box, be sure to specify the name of the source server.

Configuring Live Migration in Hyper-V Manager

To configure live migration in Hyper-V Manager, follow these steps:

Step 1.   Open **Hyper-V Manager** and from **Server Manager**, select **Tools > Hyper-V Manager.**

Step 2.   In the **Navigation** pane, select one of your servers.

Step 3.   In the **Action** pane, select **Hyper-V Settings > Live Migrations.**

Step 4.   In the **Live Migrations** pane, check **Enable incoming and outgoing live migrations.**

Step 5.   Under **Simultaneous live migrations**, specify a different number if you do not want to use the default of 2.

Step 6.   Under **Incoming live migrations**, if you want to use specific network connections to accept live migration traffic, click **Add** to type the IP address information. Otherwise, click **Use any available network for live migration** and click **OK.**

Step 7. To choose Kerberos and performance options, expand **Live Migrations** and then select **Advanced Features**.

Step 8. If you have configured constrained delegation, under **Authentication protocol**, select **Kerberos**.

Step 9. Under **Performance options**, review the details and choose a different option if it is appropriate for your environment and click **OK**.

Step 10. Select your other server in Hyper-V Manager and repeat these steps.

Configuring Live Migration in PowerShell

You can use three cmdlets in Windows PowerShell for live migration on non-clustered hosts:

- **Enable-VMMigration**, which has the following syntax:

```
Enable-VMMigration [-Passthru] [[-ComputerName] <String[]>]
   [[-Credential] <PSCredential[]>] [-WhatIf] [-Confirm]
   [<CommonParameters>]
```

- **Set-VMMigrationNetwork**, which has the following syntax:

```
Set-VMMigrationNetwork [-ComputerName <String[]>] [-Credential
   <PSCredential[]>] [-Subnet] <String> [[-NewSubnet] <String>]
   [-NewPriority <UInt32>] [-Passthru] [-WhatIf] [-Confirm]
   [<CommonParameters>]
```

- **Set-VMHost**, which has the following syntax:

```
Set-VMHost [[-ComputerName] <String[]>] [[-Credential]
   <PSCredential[]>] [-MaximumStorageMigrations
   <UInt32>] [-MaximumVirtualMachineMigrations
   <UInt32>] [-VirtualMachineMigrationAuthenticationType
   <MigrationAuthenticationType>] [-UseAnyNetworkForMigration
   <Boolean>] [-VirtualMachineMigrationPerformanceOption
   <VMMigrationPerformance>] [-ResourceMeteringSaveInterval
   <TimeSpan>] [-VirtualHardDiskPath <String>]
   [-VirtualMachinePath <String>] [-MacAddressMaximum <String>]
   [-MacAddressMinimum <String>] [-FibreChannelWwnn <String>]
   [-FibreChannelWwpnMaximum <String>] [-FibreChannelWwpnMinimum
   <String>] [-NumaSpanningEnabled <Boolean>]
   [-EnableEnhancedSessionMode <Boolean>] [-Passthru] [-WhatIf]
   [-Confirm] [<CommonParameters>]
```

Here is an example:

```
Enable-VMMigration
Set-VMMigrationNetwork 172.16.1.10
Set-VMHost -VirtualMachineMigrationAuthenticationType Kerberos
```

Setting Performance Options

Note that **Set-VMHost** allows you to choose a performance option, among many other settings. Performance options include the following:

- **TCP/IP**: Copies the memory of the virtual machine to the destination server over a TCP/IP connection

- **Compression**: Compresses the memory content of the virtual machine before copying it to the destination server over a TCP/IP connection; this is the default setting

- **SMB**: Copies the memory of the virtual machine to the destination server over an SMB 3.0 connection

Implementing Shared-Nothing Live Migration

What does "shared-nothing" refer to in a *shared-nothing live migration*? It means that servers do not need to be part of a cluster, and they do not need access to shared storage. These requirements used to be in place for any live migration in Windows Server technology!

Shared-nothing live migration is a live migration, as described in the preceding section, and also a storage migration, as described in the next section. In a shared-nothing live migration, the source server copies the virtual machine's storage to the destination, in addition to its memory and system state. The source VM remains active until the complete data transfer is complete.

Remember these shared-nothing live migration prerequisites:

- The source and destination servers must be members of the same Active Directory Domain Services domain (or trusted domains).

- The source and destination servers must be using the same processor family (Intel or AMD).

- The source and destination servers must be connected by an Ethernet network running at a minimum of 1 Gbps.

- The source and destination servers should have identical virtual switches that use the same name; if they do not, the migration process is interrupted to prompt the operator to select a switch on the destination server.

You configure a shared-nothing live migration the same way you configure a non-clustered live migration, as covered in the preceding section. You select the **Move the Virtual Machine's Data to a Single Location** option on the **Choose Move Options** page.

Storage Migration

Whereas a live migration moves a virtual machine from one host to another, leaving the storage in place, a storage migration moves the storage without moving the virtual machine. This occurs while the VM is running or stopped.

You can use storage migration to move the following for a virtual machine:

- Configuration files
- Checkpoints
- Smart paging files

These files migrate to any location the user has permission to access—perhaps another disk or a directory on the same computer or a directory on a different computer.

Storage migration uses the following process:

1. The destination server creates new virtual hard disk files of sizes and types corresponding to those on the source server.

2. The VM on the source server continues to operate using its local files, but Hyper-V begins mirroring disk writes to the destination server as well.

3. While continuing to mirror writes, Hyper-V on the source server initiates a single-pass copy of the source disks to the destination; blocks that have already been written to the destination by the mirroring process are skipped.

4. When the single-pass copy is completed, and with the mirrored writes continuing, Hyper-V updates the VM configuration and begins working from the files on the destination server.

5. Once the VM is running successfully from the migrated files, Hyper-V deletes the source files.

You should note the following:

- If the source VM is stopped, the preceding procedure is not needed; Hyper-V copies the files from the source to the destination, reconfigures the VM to use the destination files, and then deletes the source files.

- You cannot migrate VMs that use pass-through disks for their storage.

- Files must use VHD or VHDX virtual hard disks.

- To perform a storage migration, use the same Move Wizard as for non-clustered live migrations and shared-nothing live migrations. On the wizard's **Choose Move Type** page, select the **Move the Virtual Machine's Storage** option. The **Choose Options for Moving Storage** page appears, with the following options:

- **Image Move All of the Virtual Machine's Data to a Single Location**: Enables you to specify one destination for all of the source VM's files

- **Image Move All of the Virtual Machine's Data to Different Locations**: Permits the selection of the file types to migrate and specifies a destination for each type

- **Image Move Only the Virtual Machine's Virtual Hard Disks**: Enables you to select which VHD/VHDX files to migrate and specify a destination for each one

Exam Preparation Tasks

As mentioned in the section "How to Use This Book" in the Introduction, you have a couple choices for exam preparation: the exercises here, Chapter 21, "Final Preparation," and the exam simulation questions in the Pearson Test Prep Software Online.

Review All Key Topics

Review the most important topics in this chapter, noted with the Key Topics icon in the outer margin of the page. Table 13-2 lists these key topics and the page number on which each is found.

Table 13-2   Key Topics for Chapter 13

Key Topic Element	Description	Page Number
List	Key considerations for Hyper-V Replica	219
Steps	Configuration of Hyper-V Replica	221
List	Live migration requirements	226
Steps	Configuring live migration	228
Steps	The storage migration process	231

Complete Tables and Lists from Memory

There are no memory tables in this chapter.

Define Key Terms

Define the following key terms from this chapter and check your answers against the glossary:

Hyper-V Replica, Extended (Chained) Replication, Live Migration, Shared-Nothing Live Migration, Storage Migration

Q&A

The answers to these questions appear in Appendix A. For more practice with exam format questions, use the Pearson Test Prep Software Online.

1. In Hyper-V Manager, what option do you select from the shortcut menu of a virtual machine for Hyper-V Replica?

2. Name at least three requirements for Live Migration.

3. What are two requirements for disks in a storage migration scenario?

This chapter covers the following subjects:

- **Implementing Failover Clustering:** Failover Clustering—in which Windows Server systems act as a single system—is one of the most exciting high-availability technologies in IT today. This section explores this technology in detail.

- **Cluster Storage:** For a failover cluster to be effective, it must have seamless access for all nodes to shared storage. This section discusses many important shared storage topics.

## CHAPTER 14

Failover Clustering

With Failover Clustering, two or more server systems (physical or virtual) run as a single entity to offer high availability and scalability to clients. Typically, these servers (or *nodes*, to use the clustering term) also run the same application, giving excellent and reliable performance metrics for clients accessing the cluster.

"Do I Know This Already?" Quiz

The "Do I Know This Already?" quiz allows you to assess whether you should read the entire chapter. Table 14-1 lists the major headings in this chapter and the "Do I Know This Already?" quiz questions covering the material in those headings so you can assess your knowledge of these specific areas. The answers to the "Do I Know This Already?" quiz appear in Appendix A, "Answers to the 'Do I Know This Already?' Quizzes and Q&A Questions."

Table 14-1 "Do I Know This Already?" Foundation Topics Section-to-Question Mapping

Foundation Topics Section	Questions
Implementing Failover Clustering	1–4
Cluster Storage	5, 6

CAUTION The goal of self-assessment is to gauge your mastery of the topics in this chapter. If you do not know the answer to a question or are only partially sure of the answer, you should mark your answer as incorrect for purposes of the self-assessment. Giving yourself credit for an answer you correctly guess skews your self-assessment results and might provide you with a false sense of security.

1. What parameter of the **New-Cluster** cmdlet allows you to specify DNS?

    a. **administrativeaccesspoint**

    b. **resolver**

    c. **adsource**

    d. **nameserver**

2. What quorum witness type is new to Server 2016?

    a. Disk

    b. File Share

    c. Cloud

    d. Server

3. What cmdlet lets you to move a cluster out of the Mixed-OS mode?

    a. **Update-ClusterFunctionalLevel**

    b. **Update-Cluster**

    c. **Update-OS-Mode**

    d. **Update-OSMode**

4. Which of the following is not a VM state in VM resiliency?

    a. Test

    b. Unmonitored

    c. Isolated

    d. Quarantined

5. What cmdlet allows you to create a new CSV?

    a. **Update-ClusterSharedVoume**

    b. **Create-ClusterSharedVoume**

    c. **New-ClusterSharedVoume**

    d. **Add-ClusterSharedVoume**

6. Which of the following is not a requirement for a Scale-Out File Server?

    a. Shared storage

    b. Proper Failover Clustering configuration

    c. 32 GB or RAM per node

    d. Failover Clustering feature installation

Foundation Topics

Implementing Failover Clustering

Windows Server 2016 offers clustering services for amazing potential power, including support for the following:

- 64 servers

- 1024 virtual machines per node

Windows Server 2016 makes management surprisingly simple, thanks to the Failover Cluster Manager GUI and a group of Windows PowerShell cmdlets.

Hardware and Software Requirements for Failover Clustering

Because Failover Clustering is so powerful, it should come as no surprise that there are many requirements for a successful implementation, including the following:

- Nodes of the cluster should be as identical in hardware configurations as possible; this includes items such as CPU number and type and memory installations.

- Network adapters in nodes should have identical configurations.

- For full Microsoft support, systems should feature the Certified for Windows Server 2016 logo.

- All nodes should run the same OS versions and edition and should have the same updates installed.

- Separate networks are recommended for cluster traffic as well as shared storage and management traffic.

- Redundant networking equipment should be considered to help eliminate single points of failure.

Failover Cluster Manager provides the Validate Cluster Wizard to assist in ensuring a successful deployment (see Figure 14-1).

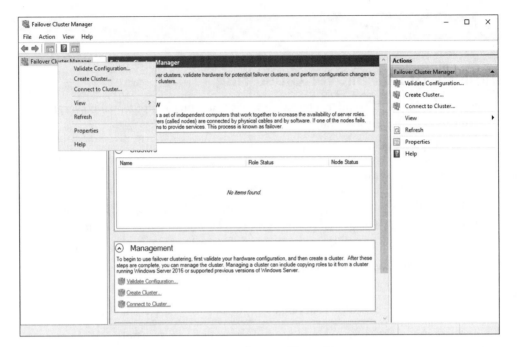

Figure 14-1   The Validate Cluster Wizard in Failover Cluster Manager

PowerShell offers the **Test-Cluster** cmdlet for the same purpose. Here is the complete syntax for this cmdlet:

```
Test-Cluster [[-Node] <StringCollection> ] [-Cluster <String>
  ] [-Disk <Object[]> ] [-Force] [-Ignore <StringCollection> ]
  [-Include <StringCollection> ] [-InputObject <PSObject> ] [-List]
  [-Pool <Object[]> ] [-ReportName <String> ] [-Confirm] [-WhatIf]
  [ <CommonParameters>]
```

Implementing Workgroup, Single-Domain, and Multi-Domain Clusters

Failover Cluster Manager is not a default management tool. Although there are plenty of PowerShell cmdlets for failover clustering configuration, the Failover Cluster Manager is extremely powerful and can complete almost all settings and configurations. To install it, follow these steps:

Step 1.   Launch **Server Manager** and select **Manage > Add Roles and Features**.

Step 2.   On the **Before You Begin** page of the **Add Roles and Features Wizard,** click **Next**.

Step 3.   On the **Select Installation Type** page, ensure that **Role-based or Feature-based installation** is selected and click **Next**.

Step 4.   On the **Select Destination Server** page, ensure that your local server is selected and click **Next**.

Step 5.   On the **Select Server Roles** page, click **Next**.

Step 6.   On the **Select Features** page, choose **Failover Clustering,** as shown in Figure 14-2.

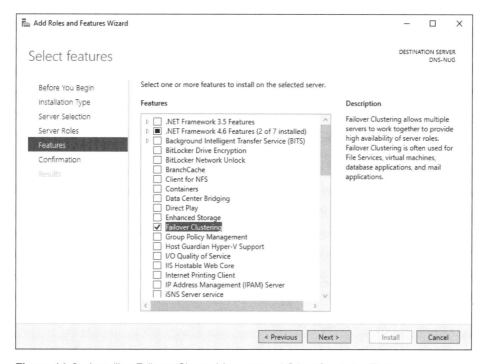

Figure 14-2   Installing Failover Cluster Manager and Other Clustering Tools

Step 7.   On the **Add Features That Are Required for Failover Clustering** window, click **Add Features** and then click **Next**.

Step 8.   Click **Install**.

Step 9.   Click **Close**.

NOTE   The installation of these management tools does not require a system reboot.

You create clusters by using the New Cluster Wizard in the Failover Cluster Manager or by using the **New-Cluster** PowerShell cmdlet. Here is the syntax for the **New-Cluster** cmdlet:

```
New-Cluster [-Name] <String> [-AdministrativeAccessPoint
  <AdminAccessPoint> {None | ActiveDirectoryAndDns | Dns |
  ActiveDirectory} ] [-Force] [-IgnoreNetwork <StringCollection>
  ] [-Node <StringCollection> ] [-NoStorage] [-S2D] [-StaticAddress
  <StringCollection> ] [ <CommonParameters>]
```

The following PowerShell example creates a four-node cluster named **pearsonrocks**, which uses the static IP address 192.168.1.1 and does not use the network 192.168.2.0/24:

```
New-Cluster -Name pearsonrocks -Node node1,node2,node3,node4
  -StaticAddress 192.168.1.1 -IgnoreNetwork 192.168.2.0/24
```

Here are the steps for creating a cluster using the Failover Cluster Wizard:

Step 1.   Launch **Server Manager** and select **Tools > Failover Cluster Manager**.

Step 2.   In the left pane, right-click the **Failover Cluster Manager** node and choose **Create Cluster.**

Step 3.   On the **Before You Begin** screen, click **Next**.

Step 4.   On the **Select Servers** screen, enter your servers and click **Next**.

Step 5.   On the **Validation Warning** screen, click **No** in order to skip validation testing and then click **Next**.

Step 6.   On the **Access Point for Administering the Cluster** screen, provide a name for the cluster and an IP address and network and then click **Next** (see Figure 14-3).

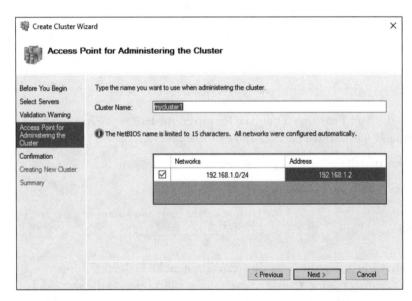

Figure 14-3   Configuring a Cluster in the Failover Cluster Manager

Step 7.   On the **Confirmation** screen, click **Next**.

Step 8.   On the **Summary** screen, click **Finish**.

Figure 14-4 shows a sample cluster created in Failover Cluster Manager.

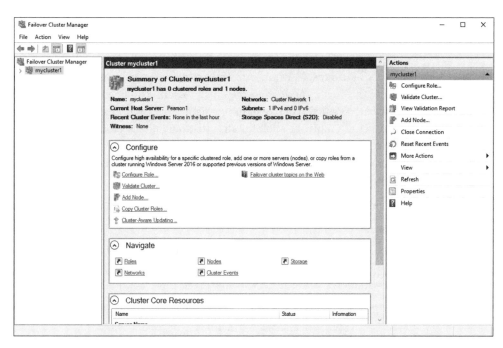

Figure 14-4   A Sample Cluster in the Failover Cluster Manager

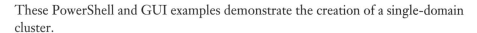

NOTE (A cluster has its own computer object in Active Directory.) This object is the Cluster Name Object (CNO). Once an application is running on the cluster nodes, the clients send their requests to the cluster itself, not to an individual server.

These PowerShell and GUI examples demonstrate the creation of a single-domain cluster.

Thanks to Windows Server 2016, it is now possible to create a cluster using servers joined to different domains; this is fittingly called a *multi-domain cluster*. You can also create a cluster using servers that are not joined to any domain; this is appropriately termed a *workgroup cluster*.

Follow these steps to create a multi-domain or workgroup cluster:

Key Topic

Step 1.   Create a local account: Specifically, create a local user account on every node, with the same user name and the same password; add the user to the local Administrators group; you can also use the built-in Administrator account as long as the password is the same on each node; if you do not use the Administrator account, you must set a registry key called

LocalAccountTokenFilterPolicy on every node, using the following command in a PowerShell session with administrative privileges:

```
new-itemproperty -path hklm:\software\microsoft\
  windows\currentversion\policies\system -name
  localaccounttokenfilterpolicy -value 1
```

Step 2. **Add DNS suffixes**: Without Active Directory, a cluster must use DNS to locate the cluster nodes and the cluster itself. You need to specify a primary DNS suffix when assigning a name to each node in the System applet of Control Panel; for a multi-domain cluster, configure the Advanced TCP/IP Settings in every node with the DNS suffixes for all the domains represented in the cluster; you can also do this by using the **Set-DnsClientGlobalSettings** PowerShell cmdlet, as follows:

```
set-dnsclientglobalsettings -suffixsearchlist @
("pearsonitcertification.com", "corp.pearsonitcetification.com",
"paris.pearsonitcertification.com")
```

Step 3. **Create the workgroup or multi-domain cluster**: Using PowerShell, use the **New-Cluster** cmdlet but include the **AdministrativeAccessPoint** parameter with the DNS value, as in this example:

```
new-cluster -name mycluster1 -node server1,server2,server3
  -administrativeaccesspoint dns
```

Configuring Quorum

Quorum in Failover Clustering prevents the dreaded "split-brain" situation, in which the cluster splits in two and each half continues to function on the network.

Consider a database application running on a split-brain cluster. Database consistency and integrity is virtually nonexistent as clients manipulate different application systems.

Quorum provides each node in the cluster with a vote, and in many cases, a witness disk adds another vote. This witness disk breaks potential ties.

All nodes monitor the continual votes from the other nodes and the witness. If a node detects that the vote tally drops below 50% +1, it removes itself from the cluster.

When you create a failover cluster, the Create Cluster Wizard or the **New-Cluster** cmdlet creates a quorum configuration that is appropriate for the cluster in most cases. Windows Server 2016 configures this based on the number of nodes and the available storage resources.

By default, each node gets one vote, and if there is an even number of nodes, the wizard or cmdlet attempts to create a witness to function as a tiebreaker. Like the nodes, the witness gets one vote.

A witness casts a vote for the continued operation of the cluster. Failover Clustering in Windows Server 2016 supports three types of witnesses:

- **Disk witness**: This is a dedicated disk in the cluster's shared storage that contains a copy of the cluster database. It is a common type for a cluster located at a single site.

- **File Share witness**: This is an SMB file share on a Windows server with a Witness.log file containing information about the cluster. It is a common type for clusters divided among multiple sites with replicated storage.

- **Cloud witness**: This new choice in Windows Server 2016 is a blob stored in the cloud using standard Microsoft Azure services. This type is designed for stretched clusters split among multiple data centers at remote sites, where it is important to keep a witness that is independent of all the data centers.

Windows Server 2016 also includes dynamic quorum management. This allows Windows Server 2016 to keep a cluster running in situations where it would stop in earlier versions of the Failover Clustering feature from Microsoft.

When a node leaves the cluster, dynamic quorum management automatically removes its vote. At that point, the functionality of the cluster relies on the quorum of the remaining votes. This feature enables a cluster to function even when all but one of the nodes fails.

You can modify the quorum configuration by running the **Configure Cluster Quorum Wizard** in Failover Cluster Manager or by using the **Set-ClusterQuorum** cmdlet in Windows PowerShell. Using these tools, you can add or change a witness and specify which nodes should have votes in the quorum.

Here is the complete syntax for the **Set-ClusterQuorum** cmdlet:

```
Set-ClusterQuorum [-AccessKey <System.String> ] [-AccountName
  <System.String> ] [-CloudWitness] [-Cluster <String> ] [-DiskOnly
  <String> ] [-DiskWitness <String> ] [-Endpoint <System.String> ]
  [-FileShareWitness <String> ] [-InputObject <PSObject> ]
  [-NoWitness] [ <CommonParameters>]
```

To run the **Configure Cluster Quorum Wizard**, follow these steps:

Step 1.   Launch **Server Manager** and **select Tools > Failover Cluster Manager**.

Step 2.   In the left pane, right-click the **Failover Cluster Manager** node and choose **Connect to Cluster** if your cluster is not visible.

Step 3.   Right-click the cluster and choose **More Actions** then **Configure Cluster Quorum Settings**.

Step 4.   On the **Before You Begin** screen of the **Configure Cluster Quorum Wizard**, click **Next**.

Step 5.   On the **Select Quorum Configuration Option** screen, select one of the three options shown in Figure 14-5:

- **Use default quorum configuration**: Enables the wizard to configure an appropriate quorum configuration for the cluster without manual input

- **Select the quorum witness**: Enables you to add a witness, remove an existing witness, and specify the type and location of the witness the quorum should use

- **Advanced quorum configuration**: Enables you to specify which nodes should have votes in the quorum; also configures the same witness settings as the **Select the quorum witness** option

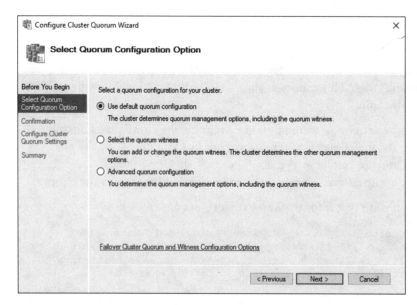

Figure 14-5   The Quorum Configuration Options

After you select the appropriate **Quorum Configuration** option, click **Next**.

Step 6.   In the **Confirmation** window, click **Next**.

Step 7.   On the **Summary** page, click **Finish**.

> **NOTE** You may have additional configuration steps, depending on your desired quorum configuration choice. For example, you may have a screen that enables the selection of the quorum witness following that configuration choice.

In most cases, Failover Clustering creates a witness when the cluster has an even number of nodes. There can only be one witness in a cluster. Microsoft recommends that you not create a witness in a situation where it would result in an even number of votes in the quorum.

When all the nodes in a cluster have access to the same shared storage, a disk witness is the recommended configuration. The Configure Storage Witness page in the Configure Cluster Quorum Wizard enables you to select the disk that should function as the witness. The witness disk can be small! In fact, a 512 MB NTFS disk is suitable.

Configuring Cluster Networking

As mentioned earlier in this chapter, you should consider using separate networks for the various traffic forms common to your cluster, which could include the following:

- Client communications
- Cluster communications
- iSCSI
- Live migration

Regarding your specific networking hardware, be sure to follow these recommendations:

- Use separate network adapters to avoid the adapter card being a single point of failure.
- Use different vendors and makes of network adapters when possible to prevent driver issues from affecting multiple adapters.
- Use separate physical switches to prevent a switch from being a single point of failure.
- Create redundant network connections whenever possible, especially for the client communication network.
- For networks without redundant connections, use NIC Teaming to provide failover capability in the event of a network adapter malfunction.

When you create a cluster, the system evaluates each of the connected networks and assigns traffic roles to them as follows:

- Any network carrying iSCSI traffic is disabled for any cluster communication.
- Networks without a default gateway address are configured for cluster communications only.
- Networks with a default gateway address are configured for both client and cluster communication.

The current states of the detected networks display on the **Networks** page of **Failover Cluster Manager**. You can also run the **Get-ClusterNetwork** cmdlet in PowerShell. It has the following syntax:

```
Get-ClusterNetwork [[-Name] <StringCollection> ] [-Cluster <String> ]
   [-InputObject <PSObject> ] [ <CommonParameters>]
```

To modify the default networking configuration using Failover Cluster Manager, follow these steps:

Step 1.   Launch **Server Manager** and select **Tools > Failover Cluster Manager**.

Step 2.   In the left pane, right-click the **Failover Cluster Manager** node and choose **Connect to Cluster** if the cluster is not visible.

Step 3.   In the left pane, double-click the cluster to expand its configuration nodes.

Step 4.   Select the **Networks** node under the cluster, as shown in Figure 14-6.

Step 5.   Right-click the network you want to modify and choose **Properties**.

Step 6.   On the **Properties** sheet, choose from the following options and then click **OK**.

- **Allow cluster communication on this network**
- **Allow clients to connect through this network**
- **Do not allow cluster communication on this network**

Figure 14-6 Modifying the Default Network Configuration

Restoring Single-Node or Cluster Configuration

Of course, failover clusters provide fault tolerance, but note that you still need a backup strategy. Whatever shared storage solution you use for a failover cluster, you should have a backup strategy in place. This is prudent even if your storage solution includes mirrors or parity-based data redundancy.

Another issue regarding backups is the cluster configuration itself. Windows Server Backup is limited in its ability to perform backups of Cluster Shared Volumes (CSVs) as part of the server backup, but it can back up the cluster database.

The cluster database is stored on each node of a cluster, as well as on a disk witness, if one exists. Cluster Service running on each node is responsible for synchronizing the most recent version of the cluster database for each node. When you perform a restore from a backup on a cluster node, you must consider whether you want to perform an authoritative restore of the cluster database.

One of the most likely disaster situations for a failover cluster environment is the loss of a single node. If one node fails, and the rest of the cluster is running, you can just perform a full restore of that node from a backup. The version of the cluster database in the backup is outdated, and Cluster Service overwrites it with the latest version as soon as the node comes up as part of the cluster. Microsoft calls this a non-authoritative backup.

You might also want to perform an authoritative restore of a cluster database. To do this with Windows Server Backup, you must perform the restore from the command prompt using the **Wbadmin.exe** program. There is no GUI option for this configuration.

Implementing Cluster-Aware Updating

Because all your cluster nodes should have exactly the same software running, it is critical to ensure that Windows updates coordinate between nodes. Cluster-Aware Updating (CAU) provides this functionality.

CAU applies updates to a cluster in a round-robin fashion called an updating run. CAU uses the following:

1. It selects a node to update.

2. It moves any existing roles off the selected node to other nodes in the cluster.

3. It places the updating node into maintenance mode.

4. It installs the required updates on the selected node and restarts it if needed.

5. It removes the node from maintenance mode.

6 It targets the next node in the cluster for this process.

CAU uses a device called the Update Coordinator to carry out these activities in the cluster. There are two operating modes for CAU:

- **Self-Updating mode**: In this mode, which lets CAU function automatically, one node has the CAU clustered role installed. When the system must update, it transfers this role to another node.

- **Remote-Updating mode**: In this mode, in which updating the cluster is a manual process, a system out of the cluster is the update coordinator. This update coordinator does not need to have Failover Clustering features installed; rather, it uses the tools under **Remote Server Administration Tools** in the **Add Roles and Features Wizard.**

CAU features the Cluster-Aware Updating console, and PowerShell offers a **Cluster-AwareUpdating** module with many cmdlets.

To ensure that a cluster supports CAU, you can either click **Analyze Cluster Updating Readiness** in the **Cluster Actions** list or run the following PowerShell cmdlet:

```
Test-CauSetup [[-ClusterName] <String> ] [[-Credential]
  <PSCredential> ] [ <CommonParameters>]
```

When the cluster is ready, you install the CAU clustered role by using **Configure Cluster Self-Updating Options** in the console. Alternatively, in PowerShell, you can use the **Add-CauClusterRole** cmdlet as follows:

```
Add-CauClusterRole [[-ClusterName] <String> ] [[-Credential]
  <PSCredential> ] [-CauPluginArguments <Hashtable[]> ]
  [-CauPluginName <String[]> ] [-ConfigurationName <String> ]
  [-DaysOfWeek <Weekdays> {None | Sunday | Monday | Tuesday |
  Wednesday | Thursday | Friday | Saturday} ] [-EnableFirewallRules]
  [-FailbackMode <FailbackType> {NoFailback | Immediate |
  Policy} ] [-Force] [-GroupName <String> ] [-IntervalWeeks
  <Int32> ] [-MaxFailedNodes <Int32> ] [-MaxRetriesPerNode
  <Int32> ] [-NodeOrder <String[]> ] [-PostUpdateScript
  <String> ] [-PreUpdateScript <String> ] [-RebootTimeoutMinutes
  <Int32> ] [-RequireAllNodesOnline] [-RunPluginsSerially]
  [-SeparateReboots] [-StartDate <DateTime> ] [-StopAfter <TimeSpan>
  ] [-StopOnPluginFailure] [-SuspendClusterNodeTimeoutMinutes <Int32>
  ] [-VirtualComputerObjectName <String> ] [-WarnAfter <TimeSpan> ]
  [-Confirm] [-WhatIf] [ <CommonParameters>]
```

NOTE   There is also a **WeeksOfMonth** option available for the cmdlet.

To manually trigger an updating run, use the **Apply Updates** option in the console or use the **Invoke-CauRun** cmdlet:

```
Invoke-CauRun [[-ClusterName] <String> ] [[-CauPluginName]
  <String[]> ] [[-Credential] <PSCredential> ] [-CauPluginArguments
  <Hashtable[]> ] [-ConfigurationName <String> ]
  [-EnableFirewallRules] [-FailbackMode <FailbackType>
  {NoFailback | Immediate | Policy} ] [-Force] [-MaxFailedNodes
  <Int32> ] [-MaxRetriesPerNode <Int32> ] [-NodeOrder <String[]>
  ] [-PostUpdateScript <String> ] [-PreUpdateScript <String>
  ] [-RebootTimeoutMinutes <Int32> ] [-RequireAllNodesOnline]
  [-RunPluginsSerially] [-SeparateReboots] [-StopAfter <TimeSpan> ]
  [-StopOnPluginFailure] [-SuspendClusterNodeTimeoutMinutes <Int32> ]
  [-WarnAfter <TimeSpan> ] [-Confirm] [-WhatIf] [ <CommonParameters>]
```

Implementing Cluster Operating System Rolling Upgrade

With Windows Server 2016, upgrading an operating system in a Hyper-V or Scale-Out File Server cluster no longer requires an administrator to take the cluster offline. Upgrading from Windows Server 2012 R2 to Windows Server 2016 is possible on a node-by-node basis, and the cluster functions normally for client access.

While a cluster functions with different operating system in use, the cluster is running in what Microsoft terms Mixed-OS mode. Follow these steps for each Windows Server 2012 R2 node to upgrade it:

Step 1.   Pause the node.

Step 2.   Drain the node of its workload by migrating clients to another node.

Step 3.   Evict the node from the cluster.

Step 4.   Reformat the system drive and perform a clean install of Windows Server 2016.

Step 5.   Configure the network and storage connections.

Step 6.   Install the Failover Clustering feature.

Step 7.   Add the newly upgraded node back to the cluster.

Step 8.   Re-implement the cluster workload.

> **NOTE**   When Windows Server 2016 systems are in a cluster with down-level operating systems, the Windows Server 2016 systems run in a compatibility mode, and Server 2016 specific features are unavailable.

Microsoft does not consider Mixed-OS mode a permanent solution and suggests that you perform all upgrades within a month or less.

Once you complete all upgrades, use the **Update-ClusterFunctionalLevel** cmdlet:

```
Update-ClusterFunctionalLevel [-Cluster <String> ] [-Force]
   [-InputObject <PSObject> ] [ <CommonParameters>]
```

Configuring Clusters Without Network Names

It is possible to create a cluster in Windows Server 2016 without a Cluster Name Object (CNO) in Active Directory even though the nodes are Active Directory participants. Windows Server calls this an Active Directory–detached cluster. This type of cluster eliminates the need for the administrator creating the cluster to have permissions for Active Directory object creation. What takes the place of Active Directory in this environment? Domain Name Services (DNS).

To create an Active Directory-detached cluster, use the **New-Cluster** PowerShell cmdlet and include the **AdministrativeAccessPoint** parameter. This time, this parameter specifies a DNS value, as shown in the following example:

```
new-cluster mycluster1 -node node1,node2 -staticaddress 10.10.10.1
   -nostorage -administrativeaccesspoint dns
```

Implementing VM Resiliency

Clustering in Windows Server 2016 offers valuable new virtual machine resiliency functionality. This is extremely beneficial in environments where localized transient failures occur as opposed to major catastrophic events. These types of smaller failures are much more common.

Single VMs might temporarily lose contact with their cluster for a variety of reasons:

- The cluster service on the VM has shut down.

- There is a memory problem.

- There is a software problem.

- Network communication disrupts.

- There is a driver issue.

- There is an IP addressing issue.

- There is a damaged network cable.

- There is a disconnected network cable.

To help administrators combat these issues, Windows Server 2016 has introduced new VM states:

- **Unmonitored**: Shows that the VM owning a role is not watched by the cluster service

- **Isolated**: Shows that the node is not an active member of the cluster but is still in possession of a role

- **Quarantine**: Shows a node that has been drained of its roles and removed from the cluster for a specified length of time after having left and reentered the cluster three times in the previous hour

You can configure the way the cluster uses these states by using the following settings in Windows PowerShell:

- **ResiliencyLevel**: With a value of 1, enables the use of the Isolated state only if the node supplies a known reason for disconnecting from the cluster; otherwise, the node fails at once; with a value of 2 (the default), enables the free use of the Isolated state and allows the node time to recover

- **ResiliencyDefaultPeriod**: Specifies how long the nodes in the entire cluster can stay in the Isolated state (in seconds); the default is 240

- **ResiliencyPeriod**: Specifies how long the nodes in a group stay in the Isolated state (in seconds); a value of -1 causes the group to revert to the **ResiliencyDefaultPeriod** setting; the default is 240

- **QuarantineThreshold**: Specifies the number of failures that a node can experience in a one-hour period before the Quarantine state; the default is 3

- **QuarantineDuration**: Specifies the length of time (in seconds) that a node stays in quarantine; the default is 7200

Cluster Storage

Some type of shared storage is a critical ingredient for successful Failover Clustering, as discussed in the following sections.

Configuring Cluster Storage

Windows Server 2016 supports several shared storage technologies, including the following:

- Fibre Channel

- Serial Attached SCSI (SAS)

- Internet SCSI (iSCSI)

If you provide a cluster with the appropriate disks, they magically appear in the Failover Cluster Manager when you choose **Add Disks** on the **Storage\Disks** page.

You can also create a clustered storage pool. Note that this is similar technology to Storage Spaces Direct, configured for a single-node system.

Clustered storage pools require the following:

- A minimum of three disks

- A minimum of 4 GB each

- Connection via SAS or iSCSI

Follow these steps to create a storage pool:

Step 1. Launch **Server Manager** and select **Tools > Failover Cluster Manager**.

Step 2. In the left pane, right-click the **Failover Cluster Manager** node and choose **Connect to Cluster** if the cluster is not visible.

Step 3. In the left pane, double-click the cluster to expand its configuration nodes.

Step 4.   Double-click **Storage** in the left pane to expand its options, as shown in Figure 14-7.

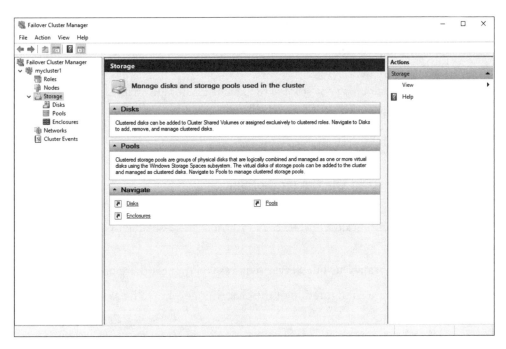

Figure 14-7   The Storage Options in Failover Cluster Manager

Step 5.   Right-click the **Pools** node under **Storage** and select **New Storage Pool** to launch the **New Storage Pool Wizard**.

Step 6.   On the **Specify a Storage Pool Name and Subsystem** page, provide a name for the pool and select the **primordial pool** that contains the disks you require.

Step 7.   On the **Select Physical Disks for the Storage Pool** page, choose the disks you want to add to the pool and specify each as either **Automatic**, **Manual**, or **Hot Spare**.

Step 8.   Click **Create**.

Configuring and Optimizing Clustered Shared Volumes (CSVs)

Using Clustered Shared Volumes (CSVs) creates a pseudo-file system (CSVFS) layered on top of the NTFS file system. This allows seamless access to shared volume data without conflicts. Note that NTFS by itself does not have this capability.

When you add a disk to a cluster, it appears in Failover Cluster Manager as Available Storage. To add the disk to a cluster, in the **Actions** pane, click **Add to Cluster Shared Volume**. Or, in PowerShell, you can use the cmdlet **Add-ClusterSharedVolume** as follows:

```
Add-ClusterSharedVolume [[-Name] <StringCollection> ] [-Cluster
    <String> ] [-InputObject <PSObject> ] [ <CommonParameters>]
```

The use of CSV mounts your storage to C:\ClusterStorage on all cluster nodes. The Disk Management snap-in depicts the storage now on all the cluster's nodes. You can also select the CSV in **Failover Cluster Manager** and click **Move > Best Possible Node**.

Implementing Scale-Out File Server (SoFS)

Scale-Out File Server (SoFS) is a clustered role that provides highly available storage for applications. Scale-Out File Servers host shares available to all cluster nodes simultaneously.

Implementing a Scale-Out File Server requires you to meet these prerequisites:

- The hardware configuration of the cluster nodes should be as identical as possible.

- All nodes should have access to shared storage using iSCSI, SAS, or Fibre Channel.

- All nodes must have the Failover Clustering feature properly implemented.

- You must fully implement Failover Clustering prior to the Scale-Out File Server configuration.

Follow these steps to install a Scale-Out File Server:

Step 1.   Launch **Server Manager** and select **Tools > Failover Cluster Manager**.

Step 2.   In the left pane, right-click the **Failover Cluster Manager** node and choose **Connect to Cluster** if the cluster is not visible.

Step 3.   In the left pane, double-click the cluster to expand its configuration nodes.

Step 4.   Right-click the **Roles** node and choose **Configure Role** to launch the **High Availability Wizard**.

Step 5.   On the **File Server Type** page, select the **Scale-Out File Server for Application Data** option and click **Next**.

Step 6. On the **Client Access Point** page, specify a name that clients use to access the role and click **Next**. The wizard creates an Active Directory Domain Services computer object using this name.

Step 7. Click **Finish**.

Follow these steps to create a file share:

Step 1. Launch **Server Manager** and select **Tools > Failover Cluster Manager**.

Step 2. In the left pane, right-click the **Failover Cluster Manager** node and choose **Connect to Cluster** if the cluster is not visible.

Step 3. In the left pane, double-click the cluster to expand its configuration nodes.

Step 4. Double-click to expand the **Roles** node, right-click the **Scale-Out File Server** role, and choose **Add File Share** to launch the **New Share Wizard**.

Step 5. On the **Select the Profile for This Share** page, click **SMB Share - Applications** and then click **Next**.

Step 6. On the **Select the Server and Path for This Share** page, click the **Scale-Out File Server** role and then click **Next**.

Step 7. In the **Share Location** box, click **Cluster Shared Volume**.

Step 8. On the **Specify Share Name** page, enter a name and description and then click **Next**.

Step 9. On the **Configure Share Settings** page, make sure to select the **Enable continuous availability** check box and be sure to clear the **Enable access-based enumeration** check box; click **Next**.

Step 10. On the **Specify Permissions to Control Access** page, click **Customize Permissions** and make sure all computer objects for the cluster have the **Full Control** permission.

Step 11. Click **Create**.

In Windows PowerShell, you can use the **New-SmbShare** cmdlet to create the share. You can use the **Set-SmbPathACL** cmdlet to set file permissions. Here is the full syntax for these cmdlets:

```
New-SmbShare [-Name] <String> [-Path] <String> [[-ScopeName] <String>
  ] [-CachingMode <CachingMode> {None | Manual | Documents | Programs
  | BranchCache | Unknown} ] [-CATimeout <UInt32> ] [-ChangeAccess
  <String[]> ] [-CimSession <CimSession[]> ] [-ConcurrentUserLimit
  <UInt32> ] [-ContinuouslyAvailable <Boolean> ] [-Description
```

```
<String> ] [-EncryptData <Boolean> ] [-FolderEnumerationMode
<FolderEnumerationMode> {AccessBased | Unrestricted} ]
[-FullAccess <String[]> ] [-NoAccess <String[]> ] [-ReadAccess
<String[]> ] [-SecurityDescriptor <System.String> ] [-Temporary]
[-ThrottleLimit <Int32> ] [-Confirm] [-WhatIf] [ <CommonParameters>]
[ <WorkflowParameters>]

Set-SmbPathAcl [-ShareName] <String> [[-ScopeName] <String> ] [
<CommonParameters>]
```

Determining Different Scenarios for the Use of SoFS Versus Clustered File Server

SoFS makes its shares available on all the cluster's nodes, meaning that any node can process disk read and write requests. However, the underlying CSVFS file system still needs a disk coordinator (that is, the node that owns the disk) to perform all metadata-related activities. The coordinator node must receive all requests to open, close, create, and rename files on an SoFS share.

Therefore, Microsoft recommends the SoFS role specifically for use on Hyper-V and SQL Server clusters. Both of those applications routinely open large files (VHDs and databases) and leaves them open for long periods. Because metadata requests are infrequent in this type of application, there is a minimum burden on the disk coordinator node.

Many other applications might cause the disk coordinator to become a bottleneck in the datacenter. This occurs when many requests need access to the file system metadata. A classic example is file server administrator functions like modifying NTFS permissions and other file system attributes.

Always consider the nature of the cluster workload before designing cluster storage. The more file management requests an application generates, the less likely it is to be suitable for a Scale-Out File Server implementation.

Determining Usage Scenarios for Implementing Guest Clustering

Guest failover clusters consist solely of virtual machines running on a single Hyper-V host server. You can create two or more identical VMs, install the Failover Clustering feature on all of them, and create a cluster out of them, just as if they were physical computers. For the shared storage that a guest cluster needs, you can use any of the standard storage area networking technologies, including Fibre Channel, SAS, or iSCSI, as pass-through disks.

Guest clusters are useful in the following scenarios:

- **Node-monitoring clusters:** Guest clusters watch resources, such as the storage subsystem, the network connectivity, and the clustered application itself, and automatically act when a problem occurs by migrating or failing over the role to another node

- **Application migration**: Guest clusters allow you to support availability by migrating the application to different nodes in the cluster.

- **Host availability**: You can create a guest cluster from virtual machines on different Hyper-V hosts; if a host experiences a failure, the nodes running on other hosts detect the absence of its VMs and bring any clustered applications that were running there online.

- **VM migration**: If you have multiple Hyper-V hosts available, you can migrate virtual machines between hosts as needed to perform maintenance tasks that require you to take a host offline temporarily.

- **Nested clustering**: It is possible to create a guest cluster within a cluster, by joining two or more physical servers into a Hyper-V cluster and then guest clustering virtual machines running on the Hyper-V host nodes. This enables the system to automatically react to the failure of a Hyper-V host by migrating its virtual machines to the other hosts; or it enables the system to automatically react to the failure of a VM by migrating its clustered applications.

Implementing a Clustered Storage Spaces Solution Using Shared SAS Storage Enclosures

Clustered storage spaces combine Storage Spaces technology with Failover Clustering. This solution offers high availability for both storage and server failures.

The solution begins with one or more SAS disk arrays. The SAS disk array might have a JBOD (just a bunch of disks) or RAID (redundant array of independent disks) configuration. If so, you need to disable this functionality for use with Storage Spaces.

To create a truly reliable solution for enterprise connectivity, there should be hardware redundancy at all levels. This includes multiple host bus adapters in each server, redundant power supplies in the disk enclosures, and even redundant disk enclosures.

You build a clustered storage space in one of two ways:

- **Image the storage pool first**: If you have an existing storage pool, or if you are building a cluster from scratch, you can create the storage pool by using Server Manager or the **New-StoragePool** cmdlet before you create the cluster; once you have created the cluster, the storage pool is available to it.

- **Image the failover cluster first**: If you have an existing cluster, you can create the storage pool in Failover Cluster Manager.

To create a clustered storage space in an existing cluster with Failover Cluster Manager, use the following steps:

Step 1. Launch **Server Manager** and select **Tools > Failover Cluster Manager**.

Step 2. In the left pane, right-click the **Failover Cluster Manager** node and choose **Connect to Cluster** if the cluster is not visible.

Step 3. In the left pane, double-click the cluster to expand its configuration nodes.

Step 4. Double-click **Storage** in the left pane to expand its options.

Step 5. Right-click the **Pools** node under **Storage** and select **New Storage Pool** to launch the **New Storage Pool Wizard**.

Step 6. On the **Specify a Storage Pool Name and Subsystem** page, specify a name for the pool and select the primordial pool that contains the disks you want to add and then click **Next**.

Step 7. On the **Select Physical Disks for the Storage Pool** page, select the check boxes for the disks you want to add to the pool. For example, to create a clustered storage pool, you must select a minimum of three disks, and for three-way mirroring, you must select a minimum of five disks. Click **Next**.

Step 8. Click **Create**.

Step 9. On the **View Results** page, select the **Create a virtual disk when this wizard closes** check box and click **Close**. The **New Virtual Disk Wizard** appears.

Step 10. On the **Select the Storage Pool** page, select the pool you just created and click **Next**.

Step 11. On the **Specify the Virtual Disk Name** page, type a name for the disk and click **Next**.

Step 12. On the **Select the Storage Layout** page, select **Simple, Mirror,** or **Parity**; if you select **Mirror** and there are five disks in the pool, a **Configure the Resiliency Settings** page appears, prompting you to choose **Two-Way Mirror** or **Three-Way Mirror**. Choose one of these options and click **Next**.

Step 13. On the **Specify the Size of the Virtual Disk** page, type a size in MB, GB, or TB or select the **Maximum Size** check box. Click **Next**.

Step 14. Click **Create**.

Step 15.   On the **View Results** page, select the **Create a volume when this wizard closes** check box and click **Close**. The **New Volume Wizard** appears.

Step 16.   On the **Select the Server and Disk** page, select your cluster and the virtual disk you just created and then click **Next**.

Step 17.   On the **Specify the Size of the Volume** page, type a volume size and click **Next**.

Step 18.   On the **Assign to Drive Letter or Folder** page, select a drive letter or a folder where you want to mount the volume and click **Next**.

Step 19.   On the **Select File System Settings** page, select the **NTFS** or **ReFS** file system, specify an **allocation unit size**, type a volume label, and click **Next**.

Step 20.   Click **Create** and then click **Close**.

The resilient storage is now available to the cluster. You can create CSVs from this storage to create highly available shares using a single unified namespace.

Implementing Storage Replica

Thanks to the cluster-aware Storage Replica functionality of Windows Server 2016, you can create a stretch cluster. This is a cluster that divides between two or more sites, without shared storage connecting the sites.

Each site has shared storage for nodes, but each site does not have access to the storage at the other site. However, for the two sites to function as a true failover cluster, they must have the same data. Storage Replica can replicate the data between the two sites, either synchronously or asynchronously. For more information on Storage Replica, see Chapter 5, "Server Storage."

Implementing Shared VHDX as a Storage Solution for Guest Clusters

You can use the shared storage offered by a physical cluster to create a shared VHDX file for a guest cluster. In such a scenario, you have two or more physical Hyper-V servers functioning as nodes in a failover cluster. These physical servers connect to shared storage hardware, using iSCSI, SAS, or Fibre Channel. You configure the shared storage as Clustered Shared Volumes or SMB 3.0 shares.

To create a guest cluster, each of the Hyper-V servers hosts a virtual machine. To create the shared storage needed by the guest cluster, you create a shared VHDX file on the physical cluster's CSVs.

Windows Server 2016 supports two types of shared virtual hard disk files:

- **VHDX**: Files created on a shared storage infrastructure are shared between virtual machines in a guest cluster; while Serer 2016 supports VHDX, VHD sets are now recommended.

- **VHD set**: A VHD set consists of a 260 KB VHDS file, which has metadata, and an AVHDX file, which has the actual data. VHD sets offer online resizing capabilities and support for host-based backups that VHDX files lack.

To create a new shared VHDX or VHD set file for a guest cluster, you open the **Settings** dialog box in **Failover Cluster Manager**, select the **SCSI Controller**, select **Shared Drive**, and click **Add**. You can then launch and run the **New Virtual Hard Disk Wizard**, just as you would on a non-clustered Hyper-V server. The only difference is that you see a **Choose Disk Format** page, on which you specify whether to create a VHDX or VHD set file.

Exam Preparation Tasks

As mentioned in the section "How to Use This Book" in the Introduction, you have a couple choices for exam preparation: the exercises here, Chapter 21, "Final Preparation," and the exam simulation questions in the Pearson Test Prep Software Online.

Review All Key Topics

Review the most important topics in this chapter, noted with the Key Topics icon in the outer margin of the page. Table 14-2 lists these key topics and the page number on which each is found.

Table 14-2 Key Topics for Chapter 14

Key Topic Element	Description	Page Number
List	Requirements for clustering	237
Steps	Create multi-domain or workgroup clusters	241
List	Types of quorum witnesses	243
List	Cluster networking recommendations	245
List	New VM states for resiliency	251
List	Clustered storages pool requirements	252

Key Topic Element	Description	Page Number
Steps	Creating a clustered storage pool	252
Steps	Steps for creating a Scale-Out File Server	254

Complete Tables and Lists from Memory

There are no memory tables in this chapter.

Define Key Terms

Define the following key terms from this chapter and check your answers against the glossary:

Nodes, Cluster Name Object (CNO), Quorum, Witness, Cluster-Aware Updating (CAU), Rolling Upgrade, CSVFS, Scale-Out File Server (SoFS)

Q&A

The answers to these questions appear in Appendix A. For more practice with exam format questions, use the Pearson Test Prep Software Online.

1. Name at least four requirements for successful failover clustering.

2. What cmdlet in PowerShell creates a new cluster?

3. Name three clustered storage pools requirements.

4. Name at least four usage scenarios for guest clusters.

This chapter covers the following subjects:

- **Role-Specific Settings and Continuously Available Shares**: Each role you are using in a failover cluster has unique settings based on the role's function. This section examines this fact and elaborates on a powerful setting for making shares continuously available.

- **More Management Settings and Monitoring**: There are many powerful monitors and advanced failover cluster management topics. This section examines them in detail.

## CHAPTER 15

Managing Failover Clustering

It is not really surprising that there are many management capabilities for a feature as important as failover clustering. This chapter ensures that you can precisely monitor your Windows Server 2016 failover clusters and make the most of their configurations.

"Do I Know This Already?" Quiz

The "Do I Know This Already?" quiz allows you to assess whether you should read the entire chapter. Table 15-1 lists the major headings in this chapter and the "Do I Know This Already?" quiz questions covering the material in those headings so you can assess your knowledge of these specific areas. The answers to the "Do I Know This Already?" quiz appear in Appendix A, "Answers to the 'Do I Know This Already?' Quizzes and Q&A Questions."

Table 15-1 "Do I Know This Already?" Foundation Topics Section-to-Question Mapping

Foundation Topics Section	Questions
Role-Specific Settings and Continuously Available Shares	1, 2
More Management Settings and Monitoring	3–5

CAUTION The goal of self-assessment is to gauge your mastery of the topics in this chapter. If you do not know the answer to a question or are only partially sure of the answer, you should mark your answer as incorrect for purposes of the self-assessment. Giving yourself credit for an answer you correctly guess skews your self-assessment results and might provide you with a false sense of security.

1. Which of the following would not be an option with the Virtual Machine role in Failover Cluster Manager?

   a. Monitor

   b. Start

   c. Stop

   d. Connect

2. What SMB 3.0 feature enables continuously available shares?

   a. SMB Direct

   b. SMB Scale-Out

   c. SMB Transparent Failover

   d. SMB Multichannel

3. Which is not a valid prerequisite for VM monitoring?

   a. The VM must be Generation 1.

   b. The VM must be in the same domain as the Hyper-V host.

   c. Windows Firewall must permit the monitoring rules inbound.

   d. The Hyper-V cluster administrator must be a member of the local Administrators group on the VM.

4. What cmdlet in PowerShell allows the configuration of VM monitoring?

   a. **Create-MonitoredClusterVM**

   b. **Set-ClusterVMItem**

   c. **Add-ClusterVMMonitoredItem**

   d. **Get-VMMonitoredItem**

5. What is a stretch cluster?

   a. A cluster that has nodes in two different domains

   b. A cluster that has nodes using Server 2012 and Server 2016

   c. A cluster that has nodes maxing out the RAM of a failover host

   d. A cluster that has nodes in a different geographic area

Foundation Topics

Role-Specific Settings and Continuously Available Shares

This section tackles two specific management topics: role-specific settings in a failover cluster and continuously available shares.

Role-Specific Settings

When you install cluster roles, each has its own settings that are specific to the role's function. An easy way to see this is to visit the Roles page in Failover Cluster Manager and select a role and note the specific actions possible in the Actions pane.

For example, the Virtual Machine role includes the following actions:

- **Start**

- **Stop**

- **Connect**

- **Settings**

Failover cluster roles include the following:

- **DFS Namespace Server:** A virtual view of file shares in the organization

- **DHCP Server:** Provides TCP/IP configuration information to client computers

- **Distributed Transaction Coordinator (DTC):** Supports distributed applications that perform transactions

- **File Server:** Provides a central location on the network for shared file resources accessed by users or computers

- **Generic Application:** Offers high availability for certain applications that were not designed to run on a cluster

- **Generic Script:** For scripts that run in the Windows Script Host to control applications, you can enable high availability using this role

- **Generic Service:** Offers high availability for certain services that were not designed to run in a cluster

- **Hyper-V Replica Broker:** Permits the participation of the cluster in Hyper-V Replica

- **iSCSI Target Server:** Provides SCSI storage over TCP/IP

- **iSNS Server:** Provides discovery of iSCSI Targets

- **Message Queuing:** Permits distributed applications to communicate with systems that might be temporarily offline

- **Other Server:** Provides a client access point and storage

- **Virtual Machine:** A virtual system running on a physical host

- **WINS Server:** Permits older systems to use NetBIOS for name resolution

Table 15-2 shows these roles and their required role or feature prerequisites.

Table 15-2   Failover Cluster Roles and Feature Prerequisites

Cluster Role	Role or Feature Prerequisite
DFS Namespace Server	DFS Namespaces (part of File Server role)
DHCP Server	DHCP Server role
Distributed Transaction Coordinator (DTC)	None
File Server	File Server role
Generic Application	Not applicable
Generic Script	Not applicable
Generic Service	Not applicable
Hyper-V Replica Broker	Hyper-V role
iSCSI Target Server	iSCSI Target Server (part of File Server role)
iSNS Server	iSNS Server Service feature
Message Queuing	Message Queuing Services feature
Other Server	None
Virtual Machine	Hyper-V role
WINS Server	WINS Server feature

No matter the role, be sure to verify it by following these steps:

Step 1.   Launch **Server Manager** and select **Tools > Failover Cluster Manager**.

Step 2.   In the **Roles** pane, make sure the role has the status **Running**; the Roles pane also shows the owner node.

Step 3. To test failover, right-click the role, select **Move**, and then click **Select Node**.

Step 4. In the **Move Clustered Role** dialog box, click the desired cluster node and then click **OK**.

Step 5. In the **Owner Node** column, verify that the owner node changed.

Continuously Available Shares

As you know from Chapter 14, "Failover Clustering," when you install the File Server cluster role, you have the choice of Scale-Out File Server or general use file server. Both roles allow the use of continuously available shares using Server Message Block (SMB) 3.0.

In fact, SMB 3.0 provides many enhancements, several that are ideal in clustered setups:

- **SMB Transparent Failover**: Transfers client sessions from one cluster node to another without client interruption

- **SMB Scale-out**: Enables a share to be accessible by clients from all nodes in the cluster simultaneously; note that this effectively increases the share's usable bandwidth

- **SMB Multichannel:** Allows file servers to use the bandwidth from multiple network adapters simultaneously

- **SMB Direct**: Uses Remote Direct Memory Access (RDMA) and allows SMB 3.0 to complete directory memory-to-memory data transfers between remote systems

- **SMB Encryption**: Provides end-to-end AES encryption between servers and clients

- **VSS for SMB File Shares**: Enables VSS-aware backup applications to perform application consistent shadow copies of VSS-aware server applications storing data on SMB 3.0 file shares

- **SMB Directory Leasing**: Reduces the latency for file access over high-latency WAN networks

When you create or change a file server share in Failover Cluster Manager, the New Share Wizard presents the Configure Share Settings page. The Enable Continuous Availability check box, selected by default, activates the SMB Transparent Failover feature, and the Encrypt Data Access check box enables SMB Encryption.

More Management Settings

This section describes several other important cluster management topics, including the configuration of VM monitoring, the configuration of failover and preference settings, stretch clusters, and node fairness. While you may not need all these features, you might find some of them critical in select environments.

Configuring VM Monitoring

A great management feature for failover clustering in Windows Server 2016 is the ability to monitor VMs for issues and then restart VMs or fail them over to another node.

Remember these prerequisites for VM monitoring:

- The VM must be in the same domain as the Hyper-V host.

- Windows Firewall on the VM must have inbound rules in the Virtual Machine Monitoring group enabled.

- The Hyper-V cluster administrator must be a member of the local Administrators group on the VM.

Follow these steps to configure monitoring for a VM:

Step 1.   Launch **Server Manager** and select **Tools > Failover Cluster Manager**.

Step 2.   In the **Roles** pane, select the **VM** for monitoring, and in the **Actions** page, click **More Actions** and then click **Configure Monitoring**.

Step 3.   In the **Select Services** page, select the services you want to monitor and click **OK**.

You can instead use the **Add-ClusterVMMonitoredItem** cmdlet in PowerShell. Its syntax is as follows:

```
Add-ClusterVMMonitoredItem [[-VirtualMachine] <System.String> ] [-Wait
   <System.Int32> ] [ <CommonParameters>]
```

Remember that when a service experiences an issue, the Service Control Manager follows the actions specified on the Recovery tab of the service first. This includes the following options:

- First Failure

- Second Failure

- Subsequent Failures

If the Service Control Manager cannot solve the issue, the cluster takes over and performs its own recovery actions:

- The cluster creates an entry in the hosts' System log with the Event ID 1250.

- The cluster changes the status of the VM to Application in VM Critical.

- The cluster restarts the VM on the same node.

- The cluster fails the VM over to another node.

You can change these settings by opening the Virtual Machine Cluster WMI Properties sheet and using the Policies tab.

Configuring Failover and Preference Settings

A failover occurs when a role running on a cluster node can no longer continue to run and moves to another node. This might occur because of any of the following:

- A power failure

- A software malfunction

- An administrator shutting down the node for maintenance

With a *failback*, the cluster moves the role back to the original node.

You control the settings for failover behavior by using the Roles page in Failover Cluster Manager. You use the Properties option in the Actions pane to see the Properties page.

On the General tab, you specify the node you would prefer to run the role. In the Priority drop-down list, you can specify High, Medium, or Low to indicate when the role should start in relation to the other roles in the cluster.

On the Failover tab, you can specify the maximum number of times the cluster should try to restart a role or fail it over to another node during the time interval specified by the Period setting. Notice that the Failover tab also allows failback configuration.

Implementing Stretch and Site-Aware Failover Clusters

Stretch clusters have their nodes separated by large geographic distances. They are critical because natural disasters can often affect entire geographic areas of a country.

Because it is often not practical to create shared storage accessible to all nodes in a stretch cluster, many administrators use asymmetric storage for stretch clusters. These administrators then use Storage Replica to sync data between sites.

How can the Failover Clustering feature distinguish between nodes in one geographic location versus another? Site-aware failover clustering solves this in Windows Server 2016. These clusters have fault domains based on the values of a site property for each node.

To create a site-aware cluster, you first use the **New-ClusterFaultDomain** PowerShell cmdlet to define the sites. Then you use the **Set-ClusterFaultDomain** cmdlet to assign the cluster nodes to the sites you have created. The syntax for these PowerShell cmdlets is as follows:

```
New-ClusterFaultDomain -FaultDomainType <FaultDomainType> {Unknown
   | Site | Rack | Chassis | Node} -Name <String> [-CimSession
   <CimSession[]> ] [-Description <String> ] [-FaultDomain <String> ]
   [-Flags <UInt32> ] [-Location <String> ] [-ThrottleLimit <Int32> ] [
   <CommonParameters>] [ <WorkflowParameters>]


Set-ClusterFaultDomain [-CimSession <CimSession[]> ] [-Description
   <String> ] [-FaultDomain <String> ] [-Flags <UInt32> ] [-Location
   <String> ] [-NewName <String> ] [-PassThru] [-ThrottleLimit <Int32>
   ] [ <CommonParameters>] [ <WorkflowParameters>]
```

Nodes try to fail over to the same site until there are no more nodes at the local site. Failover then targets other sites.

Because stretch clusters might have much larger latencies between sites, you must be able to change settings, including the following, to control failure detection:

- **CrossSiteDelay**: The amount of time between heartbeats sent to nodes in different sites

- **CrossSiteThreshold**: The number of missed heartbeats before the interface is considered down to nodes on dissimilar sites

You tweak these settings by using the **Get-Cluster** cmdlet in PowerShell, as shown in this example:

```
(get-cluster).crosssitedelay = 2000
```

Here is the complete syntax of the **Get-Cluster** cmdlet:

```
Get-Cluster [-Domain <string>] [<CommonParameters>]
```

Enabling and Configuring Node Fairness

Node fairness seeks to balance the distribution of workloads between nodes in a cluster. This is possible thanks to Windows Server 2016 monitoring CPU and memory usage patterns over time. Server 2016 migrates VMs to different nodes based on this captured information.

Windows Server 2016 enables node fairness by default, but you can configure whether it runs and when load balancing occurs. You can also configure the aggressiveness of the load balancing that occurs. You do this in the cluster's Properties sheet, on the Balancer tab, as shown in Figure 15-1.

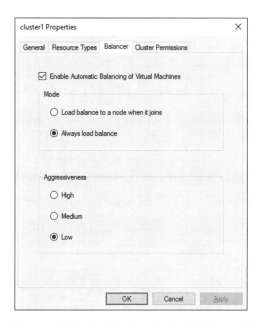

Figure 15-1   Configuring the Node Fairness Feature

You can also configure these settings with Windows PowerShell, using the following commands:

- **(Get-Cluster).AutoBalancerMode**: Specifies whether node fairness should run and how often it should balance the load, using the following values:

    - **0**: Node fairness is disabled.

    - **1**: Load balancing occurs when a node joins the cluster.

    - **2**: Load balancing occurs when a node joins the cluster and every 30 minutes thereafter; this is the default.

- **(Get-Cluster).AutoBalancerLevel**: Specifies the aggressiveness with which node fairness should evaluate the load on each node, using the following values:

  - **1 - Low**: Migrates VMs when the host is more than 80% loaded; this is the default
  - **2 - Medium**: Migrates VMs when the host is more than 70% loaded
  - **3 - High**: Migrates VMs when the host is more than 60% loaded

Exam Preparation Tasks

As mentioned in the section "How to Use This Book" in the Introduction, you have a couple choices for exam preparation: the exercises here, Chapter 21, "Final Preparation," and the exam simulation questions in the Pearson Test Prep Software Online.

Review All Key Topics

Review the most important topics in this chapter, noted with the Key Topics icon in the outer margin of the page. Table 15-3 lists these key topics and the page number on which each is found.

Table 15-3   Key Topics for Chapter 15

Key Topic Element	Description	Page Number
List	SMB 3.0 features	267
Steps	VM monitoring configuration	268
Commands	Creating a stretch cluster	270

Complete Tables and Lists from Memory

Print a copy of Appendix B, "Memory Tables" (found on the book website), or at least the section for this chapter, and complete the tables and lists from memory. Appendix C, "Memory Tables Answer Key," also on the website, includes completed tables and lists to check your work.

Define Key Terms

Define the following key terms from this chapter and check your answers against the glossary:

Server Message Block (SMB) 3.0, Failback, Stretch Cluster, Site-Aware Clusters, Node Fairness

Q&A

The answers to these questions appear in Appendix A. For more practice with exam format questions, use the Pearson Test Prep Software Online.

1. What encryption algorithm does SMB 3.0 use for SMB encryption?
2. What components of a VM do you monitor with VM monitoring?
3. What are the three options on the Recovery tab in Service Control Manager?
4. What PowerShell cmdlet do you use to create a stretch cluster site?

This chapter covers the following subjects:

- **Storage Spaces Direct:** This section discusses scenarios for using Storage Spaces Direct and how to implement this exciting new feature using Windows PowerShell.

- **Disaggregated and Hyper-Converged Storage Spaces Direct:** This part of the chapter examines two specific scenarios for usage: the disaggregated configuration and the hyper-converged approach.

## CHAPTER 16

Storage Spaces Direct

What is better than Storage Pool technology? How about Storage Pool technology that functions with clusters? It is called Storage Spaces Direct (S2D), and this chapter tells you what you need to know about this new technology.

"Do I Know This Already?" Quiz

The "Do I Know This Already?" quiz allows you to assess whether you should read the entire chapter. Table 16-1 lists the major headings in this chapter and the "Do I Know This Already?" quiz questions covering the material in those headings so you can assess your knowledge of these specific areas. The answers to the "Do I Know This Already?" quiz appear in Appendix A, "Answers to the 'Do I Know This Already?' Quizzes and Q&A Questions."

Table 16-1 "Do I Know This Already?" Foundation Topics Section-to-Question Mapping

Foundation Topics Section	Questions
Storage Spaces Direct	1–3
Disaggregated and Hyper-Converged Storage Spaces Direct	4, 5

CAUTION The goal of self-assessment is to gauge your mastery of the topics in this chapter. If you do not know the answer to a question or are only partially sure of the answer, you should mark your answer as incorrect for purposes of the self-assessment. Giving yourself credit for an answer you correctly guess skews your self-assessment results and might provide you with a false sense of security.

1. What edition of Server 2016 do you need for Storage Spaces Direct?

    a. Enterprise

    b. Datacenter

    c. Standard

    d. Advanced

2. How many nodes can take part in Storage Spaces Direct?

    a. 8

    b. 16

    c. 32

    d. 64

3. Which of the following is true about Storage Spaces Direct?

    a. Disks can be partitioned.

    b. You should use a minimum of six drives.

    c. You can have RAID running already on the disks.

    d. You should have at least four SSDs.

4. What clusters are used in disaggregated Storage Spaces Direct? Choose two.

    a. SoFS

    b. File Server

    c. App Server

    d. Hyper-V

5. What is the scenario called when the Hyper-V cluster and the storage are one?

    a. Hyper-converged

    b. Disaggregated

    c. Scale in cluster

    d. Combined

Foundation Topics

Storage Spaces Direct

Thanks to Storage Spaces Direct (S2D), in clustered Windows Server 2016 environments you can enjoy the same type of storage virtualization you enjoy in Windows 10 and Windows Server 2016. Storage can be standard Serial Attached SCSI (SAS), Serial Advanced Technology Attachment (SATA), or Non-Volatile Memory Express (NVMe) drives instead of expensive external storage arrays that are typical for shared clustered storage.

Storage Spaces Direct offers the following features:

- **Storage for Hyper-V and Microsoft Azure Stack**: The primary use cases for Storage Spaces Direct are storage for Hyper-V VMs and storage for Azure Stack; this chapter focuses on Hyper-V VMs; Azure Stack is a new hybrid cloud platform product that enables an organization to deliver Azure services from its own datacenter in a way that is consistent with Azure.

- **Hardware flexibility**: As previously mentioned, Storage Spaces Direct makes it possible to build highly available and scalable storage solutions using modern storage hardware like SATA SSD for lower cost and NVMe SSD for better performance and less CPU overhead; S2D can also use an RDMA-enabled network infrastructure for low-latency storage with less CPU overhead than with traditional Ethernet.

- **Prescriptive configurations**: Microsoft works closely with hardware partners to define and validate prescriptive server configurations for Storage Spaces Direct.

- **Varied storage configuration support**: There are numerous configuration options, including the following:

  - SSDs with traditional hard drives, where the SSDs are used as a read/write cache to accelerate I/O performance

  - All-flash configurations with NVMe SSDs and SATA SSDs for extremely high I/O performance

  - Three tiers of physical storage: NVMe SSDs, SATA SSDs, and traditional hard drives

- **Flexible deployment options**: As described in detail later in this chapter, there are two main deployment options: aggregating the Hyper-V and storage clusters into one hyper-converged cluster or disaggregating the clusters.

- **Fault tolerance**: Storage Spaces Direct is resilient to drive failures and supports three fault domain types: server, chassis, and rack.

- **Accelerated erasure coding**: Storage Spaces Direct introduces hybrid volumes, which mixes the best of mirror (performance) with the best of erasure coding (efficiency) into a single volume with automatic real-time storage tiering.

- **Efficient VM checkpoints**: S2D utilizes the new ReFSv2 file system, which combines with Hyper-V for quick and efficient VM checkpoints with little overhead and storage I/O.

- **Scalability**: Storage Spaces Direct can scale from 2 to 16 servers; you can add servers as needed, and data can be rebalanced to best utilize the additional resources.

- **Health Service**: S2D includes an intelligent built-in diagnostic engine, Health Service, that makes it possible for administrators with limited technical ability to monitor and operate the system day to day.

It is important that you understand the components that make up the new Storage Spaces Direct architecture. Figure 16-1 shows them.

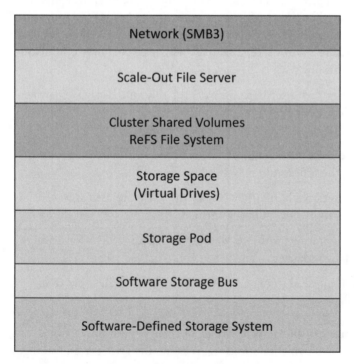

Figure 16-1   The Storage Spaces Direct Architecture

Determining Scenario Requirements for Implementing Storage Spaces Direct

Storage Spaces Direct offers many of the same benefits as Storage Spaces, such as data redundancy and tiered storage. Just like its older sibling, Storage Spaces, S2D does this in software, using standard, off-the-shelf disk drives and common networking components. This is not to say that S2D does not have any special requirements, however.

The following are some of the factors you must consider before deploying an S2D cluster:

- You find Storage Spaces Direct only in the Datacenter Edition of Windows Server 2016, not the Standard Edition; you can use S2D on a Datacenter Edition server with any of the installation options, including Server Core and Nano Server, as well as the full Desktop Experience.

- A Storage Spaces Direct cluster can consist of as many as 16 nodes, with up to 400 drives.

- Despite the capability of S2D to function with standard components, the servers in the cluster must be able to support large numbers of drives; there must also be support for multiple network interfaces.

- The recommended drive configuration for a node in an S2D cluster is a minimum of six drives, with at least two solid-state drives (SSDs) and at least four hard disk drives (HDDs).

- Whatever the form factor of the drive enclosure, internal or external, there must not be any RAID or any other such disk intelligence.

- For S2D to detect and use the disks, you must initialize them (typically using the GUID Partition Table [GPT] mode); you cannot partition these disks, however.

The key to Storage Spaces Direct is the software storage bus, a logical network conduit that connects the local data drives in all the cluster nodes. This bus theoretically falls between the servers and the disk drives inside them.

Because S2D creates a pool out of the internal storage in different computers, the server carries all storage traffic over standard Ethernet networks, using Server Message Block (SMB) 3.0 and Remote Direct Memory Access (RDMA). There is no traditional storage network fabric, such as SAS or Fibre Channel. This eliminates the distance limitations and the need for different types of cabling. Traffic management is therefore a critical part of any production S2D cluster deployment.

The physical realization of the logical software storage bus must transfer data as though the disks in the various cluster node are a single entity. In addition, the networks must carry the redundant data generated by the mirroring and parity arrangements on virtual disks created from the pool. Efficient S2D performance needs intra-node Ethernet communications that offer both high bandwidth and low latency.

At the physical layer, Microsoft recommends the use of at least two 10-Gbps Ethernet adapters per node. You should target adapters that use RDMA so that they can offload some of the processor burden from the servers.

As mentioned a moment ago, S2D uses SMB 3.0 for communication between cluster nodes. Storage Spaces Direct takes advantage of the protocol's advanced features, such as SMB Direct and SMB Multichannel. For a discussion of more of the advanced features of SMB 3.0, see Chapter 15, "Managing Failover Clustering."

Enabling Storage Spaces Direct Using Windows PowerShell

Most of the deployment process for a cluster using Storage Spaces Direct is the same as for any other cluster.

You perform the following steps:

Step 1. Install Windows Server 2016 on the cluster nodes.

Step 2. Update them identically.

Step 3. Add the Failover Clustering feature.

Step 4. Add the Hyper-V node.

Step 5. Create the cluster.

While you can use the graphical user interface of the Create Cluster Wizard in Failover Cluster Manager, you must prevent the system from automatically searching for and adding storage. Therefore, you should create the cluster in Windows PowerShell, using the **New-Cluster** cmdlet, which has the following syntax:

```
New-Cluster [-Name] <String> [-AdministrativeAccessPoint
  <AdminAccessPoint> {None | ActiveDirectoryAndDns | Dns |
  ActiveDirectory} ] [-Force] [-IgnoreNetwork <StringCollection>
  ] [-Node <StringCollection> ] [-NoStorage] [-S2D] [-StaticAddress
  <StringCollection> ] [ <CommonParameters>]
```

Here is an example of this cmdlet in use:

```
new-cluster -name MYCLUSTER1 -node server1,server2,server3,server4 -
  nostorage
```

The **NoStorage** parameter is important here, and the lack of storage generates an error during the creation of the cluster. You add the storage when you enable Storage Spaces Direct. To do this, you run the **Enable-ClusterStorageSpacesDirect** cmdlet without any parameters, as follows:

```
enable-clusterstoragespacesdirect
```

Here is the complete syntax of this cmdlet:

```
Enable-ClusterStorageSpacesDirect [-PoolFriendlyName <String>]
  [-Autoconfig <Boolean>] [-CacheState <CacheStateType>]
  [-CacheMetadataReserveBytes <UInt64>] [-CachePageSizeKBytes
  <UInt32>] [-SkipEligibilityChecks] [-CimSession <CimSession[]>]
  [-ThrottleLimit <Int32>] [-AsJob] [-WhatIf] [-Confirm]
  [<CommonParameters>]
```

This important cmdlet performs several tasks that are crucial to the S2D deployment, including the following:

- Finds disks

- Creates caches

- Creates a pool

Once Windows Server 2016 creates the storage pool, you can proceed to create the virtual disks you require (just as you do in Storage Spaces in Server Manager on a standalone server).

In Failover Cluster Manager, you select the storage pool and launch the New Virtual Disk Wizard (Storage Spaces Direct). In the wizard, you specify a size and then create a disk using the default two-way mirror resiliency setting. S2D virtual disks can support simple, mirror, and parity resiliency types, as well as customized storage tiers.

For more flexibility in creating virtual disks, you can use the **New-Volume** cmdlet in Windows PowerShell. This cmdlet can perform, in one step, tasks that at one time required several separate operations, including the following:

Step 1.   Create, partition, and format the virtual disk.

Step 2.   Convert it to the CSVFS file system.

Step 3.   Add it to the cluster.

Here is the complete syntax of the **New-Volume** cmdlet when used in conjunction with Storage Pools:

```
New-Volume [-StoragePool] <CimInstance> -FriendlyName <String>
  [-FileSystem <FileSystemType>] [-AccessPath <String>]
  [-DriveLetter <Char>] [-AllocationUnitSize <UInt32>] [-Size
  <UInt64>] [-ResiliencySettingName <String>] [-ProvisioningType
  <ProvisioningType>] [-MediaType <MediaType>]
  [-PhysicalDiskRedundancy <UInt16>] [-NumberOfColumns <UInt16>]
  [-NumberOfGroups <UInt16>] [-StorageTiers <CimInstance[]>]
  [-StorageTierFriendlyNames <String[]>] [-StorageTierSizes
  <UInt64[]>] [-WriteCacheSize <UInt64>] [-ReadCacheSize <UInt64>]
  [-UseMaximumSize] [-CimSession <CimSession>] [-ThrottleLimit
  <Int32>] [-AsJob] [<CommonParameters>]
```

For example, to create a virtual disk named **MYDISK** that uses parity resiliency and two tiers, with the default friendly names FAST for SSDs and SLOW for HDDs, you can use a command like the following:

```
new-volume -storagepool "s2d*" -friendlyname MYDISK -filesystem
  csvfs_refs-resiliencysettingname parity -storagetiersfriendlynames
  FAST, SLOW -storagetiersizes 100gb, 900gb
```

Once you have created the virtual disks, you can add them to cluster shared volumes. This makes them accessible in every node, of course.

Disaggregated and Hyper-Converged Storage Spaces Direct

This section presents two common scenarios for S2D. These are the disaggregated and hyper-converged Storage Spaces Direct implementations.

Implementing a Disaggregated Storage Spaces Direct Scenario in a Cluster

Microsoft designed Storage Spaces Direct for Hyper-V clusters. Specifically, there are two scenarios Microsoft had in mind. The first scenario is a disaggregated deployment. It features two distinct clusters. The first is a Scale-Out File Server cluster that uses Storage Spaces Direct. This cluster provides the storage for a second cluster. This is a Hyper-V cluster hosting virtual machines.

With this disaggregated Storage Spaces Direct scenario, the function of the S2D cluster is to provide the storage that the Hyper-V cluster needs for its virtual machines. You can envision the S2D cluster as a replacement for the Storage Area Network (SAN).

Because it needs two separate clusters, this model requires more servers and is more expensive to implement than the hyper-converged Storage Spaces Direct scenario. However, the advantage to this type of deployment is that the S2D cluster and the Hyper-V cluster can scale independently.

Storage Spaces Direct creates a highly scalable environment in which you can add drives to the nodes or add nodes to the cluster. Either way, S2D assimilates any new storage detected into the pool. In this disaggregated deployment, you can add storage to the S2D cluster without affecting the Hyper-V cluster. Similarly, you can add nodes to the Hyper-V cluster without affecting the storage infrastructure.

To implement the disaggregated deployment model, you perform the following:

Step 1.   Create a cluster.

Step 2.   Enable Storage Spaces Direct.

Step 3.   Create virtual disks.

Step 4.   Add the virtual disks to CSVs.

Step 5.   Add the Scale-Out File Server (SoFS) role to complete the configuration of the storage cluster.

Step 6.   Create the second cluster—a standard Hyper-V cluster that uses the shares offered by the SoFS cluster to store its virtual machines.

> **NOTE**   Some sources term this disaggregated scenario *converged* to distinguish it from the other deployment scenario, *hyper-converged*. This text and your exam prefer the term *disaggregated*.

Implementing a Hyper-Converged Storage Spaces Direct Scenario in a Cluster

Microsoft calls the second Storage Spaces Direct scenario hyper-converged. This is a fitting name because it combines Storage Services Direct with Hyper-V in a single cluster. This scenario offers the following benefits:

- Less hardware
- Less network traffic
- Less expense
- Less maintenance
- No need to configure file server permissions
- No need to monitor two clusters

Of course, the major drawback to this scenario is that you cannot scale the SoFS and Hyper-V services independently. If you want to add a server to offer more storage to the pool, you must add a node to the Hyper-V cluster as well.

Exam Preparation Tasks

As mentioned in the section "How to Use This Book" in the Introduction, you have a couple choices for exam preparation: the exercises here, Chapter 21, "Final Preparation," and the exam simulation questions in the Pearson Test Prep Software Online.

Review All Key Topics

Review the most important topics in this chapter, noted with the Key Topics icon in the outer margin of the page. Table 16-2 lists these key topics and the page number on which each is found.

Table 16-2   Key Topics for Chapter 16

Key Topic Element	Description	Page Number
List	Requirements for S2D	279
Steps	Enabling Storage Spaces Direct	280
Example	Storage Spaces Direct creation	280

Complete Tables and Lists from Memory

There are no memory tables in this chapter.

Define Key Terms

Define the following key terms from this chapter and check your answers against the glossary:

Storage Spaces Direct

Q&A

The answers to these questions appear in Appendix A. For more practice with exam format questions, use the Pearson Test Prep Software Online.

1. Name three requirements for S2D.

2. What PowerShell cmdlet allows you to implement S2D?

This chapter covers the following subjects:

- **Moving VMs**: This part of the chapter examines live migrations, quick migrations, and storage migrations.

- **More VM Management**: This section examines importing, exporting, and copying VMs as well as the features Network Health Protection and Drain on Shutdown.

## CHAPTER 17

Managing VM Movement

The ability to quickly and efficiently move VMs is a very powerful part of a high-availability (HA) solution. This chapter explores this important topic in detail.

"Do I Know This Already?" Quiz

The "Do I Know This Already?" quiz allows you to assess whether you should read the entire chapter. Table 17-1 lists the major headings in this chapter and the "Do I Know This Already?" quiz questions covering the material in those headings so you can assess your knowledge of these specific areas. The answers to the "Do I Know This Already?" quiz appear in Appendix A, "Answers to the 'Do I Know This Already?' Quizzes and Q&A Questions."

Table 17-1 "Do I Know This Already?" Foundation Topics Section-to-Question Mapping

Foundation Topics Section	Questions
Moving VMs	1, 2
More VM Management	3, 4

CAUTION The goal of self-assessment is to gauge your mastery of the topics in this chapter. If you do not know the answer to a question or are only partially sure of the answer, you should mark your answer as incorrect for purposes of the self-assessment. Giving yourself credit for an answer you correctly guess skews your self-assessment results and might provide you with a false sense of security.

1. What PowerShell cmdlet allows you to set a VM for high availability?

   a. **Add-VMHA**

   b. **Add-ClusterVMHA**

   c. **Add-ClusterVirtualMachineRole**

   d. **Add-ClusterVM**

2. Which of the following is a useful feature of Quick Migration that Live Migration does not offer?

   a. Moving a VM and the storage at the same time

   b. Moving a VM with no pause at all

   c. Moving a stopped VM

   d. Moving a running VM

3. What PowerShell cmdlet performs the export of a VM?

   a. **Export-VM**

   b. **Send-VM**

   c. **Place-VM**

   d. **Set-VMNode**

4. What Drain on Shutdown status code means enabled?

   a. 0

   b. 1

   c. 2

   d. 3

Foundation Topics

Moving VMs

A critical administrative task in the modern datacenter is moving virtual machines (VMs). It is important to be able to move VMs themselves and their storage quickly and efficiently. The following sections review how to do this and elaborate on parts of the process not covered elsewhere in this text.

Performing a Live Migration

When you create a Virtual Machine role on a cluster, you create the VM and then configure it for high availability using the High Availability Wizard or the **Add-ClusterVirtualMachineRole** PowerShell cmdlet. When you do so, you enable Live Migration for the role.

Here is the complete syntax of the **Add-ClusterVirtualMachineRole** cmdlet:

```
Add-ClusterVirtualMachineRole [[-VMName] <String> ] [-Cluster <String>
] [-InputObject <PSObject> ] [-Name <String> ] [-VirtualMachine
<String> ] [-VMId <Guid> ] [ <CommonParameters>]
```

There is no need to manually configure the Hyper-V server to enable Live Migration or select an authentication protocol. Once you create the virtual machine in the cluster, performing a live migration is simply a matter of right-clicking the VM on the **Roles** page and, from the context menu, selecting **Move** and then **Live Migration**. You can let the cluster choose the best node or select any of the nodes in the cluster as the target.

To start a live migration in PowerShell, you use the **Move-ClusterVirtualMachineRole** cmdlet, as in the following example:

```
Move-ClusterVirtualMachineRole -name MYCLUSTER1 -node server2
```

Here is the complete syntax for the cmdlet:

```
Move-ClusterVirtualMachineRole [[-Name] <String> ] [[-Node] <String>
] [-Cancel] [-Cluster <String> ] [-IgnoreLocked] [-InputObject
<PSObject> ] [-MigrationType <NativeGroupHelp+VmMigrationType>
{TurnOff | Quick | Shutdown | ShutdownForce | Live} ] [-VMId <Guid> ]
[-Wait <Int32> ] [ <CommonParameters>]
```

Performing a Quick Migration

Even though Live Migration is king, Windows Server 2016 still includes Quick Migration. Quick Migration is still useful in some situations. One nice feature of a quick migration is that the VM does not need to be running, as it does with a live migration.

Unfortunately, moving VMs with Quick Migration is not instantaneous, as it is with Live Migration. There is a very brief pause in processing. Just as with a live migration, the data files do not move during a quick migration. In practice, administrators typically use Quick Migration only when they cannot perform a live migration.

A quick migration of a running Virtual Machine role proceeds as follows:

1. The cluster pauses the Virtual Machine role, suspending the I/O and CPU functions of the VM.

2. The cluster saves the source VM's memory contents and system state to shared storage and places the VM into the Saved state.

3. The cluster copies the symbolic link specifying the location of the source VM's files to the destination node and transfers ownership of the source VM's files to the destination VM.

4. The cluster removes the symbolic link from the source VM.

5. The cluster resumes the role from the Saved state, copying the memory contents and the system state from shared storage to the destination VM, now running on the destination node.

The fundamental difference between Quick Migration and Live Migration is that Quick Migration copies the VM's memory first to disk and then from disk to the destination, whereas Live Migration copies the memory directly from the source to the destination. The length of the pause in a quick migration depends on the size of the VM's memory and the performance of the storage subsystem.

The only data copied directly from the source to the destination VM is the tiny symbolic link.

When the VM stops, a quick migration needs only the transfer of the symbolic link from the source to the destination. In this case, the process is instantaneous.

The effect of the pause on the clustered role depends on the applications running on the VM. Some applications can recover easily from a pause of a few seconds, while others might not.

The process of performing a quick migration is almost identical to the process of performing a live migration. You right-click the VM on the Roles page and, from the context menu, select Move and then Quick Migration, and then you choose the desired destination node. As the migration proceeds, you can see the role enter the Saved state and then the Starting state as the role is resumed.

Performing a Storage Migration

Live Migration and Quick Migration move the memory contents and the system state from one virtual machine to another. They do not move the virtual hard disk files that the VM uses to store its operating system, application files, and data.

In a failover cluster, these files should be placed on shared storage, so the destination VM already has access to them. Storage Migration has the opposite effect: It moves a VM's virtual hard disk files but not its memory and system state.

There are few limitations on Storage Migration:

- The virtual machine does not have to be part of a cluster, so you see it implemented in Hyper-V as well as Failover Clustering.

- On a standalone Hyper-V server, you can move the files to any destination you have permission to access, including a different location on the same computer. This is helpful because it updates the VM with the new locations of the files as it migrates them.

In Hyper-V, you use the Move Wizard to perform storage migrations, but you can also use a tool in Failover Cluster Manager. When you right-click a virtual machine cluster role and click Move and then Virtual Machine Storage, the Move Virtual Machine Storage dialog box appears. In this dialog box, you can select any of the virtual machine's stored resources—including individual VHD and VHDX files, checkpoints, and smart paging files—and you can drag and drop them to a location anywhere in cluster storage. A new Destination Folder Path value appears, specifying where the tool will move the file. When you have selected destinations for all the files you want to move, you can click the Start button to close the dialog box and begin the storage migration process.

More VM Management

There are a few VM management tasks we have not explored yet in this chapter. These include importing, exporting, and copying VMs, and the Health Protection and Drain on-Shutdown features. The following sections cover these important tasks.

Importing, Exporting, and Copying VMs

In Hyper-V, you need to export and import VMs for a variety of useful purposes. Hyper-V Manager offers access to an Export Virtual Machine dialog box and an Import Virtual Machine Wizard, but Failover Cluster Manager has no such interface.

You can use the **Export-VM** and **Import-VM** cmdlets in Windows PowerShell to effectively clone a clustered virtual machine. To export a virtual machine, running or stopped, you use the **Export-VM** cmdlet as follows:

```
Export-VM -name myclustervm1 -path z:\vm
```

Here is the complete syntax of the **Export-VM** cmdlet:

```
Export-VM [-CimSession <CimSession[]>] [-ComputerName <String[]>]
  [-Credential <PSCredential[]>] [-Name] <String[]> [-Path] <String>
  [-AsJob] [-Passthru] [-CaptureLiveState <CaptureLiveState>]
  [-WhatIf] [-Confirm] [<CommonParameters>]
```

You can run the cmdlet from any node in the cluster, but if you specify a local, unshared disk for the **-Path** parameter, the VM exports to the specified path on the node where it is running. Obviously, specifying shared storage for the **-Path** value is preferred.

To import the virtual machine into the Hyper-V host, you copy the files to the host's default folders and generate a new security identifier (SID) for the VM. To prevent conflicts, you can use the **Import-VM** cmdlet in the following manner:

```
Import-VM -path "z:\vm\virtual machines\
  5ae40946-3a98-428e-8c83-081a3c68d17a.xml" -copy -generatenewid
```

Here is the complete syntax for the **Import-VM** cmdlet:

```
Import-VM [-CimSession <CimSession[]>] [-ComputerName <String[]>]
  [-Credential <PSCredential[]>] [-Path] <String>
  [[-VhdDestinationPath] <String>] [-Copy] [-VirtualMachinePath
  <String>] [-SnapshotFilePath <String>] [-SmartPagingFilePath
  <String>] [-VhdSourcePath <String>] [-GenerateNewId] [-AsJob]
  [-WhatIf] [-Confirm] [<CommonParameters>]
```

When the process is complete, you have a new virtual machine on that host. If you configure the Hyper-V host to store VM files on shared storage by default, you can then use Failover Cluster Manager to add that VM as a Virtual Machine role and configure it for high availability.

Configuring VM Network Health Protection

Network Health Protection is a feature that detects whether a VM on a cluster node has a functional connection to a designated network. If it does not, the cluster automatically live migrates the VM role to another node that does have a connection to that network.

Without this feature, clustered virtual machines can lose contact with the network and continue to run as though nothing is wrong. If the problem is a simple one, such as an unplugged cable, other nodes in the cluster might still have access to that network, and migrating the VM to one of those nodes can keep it operational until you repair the network fault.

Windows Server 2016 enables Network Health Protection by default, but there are situations in which you might not want a live migration to occur automatically. For example, if you configure the cluster nodes with connections to redundant networks, you might not want live migrations to occur in response to one network's failure.

To control whether Network Health Protection applies, open the Settings dialog box for the VM, either in Failover Cluster Manager or Hyper-V Manager, and expand the network adapter offering the connection to the network in question to display the Advanced Features option, as shown in Figure 17-1.

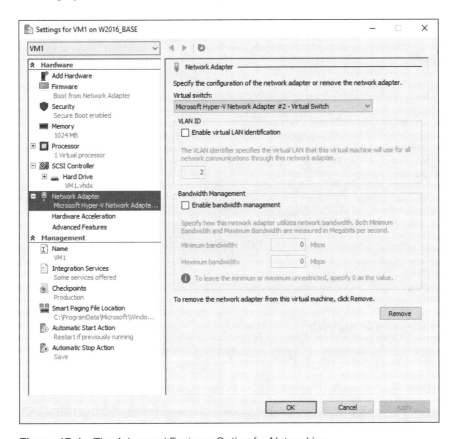

Figure 17-1   The Advanced Features Option for Networking

Select the Advanced Features option to view its settings. When you clear the Protected Network check box, you prevent live migrations from occurring due to faults detected on that network. Figure 17-2 shows this.

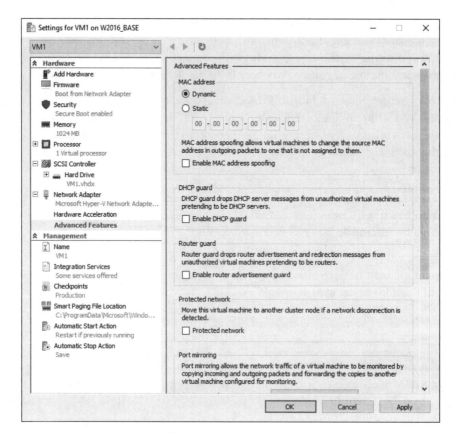

Figure 17-2 Disabling the VM Network Health Protection Feature

Configuring Drain on Shutdown

When you want to shut down a cluster node holding VMs for maintenance or any other reason, the proper procedure is to drain the roles off the node (that is, live migrate them to other nodes) before you shut down the machine.

In Failover Cluster Manager, you do this by selecting a node and clicking Pause and then Drain Roles in the Actions pane. If you click the Roles tab at the bottom of the page, you should see that each one is live migrated to another node in the cluster.

In PowerShell, you can drain a node by using the **Suspend-ClusterNode** cmdlet. Here is the complete syntax for this cmdlet:

```
Suspend-ClusterNode [[-Name] <StringCollection> ] [[-TargetNode]
<String> ] [-Cluster <String> ] [-Drain] [-ForceEvacuation]
[-InputObject <PSObject> ] [-Wait] [ <CommonParameters>]
```

At one time, if you did not drain the node and just shut it down with the roles running, Windows Server 2016 placed the roles into a Saved state, causing a service outage until the VMs could be moved to another node and resumed.

Now, Windows Server 2016 Failover Clustering includes a feature called Drain on Shutdown, which automatically live migrates all the roles on a node before shutting down the system.

It is worth noting, however, that Microsoft still recommends pausing a node and draining it before initiating a shutdown.

Drain on Shutdown is enabled by default, as you can tell by running the **(Get-Cluster).DrainOnShutdown** command. The value **1** indicates that the feature is enabled, and **0** indicates disabled. To disable Drain on Shutdown, you therefore use the following command:

```
(get-cluster).drainonshutdown = 0
```

Exam Preparation Tasks

As mentioned in the section "How to Use This Book" in the Introduction, you have a couple choices for exam preparation: the exercises here, Chapter 21, "Final Preparation," and the exam simulation questions in the Pearson Test Prep Software Online.

Review All Key Topics

Review the most important topics in this chapter, noted with the Key Topics icon in the outer margin of the page. Table 17-2 lists these key topics and the page number on which each is found.

Table 17-2 Key Topics for Chapter 17

Key Topic Element	Description	Page Number
Command	Enabling the Live Migration role	289
Steps	The quick migration process	290
Command	Verifying Drain on Shutdown	295

Complete Tables and Lists from Memory

There are no memory tables in this chapter.

Define Key Terms

Define the following key terms from this chapter and check your answers against the glossary:

Quick Migration, Storage Migration, Network Health Protection, Drain on Shutdown

Q&A

The answers to these questions appear in Appendix A. For more practice with exam format questions, use the Pearson Test Prep Software Online.

1. What are the main differences between a live migration and a quick migration?

2. Where in the network adapter properties do you find the Network Health Protection option?

This chapter covers the following subjects:

- **Installing and Configuring NLB**: In this section, you see how to install and configure Network Load Balancing (NLB) prerequisites and NLB itself.

- **More NLB Configurations**: This section examines affinity, port rules, cluster operation mode, and upgrading an NLB cluster.

## CHAPTER 18

Network Load Balancing (NLB)

Are you ready to do more than just provide failover with your Windows Server 2016 cluster? How about distributing the load between nodes? This is the job of Network Load Balancing (NLB).

"Do I Know This Already?" Quiz

The "Do I Know This Already?" quiz allows you to assess whether you should read the entire chapter. Table 18-1 lists the major headings in this chapter and the "Do I Know This Already?" quiz questions covering the material in those headings so you can assess your knowledge of these specific areas. The answers to the "Do I Know This Already?" quiz appear in Appendix A, "Answers to the 'Do I Know This Already?' Quizzes and Q&A Questions."

Table 18-1 "Do I Know This Already?" Foundation Topics Section-to-Question Mapping

Foundation Topics Section	Questions
Install and Configure NLB	1, 2
More NLB Configurations	3, 4

CAUTION The goal of self-assessment is to gauge your mastery of the topics in this chapter. If you do not know the answer to a question or are only partially sure of the answer, you should mark your answer as incorrect for purposes of the self-assessment. Giving yourself credit for an answer you correctly guess skews your self-assessment results and might provide you with a false sense of security.

1. Which of the following is not a valid prerequisite for NLB?

    a. All hosts in the cluster must have DHCP assigned addresses.

    b. All hosts should possess an identical user account.

    c. All hosts connect to the same subnet.

    d. There must be support for up to 32 hosts.

2. After you install the NLB feature, what management tool is available from Server Manager?

    a Network Load Balancing Manager

    b. Application Balancing Manager

    c. Storage Manager

    d. Cluster Manager

3. Which of the following is not a port filtering rule in NLB?

    a. Disable

    b. Single

    c Cluster Only

    d. Multiple Host

4. What upgrade type for an NLB cluster provides the least downtime?

    a. Dynamic upgrade

    b. Static upgrade

    c. Rolling upgrade

    d. Simultaneous upgrade

Foundation Topics

Installing and Configuring NLB

How do you get ready for a Network Load Balancing cluster, and how do you install one? The following sections tell all.

Configuring NLB Prerequisites

Keep these key facts in mind about a Network Load Balancing (NLB) cluster:

- It can consist of 2 to 32 servers (hosts). (Note that you do not call them *nodes*.)

- Each host runs a separate copy of the desired application. NLB uses TCP/IP addressing to send incoming client requests to the different hosts and balance the load among them. NLB is best suited for stateless applications, such as web servers, with variable client loads.

- As traffic increases, it is possible to add hosts to the cluster to increase its capacity.

- You can easily remove hosts as needed when client requests diminish. NLB hosts exchange messages called *heartbeats* once a second. Heartbeats are critical, allowing hosts to track the availability of other hosts; when the heartbeats from a single host stop for a given length of time, the other hosts remove that host from the cluster.

- Any time a cluster adds or removes a host, the NLB cluster performs a process known as *convergence*. During convergence, the cluster evaluates current cluster membership and determines how the cluster should distribute client requests. The NLB cluster has its own virtual identity on the network, with a name and IP address that clients use to connect to the application; note that this is a common service model today: You connect to an Internet resource and access content from one of any number of nodes in a cluster.

The NLB cluster is actually much simpler than the failover clusters to which you are accustomed. Because the applications needed run on all hosts, there is no need for a quorum and other such complications.

The main features of NLB are as follows:

- Creating the NLB cluster requires no hardware changes.

- NLB tools allow you to configure and manage multiple clusters and all the hosts from a single remote or local computer.

- Clients can access a cluster by using a single, logical Internet name and virtual IP address, which is known as the cluster IP address. NLB allows multiple virtual IP addresses for multihomed servers.

- NLB can be bound to multiple network adapters, which enables you to configure multiple independent clusters on each host. Support for multiple network adapters differs from virtual clusters in that virtual clusters allow you to configure multiple clusters on a single network adapter.

- You do not need to make any modifications to server applications so that they can run in an NLB cluster.

- NLB can be configured to automatically add a host to the cluster if that cluster host fails and is subsequently brought back online. The added host can start handling new server requests from clients.

- You can take computers offline for preventive maintenance without disturbing the cluster operations on the other hosts.

Keep in mind these prerequisites for NLB:

- NLB clusters can support up to 32 hosts.

- In general, no shared storage or other specialized hardware is required for NLB.

- Unlike with a failover cluster, the computers you use to create NLB hosts need not be identical.

- All the hosts in an NLB cluster must be connected to the same subnet.

- Network latency must be minimized to allow the convergence process to proceed normally.

- To provide site-based fault tolerance, in the event of a large-scale disaster, best practice is to create separate NLB clusters at different locations and use another mechanism to distribute client requests between the two sites; DNS round-robin is a common practice.

- The NLB hosts can have as many network interface adapters as needed for other purposes, but the network adapters used for NLB must all use either multicast or unicast transmissions.

- While other versions of Windows Server support NLB, best practice is to have all the hosts in an NLB cluster run the same version and the same edition of Windows Server.

- All hosts in an NLB cluster must have static IP addresses.

- All hosts in an NLB cluster should have an identical user account, with membership in the local Administrators group, which the Network Load Balancing Manager uses to access them.

Installing NLB Nodes

Network Load Balancing, like Failover Clustering, is a feature included in Windows Server 2016. You must install the feature on all servers that will function as NLB hosts by using the Add Roles and Features Wizard in Server Manager. To do so, follow these steps:

Step 1. Launch **Server Manager** and choose **Manage > Add Roles and Features**.

Step 2. On the **Before You Begin** page, click **Next**.

Step 3. Choose **Role-based or Feature-based Installation** and then click **Next**.

Step 4. Select your local server from the **Select Destination Server** page and then click **Next**.

Step 5. On the **Server Roles** page, click **Next**.

Step 6. On the **Features** page, select **Network Load Balancing** (see Figure 18-1).

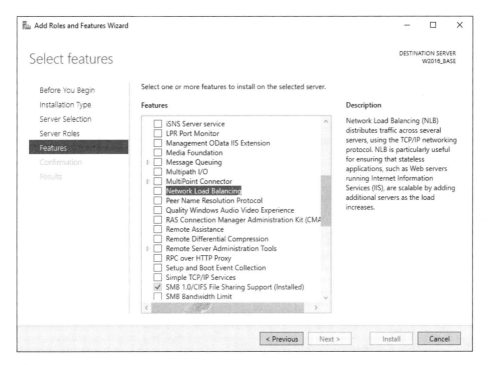

Figure 18-1 Installing NLB

Step 7. Click **Add Features** to include the management tools.

Step 8. Click **Next**.

Step 9. On the **Confirmation** page, click **Install**.

Step 10. Click **Close** when the installation completes.

You can also install Network Load Balancing by using the **Install-WindowsFeature** cmdlet in Windows PowerShell, as in this example:

```
install-windowsfeature -name nlb –includemanagementtools
```

Another option is to install the tools only on your workstation, so you can manage the NLB cluster remotely:

```
install-windowsfeature -name rsat-nlb
```

Here is the complete syntax of the **Install-WindowsFeature** cmdlet:

```
Install-WindowsFeature [-Name] <Feature[]> [-Restart]
  [-IncludeAllSubFeature] [-IncludeManagementTools] [-Source
  <String[]>] [-ComputerName <String>] [-Credential <PSCredential>]
  [-LogPath <String>] [-WhatIf] [-Confirm] [<CommonParameters>]
```

After NLB is installed, follow these steps:

Step 1. Launch the **Network Load Balancing Manager** console from the **Tools** menu in **Server Manager** (see Figure 18-2).

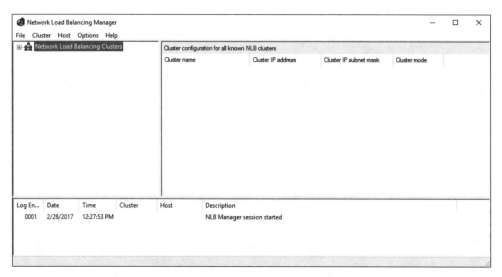

Figure 18-2 The Network Load Balancing Manager

Step 2. Select **Cluster > New**.

Step 3. On the **New Cluster: Connect** page, in the **Host** text box type the name of the first host you want to add to the cluster and then click **Connect**.

Step 4. Select the interface the host will use for the cluster.

Step 5.   On the **New Cluster: Host Parameters** page, select a value from the **Priority (Unique Host Identifier)** drop-down list, as shown in Figure 18-3. This value must be unique on each host you install; any traffic that does not conform to the port rules configured for the cluster will be forwarded to the host with the lowest priority value.

Figure 18-3   The **New Cluster: Host Parameters** Window

Step 6.   On the **New Cluster: Cluster IP Addresses** page, click **Add**.

Step 7.   In the **Add IP Address** dialog box, specify the **IPv4 Address** and **Subnet Mask** values that the cluster will use and click **OK**.

Step 8.   On the **New Cluster: Cluster Parameters** page, specify the **Full Internet Name** value for the cluster.

Step 9.   In the **Cluster Operation Mode** box, select one of the following values: **Unicast**, **Multicast**, or **IGMP Multicast**.

Step 10.   On the **New Cluster: Port Rules** page, click **Edit** to modify the default port rule.

Step 11.   In the **Add/Edit Port Rule** dialog box, modify the **Port Range** settings to specify the port(s) for the application the cluster will be running.

Step 12.   In the **Filtering Mode** area, select one of the options and click **OK** to revise the settings in the port rule.

Step 13.   Click **Finish**.

To add additional hosts to the cluster, select the server in the console and click **Cluster** and then **Add Host To Cluster**, as shown in Figure 18-4.

Figure 18-4   Adding Hosts to a Cluster

For each host you add, you must configure only the Connect, Host Parameters, and Port Rules pages. As you add each host, the cluster converges, and eventually all the hosts are recognized and incorporated into the cluster.

More NLB Configurations

As you might guess, many more configurations are possible for NLB, which is an important Windows Server 2016 feature. The following sections cover them.

Configuring Affinity

When you configure the Filtering Mode setting in a port rule, you specify how the cluster handles the traffic conforming to that port rule as follows:

- **Multiple Host**: Traffic conforming to that rule distributes among all the hosts of the cluster.

- **Single**: You are essentially using NLB as a failover cluster for that rule; only the host with the lowest priority value handles traffic for that rule.

- **Disable**: The cluster does not accept any traffic conforming to the rule.

To access these options, choose Cluster Properties from the Server options then choose the Port Rules tab. Figure 18-5 shows the filtering modes available in the Add/Edit Port Rules window.

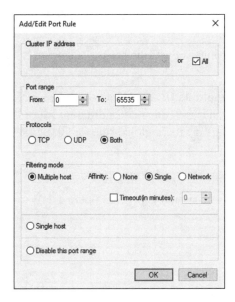

Figure 18-5   Filtering Modes

Some transactional traffic struggles with the Multiple Host setting. A great example is traffic that needs to be session-based, such as some e-commerce traffic. The Affinity settings for the Multiple Hosts option address this challenge.

You choose an Affinity setting to specify how the cluster should react to repeated requests from the same client. The available settings are as follows:

- **None**: Incoming requests from the same IP address can be handled by any host.

- **Single**: All traffic coming from a single IP address is sent to the same host.

- **Network**: All traffic originating from the same Class C network is sent to the same host.

Select the Timeout check box to specify the maximum amount of time that can pass between connections before the affinity rule no longer applies.

Configuring Port Rules

Port rules define what types of TCP/IP traffic the NLB cluster processes and the instructions for each type. When you first create a cluster, the default port rule admits traffic using all IP addresses and all ports. You can modify this rule as needed and create others to specify different settings for different types of traffic.

In addition to the Filter Mode and Affinity settings, a port rule has the following settings available (refer to Figure 18-5):

- **Cluster IP address**: A cluster can have multiple IP addresses, representing different services. By selecting a specific address, you create a different rule for each service; selecting the **All** check box creates a global rule for all the IP addresses in the cluster.

- **Port range**: A cluster can provide services that use different ports.

- **Protocols**: You can specify whether the rule should apply to TCP or UDP traffic.

Configuring Cluster Operation Mode

The Cluster operation mode setting in the cluster Properties dialog box determines what kind of TCP/IP traffic the cluster hosts should use (see Figure 18-6).

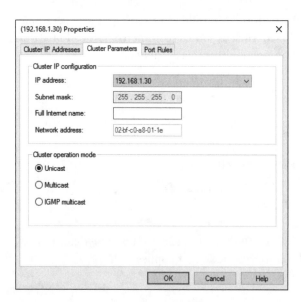

Figure 18-6   The Cluster Operation Mode Settings

Unicast is a TCP/IP transmission addressed for a single destination. Multicast is a transmission sent to multiple destinations, using a special multicast IP address. The MAC address is a unique 6-byte value encoded into network interface adapters at the factory. When you select the unicast mode for a cluster, NLB replaces the hardware MAC address on the interface you select for each host with the cluster's virtual MAC address. This causes traffic addressed to the cluster to go to all its hosts. This practice also confuses the network switches, which are unable to determine which port the cluster MAC address belongs to and therefore must forward the traffic out through all its ports, flooding the network in the process.

Unicast mode also prevents cluster hosts from communicating with each other using their designated cluster adapters. Because all the hosts use the same MAC address, outgoing traffic loops back and never reaches the network. You should therefore install a second network adapter in each host if you plan to use unicast mode and require normal communication between the hosts.

When you select the multicast option, NLB adds a second MAC address to the network interface on each host, which is a multicast MAC address that does not replace the original one. Because each host retains its unique MAC address, there is no need for a second network adapter. The multicast option also causes switch flooding, by default, but there are solutions for it. The IGMP multicast option uses Internet Group Management Protocol to program the switches so that traffic destined for the cluster's MAC address is only forwarded out through the switch ports connected to NLB hosts. You can also create a virtual local area network (VLAN) in the switch that achieves the same results.

Multicast mode is the preferable option, except in cases when the network hardware does not support multicast transmissions or the use of multicasts seriously diminishes cluster performance.

Upgrading an NLB Cluster

There are two ways to upgrade an existing Windows Server NLB cluster to the Windows Server 2016 version:

- **Simultaneous upgrade**: With this upgrade approach, you bring down the entire NLB cluster, upgrade all the hosts, and then bring up the cluster again. This entails a significant amount of downtime for the clustered application.

- **Rolling upgrade**: With this upgrade approach, you remove the hosts from the cluster, one at a time, upgrade each one, and then add each one back to the cluster. NLB accommodates the addition and removal of hosts, so the cluster converges each time you remove or add one of the servers.

Exam Preparation Tasks

As mentioned in the section "How to Use This Book" in the Introduction, you have a couple choices for exam preparation: the exercises here, Chapter 21, "Final Preparation," and the exam simulation questions in the Pearson Test Prep Software Online.

Review All Key Topics

Review the most important topics in this chapter, noted with the Key Topics icon in the outer margin of the page. Table 18-2 lists these key topics and the page number on which each is found.

Table 18-2   Key Topics for Chapter 18

Key Topic Element	Description	Page Number
List	NLB prerequisites	302
Steps	Completing the NLB install	304
List	The Affinity settings in NLB	307

Complete Tables and Lists from Memory

There are no memory tables in this chapter.

Define Key Terms

Define the following key terms from this chapter and check your answers against the glossary:

Network Load Balancing (NLB) Cluster, Affinity, Port Rules, Cluster Operation Mode, Simultaneous Upgrade, Rolling Upgrade

Q&A

The answers to these questions appear in Appendix A. For more practice with exam format questions, use the Pearson Test Prep Software Online.

1. What port filtering mode setting can benefit from affinity?

2. What affinity rule ensures that all traffic from the same IP address is sent to a single host?

This chapter covers the following subjects:

- **Windows Server Update Services:** This section examines WSUS in detail, including its implementation, the configuration of groups, and patch management.

- **Windows Defender:** This section covers the implementation of Windows Defender and how to integrate it with WSUS.

- **Backup and Restore:** This part of the chapter covers backup and restore operations using Windows Server Backup and covers backup strategies for different Windows Server roles and workloads.

## CHAPTER 19

Maintaining Servers

To keep your Windows Server 2016 machines running properly and to recover from potentially bad situations, you need to learn about updates, Windows Defender, and backups. This chapter covers these topics and more.

"Do I Know This Already?" Quiz

The "Do I Know This Already?" quiz allows you to assess whether you should read the entire chapter. Table 19-1 lists the major headings in this chapter and the "Do I Know This Already?" quiz questions covering the material in those headings so you can assess your knowledge of these specific areas. The answers to the "Do I Know This Already?" quiz appear in Appendix A, "Answers to the 'Do I Know This Already?' Quizzes and Q&A Questions."

Table 19-1 "Do I Know This Already?" Foundation Topics Section-to-Question Mapping

Foundation Topics Section	Questions
Windows Server Update Services	1, 2
Windows Defender	3, 4
Backup and Restore	5, 6

CAUTION The goal of self-assessment is to gauge your mastery of the topics in this chapter. If you do not know the answer to a question or are only partially sure of the answer, you should mark your answer as incorrect for purposes of the self-assessment. Giving yourself credit for an answer you correctly guess skews your self-assessment results and might provide you with a false sense of security.

1. What is the minimum hard disk space requirement for WSUS?

   a. 500 MB

   b. 1 GB

   c. 20 GB

   d. 100 GB

2. Where do you specify the WSUS location in Group Policy?

   a. Windows Server Update Services Location

   b. Internal Update Server

   c. Specify Intranet Microsoft Update Service Location

   d. WSUS Database

3. What management component is not typically used to control Windows Defender in a server environment?

   a. PowerShell

   b. WMI

   c. XML

   d. Group Policy

4. What method in a server environment permits the automatic download and installation of Windows Defender updates? Choose Three.

   a. Windows Update in Control Panel

   b. Group Policy

   c. AUOptions Registry Key

   d. WinDefend.exe

5. Which of the following destinations does Windows Server Backup support? Choose three.

   a. Internal hard drive

   b. Writable DVD

   c. Remote tape

   d. Network share

6. What type of Active Directory restore do you use if you are recovering a deleted AD object?

   a. Base restore

    b. Authoritative

   c. Nonauthoritative

   d. Partial restore

Foundation Topics

Windows Server Update Services

Windows Server Update Services (WSUS) permits you to deploy the latest Microsoft product updates in a more controlled and flexible manner than how clients and servers might ordinarily receive these enhancements. WSUS is a Windows Server role that you install to manage and distribute updates. A WSUS server can be the update source for other WSUS servers in an organization. The server that acts as an update source is an *upstream server*.

In a WSUS implementation, at least one WSUS server in the network must connect to Microsoft Update to get available update information.

Implementing Windows Server Update Services (WSUS) Solutions

 Here are the system requirements for WSUS:

- **Processor:** 1.4 gigahertz (GHz) x64 processor (2 GHz or faster is recommended).

- **Memory:** WSUS requires an additional 2 GB of RAM over what is required by the server and all other services or software.

- **Available disk space:** 20 GB (40 GB or greater is recommended).

- **Network adapter:** 100 megabits per second (Mbps) or greater.

The following are also required in some cases:

- For viewing reports, WSUS requires Microsoft Report Viewer Redistributable 2008.

- Microsoft .NET Framework 4.0 must be installed on the server where the WSUS server role will be installed.

- The account you plan to use to install WSUS must be a member of the Local Administrators group.

During the installation of WSUS, the following are also installed:

- .NET API and Windows PowerShell cmdlets
- Windows Internal Database (WID), which is used by WSUS
- Services used by WSUS, including the following:

    - Update service

    - Reporting web service

    - Client web service

    - Simple Web Authentication web service

    - Server Synchronization service

    - DSS Authentication web service

You can install the WSUS role on a computer that is separate from the database server computer. In this case, the following additional criteria apply:

- The database server cannot be configured as a domain controller.
- The WSUS server cannot run Remote Desktop Services.
- The database server must be in the same Active Directory domain as the WSUS server, or it must have a trust relationship with the Active Directory domain of the WSUS server.
- The WSUS server and the database server must be in the same time zone or must be synchronized to the same coordinated universal time (Greenwich Mean time) source.

To install the WSUS server role, follow these steps:

Step 1. Log on to the server on which you plan to install the WSUS server role by using an account that is a member of the Local Administrators group.

Step 2. In **Server Manager**, click **Manage > Roles and Features**.

Step 3. On the **Before you begin** page, click **Next**.

Step 4. In the **Select installation type** page, confirm that the **Role-based** or **feature-based installation** option is selected and click **Next**.

Step 5. On the **Select destination server** page, choose where the server is located (from a server pool or from a virtual hard disk) and then choose the server on which you want to install the WSUS server role and click **Next**.

Step 6. On the **Select server roles** page, select **Windows Server Update Services**, add features that are required for Windows Server Update Services, and click **Add Features**, as shown in Figure 19-1, and then click **Next**.

Figure 19-1 Adding Feature to the WSUS Install

Step 7. On the **Select features** page, keep the default selections and click **Next**.

Step 8. On the **Windows Server Update Services** page, click **Next**.

Step 9. On the **Select role services** page, leave the default selections and click **Next**.

Step 10. On the **Content location selection** page, type a valid location to store the updates, as shown in Figure 19-2, and click **Next**.

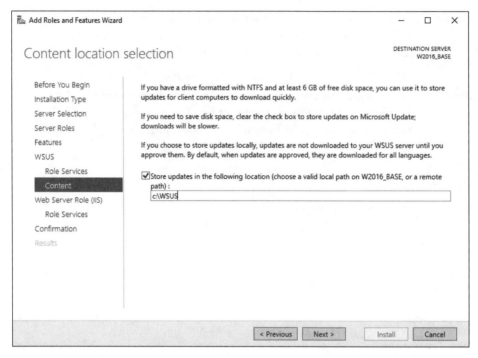

Figure 19-2   Providing a Storage Location for the Updates

Step 11.   On the **Web Server Role (IIS)** page that appears, review the information and then click **Next**.

> **NOTE**   WSUS only needs the default Web Server role configuration. If you are prompted for added Web Server role configuration while setting up WSUS, you can safely accept the default values and continue setting up WSUS. If you plan to install SQL Server for WSUS support, you must select that option here.

Step 12.   On the **Select the role services to install for Web Server (IIS)** page, keep the defaults and click **Next**.

Step 13.   On the **Confirm installation selections** page, review the selected options and click **Install**.

Step 14.   Once WSUS installation is complete, in the results window on the **Installation progress** page, click the **Launch Post-Installation** tasks link, as shown in Figure 19-3.

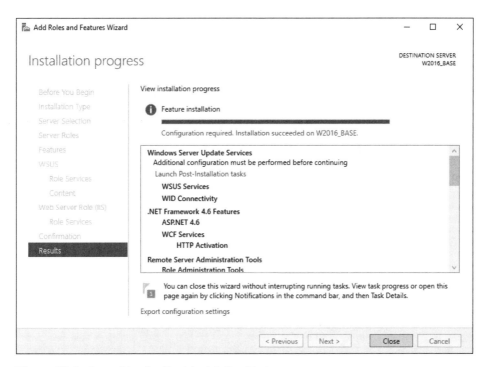

Figure 19-3   Launching the Post-installation Tasks

Step 15.   Click **Close**.

Configuring WSUS Groups

Computer groups are an important part of WSUS deployments. Computer groups allow you to test and target updates to specific computers. There are two default computer groups:

- All computers
- Unassigned computers

By default, when each client computer first contacts the WSUS server, the server adds that client computer to both groups.

You can create as many custom computer groups as you need to manage updates in your organization. It is a best practice to create at least one computer group to test updates before you deploy the updates to other computers.

Use the following steps to complete the configuration of WSUS, create a new group, and assign a computer to this group:

Step 1.   In **Server Manager,** select **Tools > WSUS Administration Console**.

Step 2.   On the **Before You Begin** page of the Configuration Wizard, click **Next**.

Step 3.   Decide whether to join the **Microsoft Update Improvement Program** and click **Next**.

Step 4.   In the **Choose Upstream Server** dialog, shown in Figure 19-4, choose the upstream server to sync from or use the Microsoft Update Internet service.

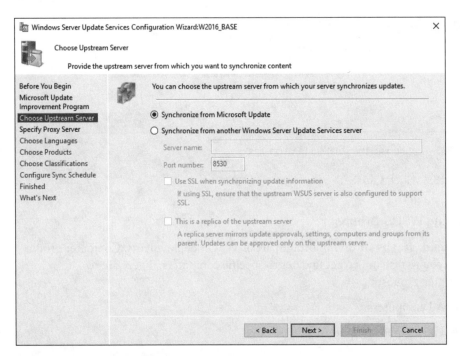

Figure 19-4   Selecting the Upstream Server

Step 5.   On the **Specify the Proxy Server** page, configure any required proxy server settings and click **Next**.

Step 6.   On the **Connect to Upstream Server** page, choose **Start Connecting** in order to contact the upstream server. Completing this process could take a few minutes.

Step 7.   Click **Next**.

Step 8. Choose the **languages** you want installed and click **Next**.

Step 9. Select the **products** for which you want updates and click **Next**.

Step 10. In the **Choose Classifications** window, select the updates you want for the products you have selected in the previous page and click **Next**.

Step 11. Set the **sync schedule** and click **Next**.

Step 12. Choose **Begin Initial Synchronization** and click **Next**.

Step 13. On the **What's Next** page, click **Finish**.

Step 14 In the **WSUS Administration Console**, under **Update Services**, expand **WSUS server**, expand **computers**, right-click **All computers**, and then click **Add computer group**.

Step 15. In the **Add computer group** dialog box, for **Name**, specify the name of the new group and then click **Add**.

Step 16. Click **Computers** and then select the computers that you want to assign to this new group.

Step 17. Right-click the computer names you selected in step 16 and then click **Change membership**.

Step 18. In the **Set Computer Group Membership** dialog box, select the test group you created and then click **OK**.

Once you create groups, you can move your computers from the Unassigned Computers group to the group of your choice using one of two methods:

- **Server-side targeting**: Right-click the system in the Update Services console and choose Change Membership.

- **Client-side targeting**: Use Group Policy to cause systems to automatically add themselves to the group you want updated; the Group Policy setting is Enable Client-Side Targeting.

Managing Patches in Mixed Environments

One of the main reasons administrators tend to consider WSUS a cherished element of their enterprise deployment is its ability to aid in update testing in mixed environments. A mixed environment refers to the typical situation in which many different versions and editions of Windows exist, and the different versions are running on many different types of hardware in many different types of configurations.

WSUS lets you group different types of systems together, test the Microsoft updates and patches against systems, and wait some time before deploying the updates enterprise wide. In fact, it is conceivable that an enterprise wide update may never even occur for various reasons. You might wonder if this is an unnecessarily paranoid reaction. Surely, Microsoft tests these updates thoroughly. Microsoft does test them. However, Microsoft would never be able to test against the incredible number of different options that might exist within your corporate walls. Imagine all the different hardware configurations, driver downloads, and application combinations possible!

When you are sure updates are ready for your servers and workstations, you enable these clients to receive them from WSUS. You configure this through Group Policy, as shown in Figure 19-5, via the path Computer Configuration\Administrative Templates\Windows Components\Windows Update.

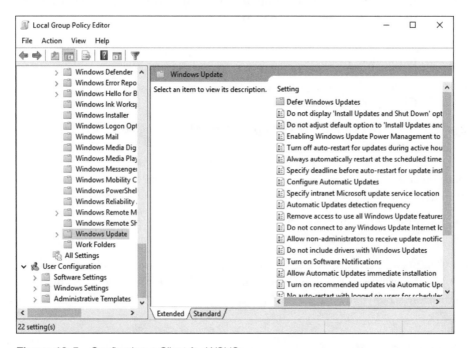

Figure 19-5   Configuring a Client for WSUS

The main settings for WSUS client behavior are Configure Automatic Updates and Specify Intranet Microsoft Update Service Location. You can also set these options to help control WSUS client behavior:

- **Automatic Updates Detection Frequency**
- **Allow Signed Updates from an Intranet Microsoft Update Service Location**

You also need to consider the following:

- What to do about restart? You can configure parameters such as the following:

  - **Delay Restart for Scheduled Installations**

  - **Re-Prompt for Restart with Scheduled Installations**

  - **No Auto-Restart with Logged On Users for Scheduled Automatic Updates Installations**

- What if the target system is shut down for the scheduled update time? Group Policy settings here include the following:

  - **Enabling Windows Update Power Management to Automatically Wake Up the System to Install Scheduled Updates**

  - **Reschedule Automatic Updates Scheduled Installations**

Windows Defender

Windows Server 2016 now includes Windows Defender, which is malware protection that actively protects Windows Server 2016 against known malware and can regularly update antimalware definitions through Windows Update. If you are familiar with Windows clients, you are already familiar with Windows Defender. While Windows Defender had a much-maligned start, thanks to cloud-based data on malware, its effectiveness is ever increasing.

Implementing an Antimalware Solution with Windows Defender

By default, Microsoft installs and enables Windows Defender on most Windows Server 2016 versions.

You manage Windows Defender using the following:

- WMI
- Windows PowerShell
- Group Policy

If your installation of Windows Server 2016 does not have Defender, use the **Add Roles and Features Wizard** or the **Install-WindowsFeature** cmdlet, as in this example:

```
Install-WindowsFeature -Name Windows-Defender-GUI
```

To disable Windows Defender, uninstall it by using the Remove Roles and Features Wizard or using the Uninstall-WindowsFeature cmdlet, as in this example:

```
Uninstall-WindowsFeature -Name Windows-Server-Antimalware
```

To verify that Windows Defender is running on the server, run the following command from a command prompt:

```
sc query Windefend
```

The **sc query** command returns information about the Windows Defender service. If Windows Defender is running, the **STATE** value displays **RUNNING**, as shown in Figure 19-6.

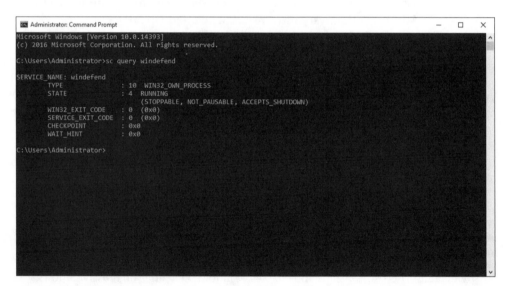

Figure 19-6   Verifying the Windows Defender Service

Integrating Windows Defender with WSUS and Windows Update

To receive updated antimalware definitions (which is critical if the service is to be of real use), you must have the Windows Update service running. If you use Windows Server Update Services (WSUS), make sure to approve updates for Windows Defender definitions.

Remember that, by default, Windows Update does not download and install updates automatically on Windows Server 2016. You can change this configuration by using one of the following methods:

- **Windows Update in Control Panel, Install updates automatically**: Selecting this option results in all updates automatically being installed, including Windows Defender definition updates. Selecting **Download updates but let me choose whether to install them** allows Windows Defender to download and install definition updates automatically, but other updates do not install automatically.

- **Group Policy**: Use the following path: **Administrative Templates\Windows Components\Windows Update\Configure Automatic Updates**.

- **AUOptions registry key**: The following two values allow Windows Update to automatically download and install definition updates:

  - **Install updates automatically**

  - **Download updates but let me choose whether to install them**

To ensure that you support protection against malware, Microsoft recommends the following services:

- Windows Defender Network Inspection service

- Windows Error Reporting service

- Windows Update service

Table 19-2 lists the services for Windows Defender and the dependent services.

Table 19-2 Windows Defender Services

Service Name	File Location	Description
Windows Defender service (Windefend)	C:\Program Files\Windows Defender\MsMpEng.exe	This is the main Windows Defender service that needs to be running at all times.
Windows Defender Network Inspection service (Wdnissvc)	C:\Program Files\Windows Defender\NisSrv.exe	This service is invoked when Windows Defender encounters a trigger to load it.
Windows Error Reporting service (Wersvc)	C:\WINDOWS\System32\svchost.exe -k WerSvcGroup	This service sends error reports to Microsoft.

Service Name	File Location	Description
Windows Firewall (MpsSvc)	C:\WINDOWS\ system32\svchost.exe -k LocalServiceNoNetwork	We recommend leaving the Windows Firewall service enabled.
Windows Update (Wuauserv)	C:\WINDOWS\system32\ svchost.exe -k netsvcs	Windows Update is needed to get definition updates and antimalware engine updates.

Backup and Restore

Many times in this text, we have talked about high-availability features. In fact, this is the number-one tested topic by far in the exam. However, none of the high-availability solutions replaces the need for backup.

Windows Server 2016 includes a backup software program that you can use to back up your volumes. Backup destinations include the following:

- Internal hard drive
- External hard drive
- Writable DVD drive
- Network share

Keep the following in mind regarding Windows Server Backup:

- **Drive support**: Windows Server Backup does not support tape or optical drives that are not accessible through the file system.
- **Scheduling**: Windows Server Backup can schedule only a single job and is limited to running the job either daily or multiple times per day.
- **Job types**: Windows Server Backup does not enable you to perform full, incremental, and differential backups on a per-job basis.
- **Different backup format**: Windows Server Backup writes its backup files in VHDX (virtual hard disk) format, which makes them accessible using Hyper-V or the Disk Management snap-in.

You install Windows Server Backup by using the Add Roles and Features Wizard in Server Manager or the Install-WindowsFeature cmdlet in Windows PowerShell. When you install this feature, you also install the Windows Server Backup console. Figure 19-7 shows the installation of the feature in the Add Roles and Features Wizard.

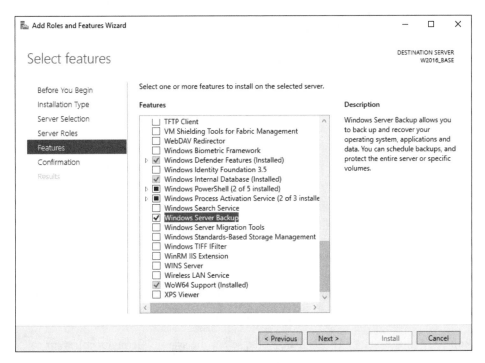

Figure 19-7   Adding the Windows Server Backup Feature

To create a single backup job using a local disk as the job destination, follow these steps:

Step 1.   Open the **Windows Server Backup** console by selecting the **Tools** menu in **Server Manager** and then, in the **Actions** pane with **Local backup** selected, click **Backup once** to launch the **Backup Once Wizard**.

Step 2.   On the **Backup Options** page, leave the **Different options** option selected, as shown in Figure 19-8.

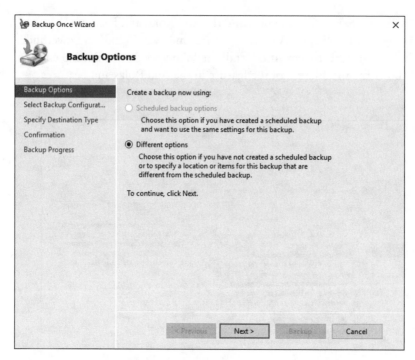

Figure 19-8   Using the Backup Once Wizard

Step 3.   On the **Select Backup Configuration** page, select the **Custom** option.

Step 4.   On the **Select Items for Backup** page, click **Add Items**.

Step 5.   In the **Select Items** dialog box, select the system elements you want to back up.

Step 6.   On the **Specify Destination Type** page, leave the **Local drives** choice selected.

Step 7.   On the **Select Backup Destination** page, use the **Backup destination** drop-down list to select the volume where you want the program to store the backups.

Step 8.   On the **Confirmation** page, click **Backup** to begin the job.

Note that you can also create a scheduled backup job. To do so, open the Windows Server Backup console and, in the Actions pane, click Backup Schedule to launch the Backup Schedule Wizard.

To perform a restore of selected files or folders, open the Windows Server Backup console and, in the Actions pane, click Recover to launch the Recovery Wizard.

The sections that follow detail the important considerations for important backup tasks related to different Windows Server roles and workloads, including the Hyper-V host, Hyper-V guests, Active Directory, file server, and web server, using Windows Server 2016 native tools and solutions.

Hyper-V Host and Hyper-V Guest

You can approach Hyper-V backup two ways:

- You can back up virtual machines as though they are separate systems, by running Windows Server Backup in the guest operating system.

- You can back them up as part of the host server, by backing up the virtual machine files and the virtual hard disks.

Backing up virtual machines from the Hyper-V host uses the Hyper-V Volume Shadow Copy Requestor service in the guest operating system to enable the host to back up the VM while it is running. The requestor service in the guest communicates with the Volume Shadow Copy Service (VSS) in the host, enabling it to back up the virtual machine configuration files, the virtual hard disks, and any checkpoints associated with the VM. You can then restore the virtual machine from the host, if needed, without having to first configure it in Hyper-V.

Windows Server Backup includes support for the VSS writer and the guest requestor service, making it a simple matter to back up virtual machines and their host settings. When you create a backup of a Hyper-V host, the Select Items dialog box includes a Hyper-V item that enables you to select the host components and the individual VMs running on the server.

Active Directory

Most administrators do not overly concern themselves with the concept of restoring Active Directory from backup. Why? They always have at least two domain controllers in their enterprise. If one has a catastrophic failure, they implement another server, promote it, and have Active Directory synchronize to it.

If you perform a scheduled backup of an Active Directory domain controller, sure enough, you back up Active Directory. You also back up Active Directory if you are specially backing up the system state on a server backup.

If you perform a full restoration of a server backup, you do restore the system state and, thus, Active Directory. But what about selectively restoring just the system state? You can do this by using the **Wbadmin.exe** command-line tool.

Table 19-3 shows the subcommands available with **Wbadmin**. Note that the **systemstaterecovery** option is particularly relevant for this discussion.

Table 19-3 Subcommands for Wbadmin

Subcommand	Description
Wbadmin enable backup	Configures and enables a regularly scheduled backup
Wbadmin disable backup	Disables daily backups
Wbadmin start backup	Runs a one-time backup
Wbadmin stop job	Stops the running backup or recovery operation
Wbadmin get versions	Lists details of backups recoverable from the local computer or, if another location is specified, from another computer
Wbadmin get items	Lists the items included in a backup
Wbadmin start recovery	Runs a recovery of the volumes, applications, files, or folders specified
Wbadmin get status	Shows the status of the running backup or recovery operation
Wbadmin get disks	Lists disks that are now online
Wbadmin start systemstaterecovery	Runs a system state recovery
Wbadmin start systemstatebackup	Runs a system state backup
Wbadmin delete systemstatebackup	Removes one or more system state backups
Wbadmin start sysrecovery	Runs a recovery of the full system (at least all the volumes that hold the operating system's state)
Wbadmin restore catalog	Recovers a backup catalog from a specified storage location in the case where the backup catalog on the local computer has been corrupted
Wbadmin delete catalog	Removes the backup catalog on the local computer

There are two types of system state restores:

- **Non-authoritative**: Non-authoritative restores replace Active Directory from the backup but then allow its overwriting from the Active Directory synchronization process from other domain controllers.

- **Authoritative**: Authoritative restores require you to restart the computer in Directory Services Restore mode by pressing F8 during boot. You then restore the system state by using **Wbadmin** followed by **Ntdsutil.exe** to specify Active Directory objects to selectively restore.

File Servers and Web Servers

While backing up file servers is straightforward using the backup and restore steps described earlier in this chapter, backup of a web (IIS) server needs some discussion. Keep the following in mind:

- Static files (such as local HTML files) are not a problem for Windows Server Backup.

- Web servers connected to backend databases (such as Microsoft SQL Server) might be accessing databases stored on other servers. Windows Server Backup performs VSS backups of SQL Server databases for this purpose.

- Configuration files (XML) for an IIS web server are located in Windows\ System32\intserv; you must remember to back up these files to properly backup IIS.

Exam Preparation Tasks

As mentioned in the section "How to Use This Book" in the Introduction, you have a couple choices for exam preparation: the exercises here, Chapter 21, "Final Preparation," and the exam simulation questions in the Pearson Test Prep Software Online.

Review All Key Topics

Review the most important topics in this chapter, noted with the Key Topics icon in the outer margin of the page. Table 19-4 lists these key topics and the page number on which each is found.

Table 19-4 Key Topics for Chapter 19

Key Topic Element	Description	Page Number
List	WSUS requirements	315
List	WSUS client settings	322
Steps	Create a single backup job	327

Complete Tables and Lists from Memory

Print a copy of Appendix B, "Memory Tables" (found on the book website), or at least the section for this chapter, and complete the tables and lists from memory. Appendix C, "Memory Tables Answer Key," also on the website, includes completed tables and lists to check your work.

Define Key Terms

Define the following key terms from this chapter and check your answers against the glossary:

Windows Server Update Services (WSUS), WSUS Groups, Windows Defender, Windows Server Backup

Q&A

The answers to these questions appear in Appendix A. For more practice with exam format questions, use the Pearson Test Prep Software Online.

1. Name at least two criteria that must be met if a database server for WSUS is separate from the WSUS role.

2. Name at least one service Microsoft recommends for protection against malware.

3. What format does Windows Server Backup use for backups?

This chapter covers the following subjects:

- **Performance Monitor:** This intense GUI tool offers incredible monitoring capabilities for your system. This section of the chapter details this.

- **Resource Monitor:** Need quick, but accurate, information about the performance of your system? Resource Monitor provides this, and more.

## CHAPTER 20

Monitoring Servers

This chapter ensures that you are proficient in the use of both Performance Monitor and Resource Monitor.

"Do I Know This Already?" Quiz

The "Do I Know This Already?" quiz allows you to assess whether you should read the entire chapter. Table 20-1 lists the major headings in this chapter and the "Do I Know This Already?" quiz questions covering the material in those headings so you can assess your knowledge of these specific areas. The answers to the "Do I Know This Already?" quiz appear in Appendix A, "Answers to the 'Do I Know This Already?' Quizzes and Q&A Questions."

Table 20-1 "Do I Know This Already?" Foundation Topics Section-to-Question Mapping

Foundation Topics Section	Questions
Performance Monitor	1, 2
Resource Monitor	3, 4

CAUTION The goal of self-assessment is to gauge your mastery of the topics in this chapter. If you do not know the answer to a question or are only partially sure of the answer, you should mark your answer as incorrect for purposes of the self-assessment. Giving yourself credit for an answer you correctly guess skews your self-assessment results and might provide you with a false sense of security.

1. What counter does Performance Monitor display by default?

    a. Disk Faults/Sec

    b. Total Pages/Sec

    c. % Processor Time

    d. Total Avail Memory

2. What Performance Monitor tool is often used to create baselines?

    a. Report Export

    b. Alerts

    c. Graphing

    d. Data Collection Set

3. What tab appears when you first launch Resource Monitor in its default configuration?

    a. Memory

    b. Network

    c. Overview

    d. CPU

4. What visual representation does Resource Monitor use when information is filtered?

    a. A red filter label

    b. A green highlight

    c. An exclamation point

    d. An orange bar

Foundation Topics

Performance Monitor

You use Windows Performance Monitor to examine how programs and services you run affect your server's performance. You can do this in real time and by collecting log data for later analysis.

Windows Performance Monitor uses performance counters, event trace data, and configuration information. You can combine all this information into Data Collector Sets.

Performance counters are measurements of system state or activity. These measurements might be from the operating system or from individual applications. Windows Performance Monitor pulls the current values of performance counters at specified time intervals.

Performance Monitor collects event trace data from trace providers, which are components of the operating system or of individual applications that report actions or events. Performance Monitor can collect output from multiple trace providers and combine it into a trace session.

Performance Monitor collects configuration information from key values in the Windows registry. Performance Monitor can also record the value of a registry key at a specified time or interval as part of a log file.

Monitoring Workloads Using Performance Monitor

To launch Performance Monitor, enter Performance Monitor in the Search area. Note that Performance Monitor launches in a Microsoft Management Console (MMC) with the Performance node selected, as shown in Figure 20-1. This view gives an overview of Performance Monitor and an important System Summary area where you can quickly view key system performance metrics.

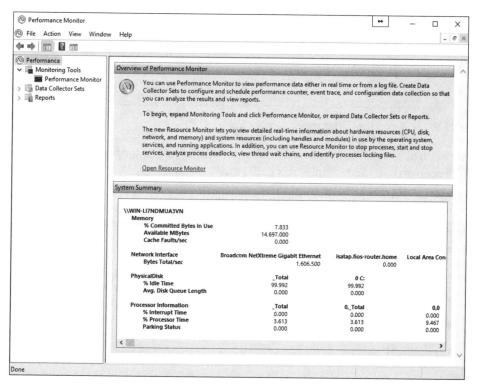

Figure 20-1   Launching Performance Monitor

To see the Performance Monitor tool itself, click Performance Monitor in the Monitoring Tools node, as shown in Figure 20-2.

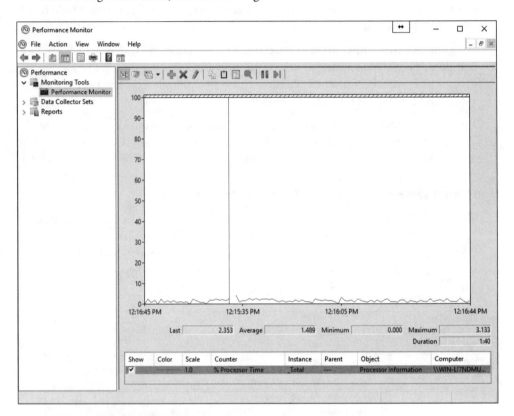

Figure 20-2   Selecting the Performance Monitor Tool

Notice that, by default, Performance Monitor displays a graph of the single counter % Processor Time and samples this data every 1 second.

At the top of the graph are the following buttons:

- View Current Activity
- View Log Data
- Change Graph Type
- Add
- Delete
- Highlight

- Copy Properties
- Paste Counter List
- Properties
- Zoom
- Freeze Display
- Update Data

Right-clicking in the graph produces the following powerful shortcut menu items:

- **Add Counters:** Permits the addition of more counters to monitor other elements of server performance
- **Save Settings As:** Allows current settings to be saved
- **Save Image As:** Permits the saving of the graph as an image file
- **Save Data As:** Permits the saving of the data captured by the graph
- **Clear:** Clears the current graph settings
- **Zoom To:** Allows the zooming to a time period on the graph
- **Show Selected Counters:** Allows the display of selected performance monitor counters on the graph
- **Hide Selected Counters:** Hides the display of selected performance monitor counters on the graph
- **Scale Selected Counters:** Allows the adjustment of the time scale for selected counters
- **Remove All Counters:** Removes all the counters added to the graph
- **Properties:** Provides access to additional settings for the graph

Configuring Data Collector Sets

A Data Collector Set allows the capture of key Performance Monitor data for later review. This can be critical for many performance monitoring tasks, including the creation of a baseline. A baseline allows you to get a snapshot of server performance under various conditions. At the very least, most administrators like to get a snapshot of performance during "normal" workloads so they can easily see if something is abnormal with a server. After all, how can you identify abnormal performance if you do not know what normal performance looks like?

Follow these steps to configure a Data Collector Set:

Step 1. In the **Performance Monitor MMC**, expand the **Data Collector Sets** node.

Step 2. Right-click the **User Defined** node and choose **New > Data Collector Set**.

Step 3. In the **Create New Data Collector Set Wizard**, name your **Data Collector Set**. You now have the option to choose one of the following options:

- **Create from a template (recommended)**
- **Create manually (advanced)**

Step 4. Select **Create manually (advanced)** and click **Next**.

Step 5. From the dialog box shown in Figure 20-3, select the type of data you want to include.

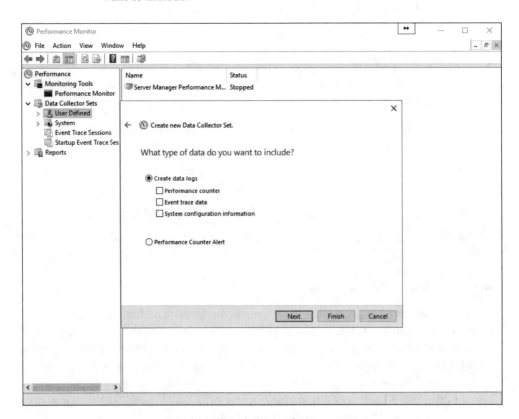

Figure 20-3   Selecting the Data for a Data Collector Set

Step 6. Choose **Performance Counter** under **Create Data Logs** and click **Next**. Event trace data and system configuration information are for special use case scenarios.

Step 7. Select the **performance counters** you want to include by using the **Add** button, choose the **sample interval** and **unit,** and click **Next**.

Step 8. Select where you want Performance Monitor to save the data and click **Next**.

Step 9. On the **Create the Data Collector Set** page, select an account for running the collector from in the **Run As** drop-down and then select from the following:

- **Open Properties for This Data Collector Set**
- **Start This Data Collector Set Now**
- **Save and Close**

Step 10. Click **Finish**.

Congratulations! Your collector is complete. You now see your collector in the User Defined node. A right-click of your collector brings up the following options:

- Start
- Stop
- Save Template
- Data Manager
- Latest Report
- New - Data Collector
- New Window from Here
- Delete
- Refresh
- Properties
- Help

Determining Appropriate CPU, Memory, Disk, and Networking Counters for Storage and Compute Workloads

The number of Performance Monitor counters you can add to a graph or Data Collector Set is truly astounding. In fact, consider that this number increases as you add server roles and features!

Here are some examples of critical counters along with desired values for general server health:

- **LogicalDisk - % Free Space**: Greater than 15%
- **PhysicalDisk - % Idle Time**: Greater than 20%
- **PhysicalDisk - Avg. Disk Sec/Read**: Less than 25 ms
- **PhysicalDisk - Avg. Disk Sec/Write**: Less than 25 ms
- **PhysicalDisk - Avg. Disk Queue Length**: Should not be larger than twice the number of physical disks
- **Memory - % Committed Bytes in Use**: Less than 80%
- **Memory - Available Mbytes**: Greater than 5% of total RAM
- **Processor - % Processor Time**: Less than 85%
- **System - Processor Queue Length**: Should be more than twice the number of CPUs
- **Network Interface - Output Queue Length**: Less than 2

Configuring Alerts

Another incredibly powerful feature of Performance Monitor is its capability to alert you when a value is outside a threshold that you define. As discussed earlier in this chapter, you can configure these alerts when you configure a Data Collector Set. (Refer to Figure 20-3 to see the choice for configuring an alert.)

When you configure alerts, the values you can enter for the thresholds vary depending on what you select for your counters. In addition, once you have your alert created, you can right-click the data collector inside the alert and choose Properties to manipulate the following tabs:

- **Alerts**
- **Alert Action**
- **Alert Task**

Figure 20-4 shows the Properties window and the Alert Task tab.

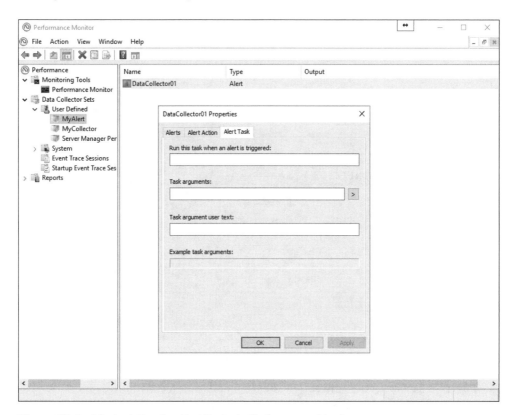

Figure 20-4   Manipulating the Alert Tasks in Performance Monitor

Resource Monitor

Resource Monitor, which has been in use in Windows clients and servers since
Windows Vista and Windows Server 2008 R2, is a powerful tool. By using this tool,
you can understand how processes and services use your server system resources.
In addition to monitoring resource usage in real time, Resource Monitor can help
analyze unresponsive processes, determine which applications are using files, and
control processes and services.

Monitoring Workloads Using Resource Monitor

To launch Resource Monitor, simply enter Resource Monitor in the Search area.
Notice that Resource Monitor launches with the Overview tab selected (see Figure
20-5). This tab gives a quick view of CPU, disk, network, and memory usage.

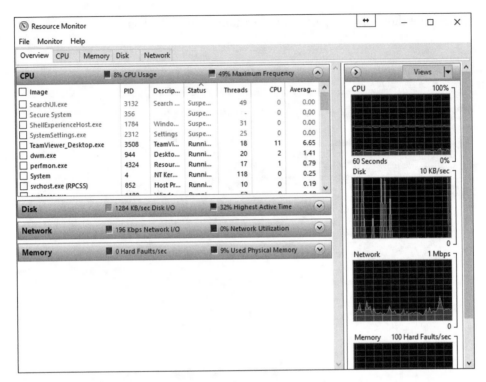

Figure 20-5   Launching Resource Monitor in Server 2016

To pause data collection and review the current data, select Monitor > Stop Monitoring. When you are ready to begin collecting data again, select Monitor > Start Monitoring.

Resource Monitor always starts in the same location and with the same display options as in the preceding session. However, at any time you can save your display state, including window size, column widths, optional columns, expanded tables, and the active tab. You can then open the configuration file to use the saved settings.

Resource Monitor includes the following elements and features:

■ **Tabs**: Resource Monitor has Overview, CPU, Memory, Disk, and Network tabs. If you filter results on one tab, only resources used by the selected processes or services display on the other tabs; Resource Monitor denotes filtered results with an orange bar below the title bar of each table. To stop filtering results while viewing the current tab, in the key table, clear the check box next to **Image** (see Figure 20-6).

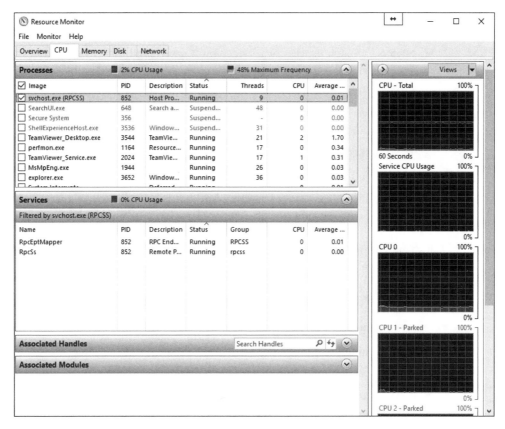

Figure 20-6 Filtering Results on a Tab

- **Tables**: Each tab in Resource Monitor includes multiple tables that offer detailed information about the resource featured on that tab. Keep in mind the following about tables:

  - To expand or collapse a table, click the arrow on the right side of the title bar of the table; not all tables are expanded by default.

  - To add or hide data columns in a table, right-click any column label and then click Select Columns; select or clear the check boxes for the columns you want displayed; not all columns are displayed by default.

  - The first table displayed is always the key table, and it always contains a complete list of processes using the resources included on that tab; for example, the key table on the Overview tab contains a complete list of processes running on the system.

  - To sort table data, click the label of the column you want to sort by; to reverse the sort order, click the column label again.

- You can filter the detailed data in tables other than the key table by one or more processes or services; to filter in the key table, select the check box next to each process or service you want to highlight; to stop filtering for a single process or service, clear its check box; to stop filtering altogether, in the key table, clear the check box next to Image.

- If you have filtered results, tables other than the key table display only data for the selected processes or services.

- To view definitions of data displayed in the tables, move the mouse pointer over the column title about which you want more information.

- A process that is no longer running but that is included in the current displayed data appears as a gray entry in a table until the data expires.

- **Chart pane**: Each tab in Resource Monitor includes a Chart pane on the right side of the window that displays graphs of the resources included on that tab. Keep in mind the following about the Chart pane:

  - You can change the size of the graphs by clicking the **Views** button and selecting a different graph size.

  - You can hide the Chart pane by clicking the arrow at the top of the pane.

  - If you have filtered results, the resources used by the selected processes or services are shown in the graphs with an orange line.

  - If you have multiple logical processors, you can choose which ones are displayed in the Chart pane; on the CPU tab, click Monitor and then click Select Processors; in the Select Processors dialog box, clear the All CPUs check box and then select the check boxes for the logical processors you want to display.

Exam Preparation Tasks

As mentioned in the section "How to Use This Book" in the Introduction, you have a couple choices for exam preparation: the exercises here, Chapter 21, "Final Preparation," and the exam simulation questions in the Pearson Test Prep Software Online.

Review All Key Topics

Review the most important topics in this chapter, noted with the Key Topics icon in the outer margin of the page. Table 20-2 lists these key topics and the page numbers on which each is found.

Table 20-2   Key Topics for Chapter 20

Key Topic Element	Description	Page Number
Steps	Creating a Data Collector Set	340
List	Key Performance Monitor counters	342

Complete Tables and Lists from Memory

This chapter does not have any memory tables.

Define Key Terms

Define the following key terms from this chapter and check your answers against the glossary:

Performance Monitor, Data Collector Set, Alert, Resource Monitor

Q&A

The answers to these questions appear in Appendix A. For more practice with exam format questions, use the Pearson Test Prep Software Online.

1. Where in Performance Monitor do you create alerts?
2. What are the five tabs in Resource Monitor?

## CHAPTER 21

Final Preparation

The first 20 chapters of this book cover the technologies, protocols, design concepts, and considerations required to be prepared to pass the Microsoft Certified Solutions Associate (MCSA) Installation, Storage, and Compute with Windows Server 2016 70-740 exam. While these chapters supply the detailed information, most people need more preparation than just reading the first 20 chapters of this book. This chapter details a set of tools and a study plan to help you complete your preparation for the exams.

This short chapter has two main sections. The first section lists the exam preparation tools useful at this point in the study process. The second section provides a suggested study plan you can use now that you have completed all the earlier chapters in this book.

NOTE Appendix B, "Memory Tables," and Appendix C, "Memory Tables Answer Key," are available on the website for this book, which you can access by going to www.pearsonITcertification.com/register, registering your book, and entering this book's ISBN: 9780789756978.

Tools for Final Preparation

The following sections provide information about available exam prep tools and how to access them.

Pearson Cert Practice Test Engine and Questions on the Website

Register this book to get access to the Pearson IT Certification test engine (software that displays and grades a set of exam-realistic, multiple-choice questions). Using the Pearson Cert Practice Test Engine, you can either study by going through the questions in Study mode or take a simulated (timed) 70-740 exam.

The Pearson Test Prep practice test software comes with two full practice exams. These practice tests are available to you either online or as an offline Windows application. To access the practice exams that were developed to accompany this book, please see the instructions in the card inserted in the sleeve in the back of this book. The card includes a unique access code that enables you to activate your exams in the Pearson Test Prep software.

Accessing the Pearson Test Prep Software Online

The online version of the Pearson Test Prep software can be used on any device that has a browser and connectivity to the Internet, including desktop machines, tablets, and smartphones. To start using your practice exams online, simply follow these steps:

Step 1. Go to http://www.PearsonTestPrep.com.

Step 2. Select **Pearson IT Certification** as your product group.

Step 3. Enter the email and password for your account. If you don't have an account on PearsonITCertification.com or CiscoPress.com, you need to establish one by going to PearsonITCertification.com/join.

Step 4. In the **My Products** tab, click the **Activate New Product** button.

Step 5. Enter the access code printed on the insert card in the back of your book to activate your product. The product is now listed in your My Products page.

Step 6. Click the **Exams** button to launch the exam settings screen and start your exam.

Accessing the Pearson Test Prep Software Offline

If you wish to study offline, you can download and install the Windows version of the Pearson Test Prep software. There is a download link for this software on the book's companion website, or you can just enter this link in your browser:

http://www.pearsonitcertification.com/content/downloads/pcpt/engine.zip

To access the book's companion website and software, simply follow these steps:

Step 1. Register your book by going to PearsonITCertification.com/register and entering the ISBN 9780789756978.

Step 2. Answer the challenge questions.

Step 3. Go to your account page and select the **Registered Products** tab.

Step 4. Click on the **Access Bonus Content** link under the product listing.

Step 5. Click the **Install Pearson Test Prep Desktop Version** link under the Practice Exams section of the page to download the software.

Step 6. Once the software finishes downloading, unzip all the files on your computer.

Step 7. Double-click the application file to start the installation and follow the onscreen instructions to complete the registration.

Step 8. Once the installation is complete, launch the application and click the **Activate Exam** button on the **My Products** tab.

Step 9. Click the **Activate a Product** button in the **Activate Product Wizard**.

Step 10. Enter the unique access code found on the card in the sleeve in the back of this book and click the **Activate** button.

Step 11. Click **Next** and then click the **Finish** button to download the exam data to your application.

Step 12. Start using the practice exams by selecting the product and clicking the **Open Exam** button to open the exam settings screen.

Note that the offline and online versions sync with each other, so saved exams and grade results recorded on one version are available to you on the other as well.

Customizing Your Exams

Once you are in the exam settings screen, you can choose to take exams in one of three modes:

- **Study mode:** Study mode allows you to fully customize your exams and review answers as you are taking the exam. This is typically the mode you use first to assess your knowledge and identify information gaps.

- **Practice Exam mode:** Practice Exam mode locks certain customization options because it presents a realistic exam experience. Use this mode when you are preparing to test your exam readiness.

- **Flash Card mode:** Flash Card mode strips out the answers and presents you with only the question stem. This mode is great for late-stage preparation, when you really want to challenge yourself to provide answers without the benefit of seeing multiple-choice options. This mode does not provide the detailed score reports that the other two modes provide, so you should not use it if you are trying to identify knowledge gaps.

In addition to these three modes, you can select the source of your questions. You can choose to take exams that cover all the chapters, or you can narrow your selection to just a single chapter or the chapters that make up specific parts in the book. All chapters are selected by default. If you want to narrow your focus to individual chapters, simply deselect all the chapters and then select only those on which you wish to focus in the Objectives area.

You can also select the exam banks on which to focus. Each exam bank comes complete with a full exam of questions that cover topics in every chapter. The two exams printed in the book are available to you, as are two additional exams of unique questions. You can have the test engine serve up exams from all four banks or just from one individual bank by selecting the desired banks in the exam bank area.

You can also make several other customizations to your exam from the exam settings screen, such as the time of the exam, the number of questions served up, whether to randomize questions and answers, whether to show the number of correct answers for multiple-answer questions, and whether to serve up only specific types of questions. You can also create custom test banks by selecting only questions that you have marked or questions for which you have added notes.

Updating Your Exams

If you are using the online version of the Pearson Test Prep software, you should always have access to the latest version of the software as well as the exam data. If you are using the Windows desktop version, every time you launch the software, it checks to see if there are any updates to your exam data and automatically down-loads any changes made since the last time you used the software. You must be con-nected to the Internet at the time you launch the software.

Sometimes, due to many factors, the exam data may not fully download when you activate an exam. If you find that figures or exhibits are missing, you may need to manually update your exams.

To update a particular exam you have already activated and downloaded, simply select the **Tools** tab and then click the **Update Products** button. Again, this is only an issue with the desktop Windows application.

If you wish to check for updates to the Pearson Test Prep exam engine software, Windows desktop version, simply select the **Tools** tab and then click the **Update Application** button to ensure that you are running the latest version of the soft-ware engine.

Premium Edition

In addition to the free practice exam provided on the website, you can purchase additional exams with expanded functionality directly from Pearson IT Certifica-tion. The Premium Edition of this title contains an additional two full practice exams and an eBook (in both PDF and ePub formats). In addition, the Premium Edition title also offers remediation for each question, pointing to the specific part of the eBook that relates to that question.

Because you have purchased the print version of this title, you can purchase the Premium Edition at a deep discount. There is a coupon code in the book sleeve that contains a one-time-use code and instructions for where you can use it to purchase the Premium Edition.

To view the Premium Edition product page, go to www.informit.com/title/9780789756978.

Memory Tables

Like most other Cert Guides from Pearson, this book purposely organizes informa-tion into tables and lists for easier study and review. Rereading these tables before the exam can be very useful. However, it is easy to skim over the tables without pay-ing attention to every detail, especially when you remember having seen a table's contents when reading the chapter.

Instead of just reading the tables in the various chapters, this book's Appendixes B and C give you another review tool. Appendix B lists partially completed versions of many of the tables from the book. You can open Appendix B (a PDF that is avail-able on the book website after registering) and print the appendix. For review, you can attempt to complete the tables. This exercise can help you focus on the review. It also exercises the memory connectors in your brain, and it makes you think about the information without as much information, which forces a little more contemplation about the facts.

Appendix C, also a PDF located on the book website, lists the completed tables to check yourself. You can also just refer to the tables printed in the book.

Chapter-Ending Review Tools

Chapters 1 through 20 each have several features in the "Exam Preparation Tasks" section at the end of the chapter. You might have already worked through these in each chapter. It can also be helpful to use these tools again as you make your final preparations for the exam.

Suggested Plan for Final Review/Study

This section lists a suggested study plan to follow from the time you finish this book until you take the MCSA 70-740 exam. Certainly, you can ignore this plan, use it as is, or take suggestions from it.

The plan involves four steps:

Step 1. **Review key topics and "Do I Know This Already?" (DIKTA) quiz questions:** You can use the table that lists the key topics in each chapter or just flip the pages, looking for key topics. Also, reviewing the DIKTA questions from the beginning of the chapter can be helpful for review.

Step 2. **Complete memory tables:** Open Appendix B from the book website and print the entire thing or just the tables by major part. Then complete the tables.

Step 3. **Review "Q&A" sections:** Go through the Q&A questions at the end of each chapter to identify areas you need more study.

Step 4. **Use the Pearson Cert Practice Test engine to practice:** You can use the Pearson Cert Practice Test engine to study by using a bank of unique exam-realistic questions available only with this book.

Summary

The tools and suggestions listed in this chapter have been designed with one goal in mind: to help you develop the skills required to pass the MCSA 70-740 exam. This book has been developed from the beginning to not just tell you the facts but also help you learn how to apply them. No matter what your experience level leading up to when you take the exam, it is our hope that the broad range of preparation tools and the structure of the book help you pass the exam with ease. We hope you do well on the exam.

Answers to the "Do I Know This Already?" Quizzes and Q&A Questions

"Do I Know This Already?" Quizzes

Chapter 1

1. B
2. D
3. B
4. A
5. D
6. C
7. B
8. B and D
9. B and C
10. B

Chapter 2

1. D
2. B
3. D
4. B
5. A
6. C
7. A
8. A
9. A
10. D

Chapter 3

1. B
2. D
3. C
4. B
5. C
6. A and D
7. C
8. A
9. C
10. A and D

Chapter 4

1. D
2. C
3. D
4. C
5. D
6. D

Chapter 5

1. C
2. D
3. B

4. C

5. A and C

6. B

Chapter 6

1. D

2. A

3. D

4. A

5. B

6. A

Chapter 7

1. B

2. B

3. C

4. A

5. D

6. B

Chapter 8

1. D

2. A

3. B

4. C

5. C

6. C

7. A

8. D

Chapter 9

1. B

2. C

3. B

4. C

5. A and D

6. D

Chapter 10

1. B

2. B and D

3. A

4. D

5. C

6. A

Chapter 11

1. A and D

2. A

3. A

4. C

5. A

6. C

7. A

8. C

Chapter 12

1. D

2. B

3. D

4. A

5. C

6. B

Chapter 13

1. A
2. A and C
3. B, C, and D
4. D
5. C
6. C
7. B
8. B

Chapter 14

1. A
2. C
3. A
4. A
5. D
6. C

Chapter 15

1. A
2. C
3. A
4. C
5. D

Chapter 16

1. B
2. B
3. B
4. A and D
5. A

Chapter 17

1. C
2. C
3. A
4. B

Chapter 18

1. A
2. A
3. C
4. C

Chapter 19

1. C
2. C
3. C
4. A, B, and C
5. A, B, and D
6. B

Chapter 20

1. C
2. D
3. C
4. D

Q&A

Chapter 1

1. Nested virtualization
2. 32 GB
3. Standard Edition
4. Upgrade and Custom
5. License conversion
6. Active Directory-based Activation and KMS

Chapter 2

1. A compute host for Hyper-V virtual machines; a storage host; a DNS server; an IIS server; a host for container apps
2. Headless; runs only 64-bit applications; cannot be an AD domain controller; Group Policy not supported; NIC teaming not supported; cannot proxy to Internet
3. VHDX
4. **-Defender**
5. PowerShell; WMI; Windows Remote Management; EMS
6. Add the IP address of your management workstation to trusted hosts; add the account to the Nano Server's administrators; enable CredSSP if using that feature

Chapter 3

1. Not UEFI compatible; migration to Azure; no OS support; unsupported boot method
2. MAP Toolkit
3. Speed; architecture; number
4. DISM
5. **/Enable-Feature**
6. **PSSession**

   Invoke-Command

Chapter 4

1. Disk Management
2. NFS Share - Advanced
3. Deny

Chapter 5

1. Hard disk drives (HDDs) and solid state drives (SSD)
2. **Connect-IscsiTarget**
3. GPT initialized disks and Datacenter Edition

Chapter 6

1. General-purpose file servers, VDI deployments, and backup targets
2. Optimization policy
3. **OptimizedFilesSavingsRate** and **SavingsRate**

Chapter 7

1. UEFI 2.3.1c, TMP v2.0, IOMMU, Generation 2, and supported OS
2. Choose the **Add Roles and Features** option from the Manage menu of Server Manager.
3. At least 4 GB of RAM; Windows Server 2016 or Windows 10 Anniversary Update; a virtual machine running Hyper-V that is the same build as the host; and an Intel processor with VT-x and EPT technology

Chapter 8

1. SCSI controller, legacy network adapter, virtual Fibre Channel adapter, and Microsoft RemoteFX 3D video adapter
2. They must be manually updated.
3. Install later, Install from a bootable image file, and Install from a network location
4. Copies of VM configuration, checkpoints, and virtual hard disk files
5. Exporting a checkpoint and exporting the virtual machine with a checkpoint
6. Set minimum and maximum memory; use dynamic memory; avoid using differencing disks if possible; use multiple Hyper-V network adapters connected to different external virtual switches; and store virtual machine files on their own volumes

Chapter 9

1. **Edit Disk**
2. Standard checkpoint
3. **New-StorageQosPolicy**

Chapter 10

1. Additional network function virtualization; container-aware virtual network features; the network controller component; SET; RDMA; and CNAs
2. Virtual Switch Manager
3. Provision enough actual bandwidth; use NIC teaming where possible; use bandwidth management; use adapters that support VMQ; and with a large number of VMs, use network virtualization for VM isolation as opposed to VLANs.

Chapter 11

1. Hyper-V containers and Windows Server containers
2. At least two
3. Server Core/Nano Server
4. **sc config** and a configuration file

Chapter 12

1. **docker ps -a**
2. Transparent
3. **-m**

Chapter 13

1. **Enable Replication**
2. A user account with permission; the Hyper-V role; source and destination machines in the same AD or that are in trusted domains; and Hyper-V management tools
3. Files must use virtual hard disks, and VMs cannot use pass-through disks.

Chapter 14

1. Identical hardware and configuration on nodes; network adapters with identical configurations; Certified for Windows Server 2016 logos; same OS versions and editions and updates; separate networks for various traffic forms recommended; redundant networking equipment recommended

2. **New-Cluster**

3. Minimum of three disks, 4 GB each, and SAS or iSCSI

4. Node monitoring; application migration; host availability; VM migration; nested clustering

Chapter 15

1. AES

2. Services

3. First Failure, Second Failure, and Subsequent Failures

4. **New-ClusterFaultDomain**

Chapter 16

1. Datacenter Edition, at least six drives, and no RAID

2. **Enable-ClusterStorageSpacesDirect**

Chapter 17

1. The Quick Migration has a delay, and the Quick Migration can move a stopped VM.

2. **Advanced Features > Protected Network**

Chapter 18

1. Multiple Host

2. Single

Chapter 19

1. That database server cannot be a domain controller; the WSUS server cannot run Remote Desktop Services; the database server must be in the AD or must be in a trusted AD; they must be in the same time zone and have the time synchronized.

2. Windows Defender Network Inspection Service; Windows Error Reporting Service; Windows Update Service

3. VHDX

Chapter 20

1. Data Collector Sets

2. Overview, CPU, Memory, Disk, and Network

Glossary

Active Directory-Based Activation A role service that allows you to use Active Directory Domain Services (AD DS) to store activation objects.

Advanced Format disk A disk that uses a 4092-byte physical sector.

Affinity The ability to control how a cluster reacts to repeated requests from the same client.

Alerts A Data Collector Set feature that allows you to configure notifications when counters breach certain thresholds.

Automatic Virtual Machine Activation A technology that allows you to install virtual machines on a properly activated Windows server without having to manage product keys for each individual virtual machine.

Azure Container Services (ACS) Clustered virtual machines for running container-based applications.

Checkpoints Point-in-time images of a virtual machine.

Chunk A section of a file that has been selected by the Data Deduplication chunking algorithm as likely to occur in other, similar files.

Chunk Store An organized series of container files in the System Volume Information folder that Data Deduplication uses to uniquely store chunks.

Cluster-Aware Updating (CAU) Windows Update technology for clusters.

Cluster Name Object (CNO) An object for the cluster in Active Directory.

Cluster Operation Mode A mode that determines whether a cluster uses unicast or multicast.

Configuration Version A virtual machine's compatibility settings.

CSVFS A pseudo file system that sits on top of NTFS in a Clustered Shared Volume (CSV).

Data Collector Set A tool that allows the collection of selected Performance Monitor data.

Datacenter Edition The most powerful edition of Server 2016.

DCB Priority-based flow control for a converged storage network.

DDA An abbreviation for Discrete Device Assignment, which permits hardware to communicate directly with a VM.

Dedup   An abbreviation for Data Deduplication that's commonly used in PowerShell, Windows Server APIs and components, and the Windows Server community.

Differencing Disk   A virtual hard disk that stores only changes from parent virtual hard disk.

DISM   An abbreviation for Deployment Imaging Servicing and Management; this command line tool has many uses including the preparation of Windows images for automated deployment in the network.

Docker   A well-known application for maintaining containers.

Docker Daemon   The actual running Docker engine on a container host.

Dockerfile   Instructions and statements for each instruction that create a Docker image.

DockerHub   A public repository for storing and sharing Docker images.

Drain on Shutdown   A new Windows Server 2016 clustering feature that automatically live migrates all the roles on a node before shutdown.

Enhanced Session Mode   A mode that permits the use of a local computer's resources.

Essentials Edition   The smallest edition of Server 2016, designed for small businesses.

Extended (Chained) Replication   Hyper-V Replica using three hosts.

External virtual switch   A switch that connects to a wired physical network.

Failback   A process in which a cluster moves a role back to the original node.

File Metadata   Metadata that describes interesting properties about the file that are not related to the main content of the file.

File Stream   The main content of a file.

File System   The software and on-disk data structure that an operating system uses to store files on storage media.

File System Filter   A plug-in that modifies the default behavior of the file system.

Gen 1 Versus Gen 2   Virtual machine type options in Hyper-V.

GUID Partition Table (GPT)   A newer partition style that supports larger disk space.

Headless   Reference to the fact that Nano Server provides no user interface.

Hyper-V Container   A container that runs in a special lightweight VM.

Hyper-V Manager   The GUI that permits the management of Hyper-V.

Hyper-V Replica   A feature that provides replication of virtual machines from one host to another for disaster recovery scenarios.

Internal Virtual Switch   A switch that is used only by the virtual machines on the host.

iSCSI Initiator   A client in the iSCSI network.

iSCSI Target   An iSCSI component that advertises storage to the iSCSI network.

iSNS   A protocol used for discovery of iSCSI resources.

Key Management Service (KMS)   A role service that allows you to activate systems within a network from a server where a KMS host has been installed.

LIS/BIS   Integration services and drivers for Linux and FreeBSD VMs.

Live Migration   The movement of a virtual machine from one host to another.

MAP   An abbreviation for Microsoft Assessment and Planning Toolkit; this collection of tools seeks to make it easy to assess the current IT infrastructure for a variety of technology migration projects; the Solution Accelerator provides a powerful inventory, assessment, and reporting tool to simplify the migration planning process.

Master Boot Record (MBR)   An older partition style that does not support disk space larger than 2 TB.

MPIO   A resiliency feature for a SAN.

Nano Server   The smallest possible installation option of Windows Server 2016, with no user interface.

Nested Virtualization   The ability to run Hyper-V virtualization from within a virtual machine.

Network Health Protection   A tool that allows dynamic monitoring of a VM to see if it has a healthy network connection.

Network Load Balancing (NLB) Cluster   A group of hosts that dynamically distribute client traffic to hosts in a cluster.

NFS   A sharing technology used by UNIX-based systems.

NIC Teaming   Using multiple NICs in parallel; this is not supported in Nano Server.

Node Fairness   A balancing technique in Windows Server 2016 which ensures that nodes in a cluster are not overtaxed with workloads.

Nodes   Members of a failover cluster.

NTFS   A common file system for Windows Server 2016.

NUMA   A computer memory design in which the memory access time depends on the memory location relative to the processor.

Optimization   A process in which a file is optimized (or deduplicated) by data deduplication if it has been chunked, and its unique chunks have been stored in the chunk store.

Optimization Policy   A policy which specifies the files that should be considered for Data Deduplication.

Pass-Through Disk   A disk that permits a VM access to the storage system of a host.

Performance Monitor   An MMC that permits careful analysis of server performance.

Port Rules   Rules that define the types of TCP/IP traffic an NLB cluster processes.

PowerShell and Desired State Configuration (DSC)   A method of deploying Server 2016 and ensuring the consistency of the deployed configurations.

PowerShell Direct   A feature that permits commands to be run against virtual machines from a local PowerShell installation.

Private Virtual Switch   A switch that does not permit communication between a host and VMs.

Quick Migration   An early form of the Live Migration that causes some delay in processing.

Quorum   A method of preventing a split-brain cluster.

RDMA   An abbreviation for Remote Direct Memory Access, which permits Hyper-V switches to use this memory feature.

ReFS   An abbreviation for Resilient File System, a new file system supported by Windows Server 2016.

Reparse Point   A special tag that notifies the file system to pass off I/O to a specified file system filter.

Resource Metering   The gathering of resource utilization data for a VM.

Resource Monitor   A basic tool for quick analysis of performance data on a Server system.

Rolling Upgrade   An update of the OS in machines of a cluster on a gradual basis.

Scale-Out File Server (SoFS)   A clustered role that provides highly available storage for applications.

Second Level Address Translation   A required feature of the processor for running Server 2016.

Server Core   An installation option for Windows Server 2016 that has no GUI.

Server Message Block (SMB) 3.0   An enhanced version of technology that makes Windows shares available on the network.

Server with Desktop Experience   An installation option of Windows Server 2016 that has a GUI.

SET   Switch Embedded Teaming, a new NIC Teaming option that provides faster performance.

Shared-Nothing Live Migration   The movement of a virtual machine and its storage from one host to another while not using clustering or shared storage.

Shared Virtual Hard Disk   A virtual hard disk used by multiple VMs.

Shielded Virtual Machine   A feature that allows the encryption of virtual machines.

Simultaneous Upgrade   An update in which the NLB cluster is brought down and then all hosts are upgraded.

Site-Aware Clusters   Clusters in which the fault domain values are used with nodes to find the site the node belongs to in a stretch cluster.

Smart Paging   Disk paging used for temporary memory.

SMB   An abbreviation for Server Message Block, a sharing technology used by Windows systems.

Standard   The typical edition of Server 2016 for most medium to large businesses.

Standard Format Disk   A disk that uses a 512-byte physical sector.

Storage Migration   The movement of a virtual machine's files from one host to another.

Storage Pool   A collection of physical disks that can be presented to users as logical disks.

Storage Quality of Service   New technology in Windows Server 2016 that enhances the IOPS of a virtual machine's access storage.

Storage Replica   Storage-agnostic data replication between servers or clusters.

Storage Spaces   A storage virtualization technology in Windows Server 2016.

Storage Spaces Direct   A technology that makes shared clustered storage directly available to clusters using Storage Space–type technology.

Stretch Cluster   A cluster with nodes in different geographic areas.

Tiered Storage   Disks of different speeds used optimally.

VHD or VHDX   An abbreviation for virtual hard disk, which is a method of installing Nano Server.

Virtual Machine Queue   A type of hardware packet filtering that delivers packets from an outside virtual machine network directly to a VM host OS.

vNIC   An abbreviation for virtual network interface card; this virtual component permits a virtual machine to connect to a network.

Volume   A Windows construct for a logical storage drive that may span multiple physical storage devices across one or more servers.

Volume Activation Services Server Role   A role that enables you to automate and simplify the issuance and management of Microsoft software volume licenses for a variety of scenarios and environments.

Windows Container Stack   Networking components that permit container network access.

Windows Server Container   A container that achieves isolation through namespace and process isolation.

Witness   A device that acts as a tie-breaker in a quorum.

Workload   An application that runs on Windows Server.

Index

G

H

X-Y-Z